The Cyprus Frenzy of 1878 and the British Press

The Cyprus Frenzy of 1878 and the British Press

Marinos Pourgouris

LEXINGTON BOOKS
Lanham • Boulder • New York • London

Published by Lexington Books
An imprint of The Rowman & Littlefield Publishing Group, Inc.
4501 Forbes Boulevard, Suite 200, Lanham, Maryland 20706
www.rowman.com

6 Tinworth Street, London SE11 5AL, United Kingdom

British Library Cataloguing in Publication Information Available

Library of Congress Cataloging-in-Publication Data
Names: Pourgouris, Marinos, author.
Title: The Cyprus Frenzy of 1878 and the British Press / Marinos Pourgouris.
Description: Lanham : Lexington Books, [2019] | Includes bibliographical references and index.
Identifiers: LCCN 2018046769 (print) | LCCN 2018051939 (ebook) | ISBN 9781498576611 (ebook) | ISBN 9781498576604 (cloth : alk. paper)
Subjects: LCSH: Cyprus—History—British rule, 1878-1960—Press coverage—Great Britain. | Foreign news—Great Britain—History—19th century. | Journalists—Cyprus—History—19th century. | Press and politics—Great Britain—History—19th century.
Classification: LCC DS54.8 (ebook) | LCC DS54.8 .P685 2019 (print) | DDC 956.93/03—dc23
LC record available at https://lccn.loc.gov/2018046769

∞ ™ The paper used in this publication meets the minimum requirements of American National Standard for Information Sciences Permanence of Paper for Printed Library Materials, ANSI/NISO Z39.48-1992.

Printed in the United States of America

To Manos

Contents

Illustrations

Acknowledgments

I am grateful to the University of Cyprus for awarding me with a two-year grant, in 2011, for the project "Literature and British Colonialism." I am particularly indebted to the graduate students who were involved in that project: Joanna Georgiou, Chrystalla Kanellidou and, especially, Maria Klonari. During researching and writing this book, I have discussed some of my findings with Pantelis Voutouris, my colleague in the Department of Byzantine and Modern Greek Studies. I appreciate his fervent encouragement and support. During my time at Brown University (2005–10) I was tremendously lucky to be part of an inspiring group of colleagues and friends who worked on Postcolonial Studies and Reception Theory: Rey Chow (now at Duke), Elliott Colla (now at Georgetown), Nauman Naqvi (now at Habib) and Ken Haynes. Our discussions have shaped my thinking and they can be traced behind the lines of this book. I am particularly indebted to Elliott Colla for sharing his immense knowledge of the Middle East with me and for our continuing collaboration. I am humbled, beyond words, by Gil Anidjar's friendship and his kind support. His ability to challenge any "given" idea raises the bar of scholarship higher. I have known Sanja Bahun (at the University of Essex) since our graduate years together and I still turn to her for advice, personal or professional. She has been tremendously supportive throughout the process of writing this book and particularly in helping me choose a good home for it. Dušan and Jakov Radunović have made me anticipate my comings and goings from Cyprus to the U.K. with eagerness. Many thanks to Andria Cleanthous, whose intervention has helped me trace some of the archival sources included in the book. Brian Hill and Eric Kuntzman, at Lexington Books, have enthusiastically embraced this project as soon as they received the manuscript. They have both guided me patiently through the nuances involved in its publication. Their professionalism and prompt responses to my many queries have made the process of publishing this manuscript a thoroughly enjoyable and exciting experience.

My partner, Yianna Ioannou, is still my most demanding reader and an unsurpassed editor of my first and final drafts. I am eternally grateful for her meticulous reading, her relentless inquiries and her unyielding support. Together we are raising a son, our beloved Manos, to whom this book is dedicated. He was born around the time I began my research for this project. I hope that, one day, once he learns to read and write, he will know that the curiosity for understanding history's "cunning passages" and "contrived corridors" stems from a similar place as our shared passion for creating, telling and listening to stories.

Introduction

Imperial Imagination and the British Press

This book focuses on what Hans Robert Jauss describes as a "synchronic cross-section of a moment" in the history of British colonialism.[1] That historical moment centers on and around the year 1878, when Great Britain acquired the Mediterranean island of Cyprus from the Ottomans. The study of colonialism from a diachronic perspective—that is, in the context of history's *longue durée*—has undoubtedly offered us important tools in the effort to understand that vast and complex mechanism that subjugated people and nations, constructed identities, divided and ruled, and, through its many historical transformations, laid the foundations that are still in place in the workings of hegemonic practices today. This project takes a different route: by focusing on a singular event—the British acquisition of Cyprus in 1878—it generally aims to "discover an overarching system of relationships in the literature of a historical moment."[2] Naturally, from the first moment the island of Cyprus entered the sphere of public discourse in Britain, it also partook in the overarching system of imperial relations: from the relationship of the Empire to the Russians or to the Ottomans, to projects such as the affordable transfer of goods from India to the Mediterranean, the Empire's attitude towards slavery, the use of foreign troops in the British army, etc. In addition to becoming a British administrative unit, the island also became part of the British colonial imaginary: it was imagined as a virgin land that offered opportunities for profit, as a desolate island whose people could now breathe freely after centuries of Ottoman subjugation, as an integral part of the glorious ancient Greek world, or even as a Christian holy site. By taking a microscopic gaze at a single historical moment, the book exposes these larger topics through specific events, whose examination raises important questions in our understanding of how colonial bureaucracy worked and, most importantly, how a hitherto unknown place became a fetishized object in the colonial imaginary.

Indeed, the acquisition of this tiny island created such sensation that it dominated public discourse and, consequently, the British press, in the second half of the year 1878. Considering how small the island is, this mania with Cyprus is astounding and revealing of the synergy between the British press and the colonial political apparatus. The role of newspapers and magazines in reporting, constructing, propagating and eventually solidifying colonial perceptions of the island was paramount. A central question that informs every chapter of this book is this: what stirred the British imagination in 1878 so that a hitherto unknown island and its people attracted, even for a brief moment, the interest of so many journalists, editors and readers?

The acquisition of Cyprus, as seen through the thousands of columns devoted to it in British newspapers and magazines, reads more like a serialized adventure story, which encompasses all those elements bound to capture the public's imagination. As most Victorian Britons saw it, here was an island that was seized from the Turks through the sheer cunning of British foreign diplomacy; an island that was in utter disarray due to centuries of mismanagement and corruption, and which could now be restored to its ancient fame; an island where the Christian population was under the rule of Ottoman Muslims and could now enter the community of Christian "civilized" nations. The most celebrated of Victorian soldiers, Sir Garnet Wolseley, was summoned to lead the historical restoration of Cyprus. Famous journalists, renowned travelers, politicians, businessmen and workers flocked to the island to be part of this glorious moment in the history of the British Empire.

The beginnings of this story are well documented. Between June 13 and July 13, 1878, the leaders of Russia, Great Britain, France, Austria-Hungary, Italy, Germany, Greece, Romania, Serbia, Montenegro and the Ottoman Empire convened in Berlin to discuss the shifting geographical and political landscape in the Balkans, following the Russo-Turkish war of 1877–78. Unbeknownst to the other delegates, at least at the opening of the Congress, the British government had already signed a secret agreement with the Ottomans, which included the transfer of control of Cyprus to England. More specifically, on June 4, 1878, Austen Henry Layard, Britain's ambassador to Turkey, and Safvet Pasha, the Ottoman Minister of foreign affairs, met in Constantinople to secretly sign the "Convention of Defensive Alliance between Great Britain and Turkey."[3] According to this agreement, as long as Russia occupied Batoum, Ardahan, and Kars, or if it attempted to capture any other territories belonging to the Ottomans, Great Britain would join Turkey "in defending them by force of arms."[4] In return, the sultan consented "to assign the Island of Cyprus to be occupied and administered by England."[5]

For political and economic reasons, the British government took extraordinary measures to keep the agreement a secret. But by early July, rumors of its acquisition had intensified, and on July 4, several newspapers, including *The Telegraph* and *The Times*, reported that "the British Government purposed asking the Porte for permission to use some parts of the island of Cyprus for depots of military stores in case of war" and that, due to the rumor of a possible British acquisition of the island, "a number of Greeks have gone to Cyprus to purchase land in anticipation of its rising in value."[6] Eventually, on July 8, *The Daily Telegraph*, "thanks to one of the extraordinary leakages from the Foreign Office which the more enterprising newspapers did not scruple to engineer, published the substance of the [June 4] Convention."[7] Under the unambiguous heading "England and Turkey-Defensive treaty-Protectorate of Asia Minor-British Occupation of Cyprus," *The Telegraph* reported that "England has concluded a Defensive Treaty with Turkey for the maintenance of the strict integrity of the Sultan's Asiatic dominions. In view of this fact, the Porte has accorded to Great Britain the right to occupy the Island of Cyprus, and this right her Majesty's Government will immediately carry into effect."[8] On the same day, *The Times* was reporting that "Her Majesty's ships *Invincible* and *Raleigh* are cruising off Cyprus, and Lord Hay's squadron has been sighted near Larnaca";[9] Ambassador Layard and the Porte were questioned about these movements, the newspaper noted, but they neither confirmed nor denied the acquisition of the island by Britain. Furthermore, Ambassador Baring, who was supposed to set off for Crete on a secret mission, was now on board the *Salamis* waiting for further instructions.

On July 8, as the British government was struggling to contain the rumors regarding Cyprus, Sir Garnet Wolseley, accompanied by his wife Louisa, or "Loo" as he affectionately called her, took an early train to the village of Datchet, near Windsor, to pay a visit to his army comrade George Greaves, who would soon join him for the Cyprus expedition. "When in the train," he wrote in his private journal, "I had told Loo that I felt tolerably sure that the secret about Cyprus would be made public that day in parliament."[10] Indeed, around lunchtime, he received a telegram from the Secretary of State for War, Colonel Frederick Stanley, instructing him to go see him at once. Wolseley left his wife behind with his friend Greaves and hurried to the War Office in London. He was soon informed that the agreement between the Sultan of Turkey and the Queen of England regarding the acquisition of the island of Cyprus would be made public that very afternoon; more importantly, he was to become the first "High Commissioner and Commander in Chief of Cyprus."[11] In the afternoon, the announcement for the acquisition of Cyprus was read in both the House of Lords and the House of Commons by Earl Granville and the Marquis of Hartington respectively. It was a prepared statement that summarized the agreement between Britain and Turkey, which included the sultan's consent "to assign the island of Cyprus to be occupied and administered by England," and concluded with the following statement, verifying the agreement with Wolseley: "Her Majesty has been pleased to appoint Sir G. Wolseley to administer the government of the island."[12]

As expected, the July 9 edition of all major and several provincial newspapers carried the headlines of England's acquisition of Cyprus, along with enthusiastic commentaries. Several editors scrambled together whatever information they could find from encyclopedias on Cyprus, including brief descriptions of the island, its geography and history. The most commonly used descriptions were the brief entries on "Cyprus" from *Chambers Encyclopaedia* and the *English Cyclopaedia*. Hence, several British newspapers' first presentation of the native Cypriotes, the Empire's new colonial subjects, included the following depiction copied from *Chambers Encyclopaedia*: "the Greek Christians, who compose the bulk of the population being indolent and spiritless, through fear of the dominant Turks, who are ignorant and fanatical."[13] Apparently, even the members of the Parliament had to look up Cyprus in the existing encyclopedias, with Earl Granville noting, in the July 19 session in the House of Lords, that "on referring to the *Encyclopaedia Britannica*, . . . there are only 15 lines which refer to the state of the Island."[14] Most newspapers, including *The Times*, published, apart from the discussion in the Parliament concerning the acquisition of Cyprus, a series of letters exchanged between Lord Salisbury, the foreign secretary, and Ambassador Layard: a justification and explanation of the agreement by Salisbury, as well as the original text of the agreement and an annex added to the agreement on July 1. Commenting on the announcement of the agreement, *The Times*' editors praised the selection of Wolseley as "Governor," noting that he "has justly won confidence by his discharge of several very responsible duties."[15]

On Wednesday, July 10, much more detailed information on Cyprus appeared in the daily press. Newspapers all over the country announced the details of the Anglo-Turkish agreement, that the occupation of Cyprus by Admiral Hay and his fleet was imminent, that Wolseley was scheduled to depart for Cyprus on Saturday, July 13, and that the Indian troops stationed in Malta were ordered to join Wolseley's fleet. They also included the first reactions of the foreign press to the acquisition. Historical and geographical information on the island poured in, with the conservative-leaning *Pall-Mall Gazette* publishing one of the most extensive articles on the history of Cyprus.[16] *The Times* coverage, in the July 10 issue, was indicative of the enormous impact the transfer of Cyprus had on the public. The newspaper's correspondents, stationed across Europe, submitted several reports detailing the explosive response of the foreign press to the news. "The Anglo-Turkish alliance," wrote the Paris correspondent, "has thrown every other topic into the background."[17] The Berlin correspondent, who was covering the ongoing Berlin Conference, wrote that the Anglo-Turkish alliance created "considerable sensation" and that "the Cyprus Treaty is the one topic of political conversation."[18] When this "grand surprise" was announced, he continues, "the English diplomacy enjoyed a *prestige* such as it has not enjoyed for a long time."[19] From Vienna, *The Times*' correspondent wrote that "the occupation of Cyprus is still the almost exclusive topic of conversation."[20] In its own commentary, the newspaper wrote that "there is certainly much to fire the imagination in the bond which practically adds Cyprus to the possessions of the English Crown. . . . The old records of our civilization begin in those lands, and the technicalities of the Eastern Question are blended with the most familiar names of Biblical Story or classic legend."[21]

There was indeed much to fire British imagination concerning Cyprus and, as expected, in the following days the issue of the island's acquisition monopolized the news. From early July until the end of 1878, the story of Cyprus unfolded in the pages of British journals and newspapers and it was mainly presented in four intertwined segments. First, there were the advertisements of products and services related to Cyprus that pointed to the intimate connection between colonial policy and capitalist ventures. Second, most of the leading newspapers sent correspondents to the island in the early days of the occupation in order to cover this historic transition. They reported back covering every minute detail: the difficulties encountered by the English Administration in Cyprus, the weather, the state of trade, deadly diseases, the character of the people, etc. Third, dozens of editorials were published in newspapers around Britain, by some of the most established scholars: from engineers to biblical scholars, doctors, Greek expatriates, politicians and travelers who shared their opinions on issues concerning Cyprus. Finally, there were the parliamentary debates between Liberals and Conservatives that covered every detail of British policy towards the island: from the existence of slavery on the island, to taxation, the suitability of ports, the number of troops deployed, the terms of the Anglo-Turkish agreement, etc. The political ramifications of the acquisition have been discussed extensively, particularly in the context of Victorian politics in the late nineteenth century.[22] What I find more pertinent, in the context of cultural history as well as the reception of Cyprus's acquisition by both the British elites and the British public, is the closer examination of the role of advertisements, editorials and newspaper correspondences in the reception and dissemination of colonial discourse.

THE FRENZY

In a letter to her brother-in-law, Harry Verney, the well-known liberal M.P., dated February 14, 1879, Florence Nightingale noted the enormous interest of the British press in Cyprus and compared it to the inadequate press coverage of the vastly more populous and significant colony of India:

> We have "annexed" Cyprus and we find in Cyprus (and we are quite surprised) a miniature of what is happening under our own eyes every day all over India, English India, among some two hundred millions of our Asiatic fellow countrymen of whom we have taken charge. And we know it not?
>
> And why do we not know it? To little atom of a Cyprus, the great newspaper sends its able "special correspondent" and we have, and we read (for the most powerful newspaper of the day, the *Times*, writes too well not to be read) three, four, five columns, or even a whole page, of large type of what is done in *Cyprus* among tens or hundreds, which we might see, if we did but look, multiplied into millions or tens of millions in *India*. (But we only see in the *Times* half a quarter of a column the smallest type about India.) Why do we not look? India is surely a more interesting and more anxious possession than Cyprus.[23]

Not a single "newspaper correspondent [was sent] to 'discover' the interior of India outside the great cities," Nightingale complains.[24] Quoting extensively from *The Times*' Cyprus correspondences, she explains that the same problems that special correspondents report in regard to Cyprus, also exist in India: the lack of infrastructure, administrative mismanagement, corruption, etc.[25] The massive interest in "pygmy Cyprus,"[26] as Nightingale describes the island, is indeed perplexing when compared to the British public's interest in other far more significant colonies. This fixation was perhaps unprecedented in the history of British colonialism. As one editor noted, under the heading "Cyprus Mania," in August 1878,

> Cyprus meets the eye everywhere at present. It forms the text for articles in newspapers, magazines, and reviews. It figures in pamphlets and in bulky books, which bear traces of haste in the manufacture. It is also largely made use of by advertisers in giving publicity to the excellence of their fragrant essences, delicious wines, and cool clothing for hot climates.[27]

Another editor wrote, also in August 1878, that the British people were talking about Cyprus everywhere: "at kettledrums, in cafes, in smoking-rooms, at dinner parties, in the clubs, at St. Stephen's, on railways, and in omnibuses."[28] The reasons behind the public's massive interest in Cyprus are, as always, varied and multifaceted. Historians of Cyprus have repeatedly noted its significance as a strategic base; indeed, the newspaper reports of the time, as well as the political debates, verify the fact that its proximity to the Suez Canal and its potential utilization as a midway point between India and Europe were important strategic factors in its acquisition. First and foremost, against the background of an economic recession in Britain, what the public saw in the occupation of Cyprus was economic opportunity: the island's relative proximity to England and its purported wealth, mobilized many entrepreneurs to seek out ways to invest in imports and exports or to open companies in Cyprus. The rising tourist industry also saw an opportunity to turn the island into a tourist haven: the opening of hotels, pubs and cafes, the import/export of alcohol or furniture, the scheduling of tours, were all considered as potentially safe ways to profit from Britain's newest acquisition.

Another important reason that fueled the fascination with Cyprus was the political landscape in 1878. On the one hand, it was natural for the ruling Disraeli government to present the acquisition of the island as a monumental victory of British diplomacy. The conservatives' celebratory tone, however, soon subsided when they came to the realization that Cyprus was not the profitable paradise they envisioned and that the treaty was perhaps more beneficial to the Ottomans than to the British: infrastructure was not existent on the island, ports were too shallow, the colonial administration was forced to aggressively collect taxes from the locals in order to pay for Ottoman loans (since revenues were not enough), an increasing number of soldiers were getting sick since they landed in Cyprus, rents skyrocketed within days of the occupation making the housing of administrative departments more costly, the transition from the Ottoman to the British legal system was more difficult than imagined, and, to make matters worse, Cypriots were complaining about mistreatment by the British administration. Most importantly, the treaty clearly stated that Britain would *administer*—not own—Cyprus on behalf of the Ottomans. By the end of 1878, what began as a monumental triumph for the Disraeli government was turning more into a diplomatic debacle and, unsurprisingly, the Liberals took advantage of the changing opinions in regard to Cyprus. Against this background, and with all eyes, in the parliament, fixed on the general election of 1880, Cyprus emerged as a heated political subject with Conservatives and Liberals competing to prove their case. Consequently, much of that great space devoted to Cyprus in newspaper columns from the summer of 1878 through 1879, is linked to its emergence as a contested political subject.

Accurate as they might be, such explanations do not fully account for the enormous public curiosity over Cyprus. The public's reaction amounted to an unparalleled frenzy, a sort of fixation more akin to a fetish, and in the context of British colonialism's cultural history, several other reasons should be considered in relation to it. First, in January 1877, a year prior to the occupation of the island, Queen Victoria was proclaimed Empress of India. Though the title was widely used in addressing the queen prior to the proclamation, its official adaptation signaled an emphatic reaffirmation of the Empire's vastness and might. It also coincided with the beginning of the Empire's sharp territorial expansion that would last until the 1920s, before its eventual decline in the period following the Great War. With the acquisition of the island in 1878, Britain became the undisputed dominant force in the Mediterranean, controlling the entire basin from Gibraltar to Malta and Cyprus.

Second, the British frenzy over Cyprus is linked to the island's symbolic historical value both as a Christian site and as part of the ancient Greek world. Unsurprisingly, one of the first books to be published, immediately after the announcement of the occupation, was the Presbyterian minister's, John Thain Davidson, *Cyprus: England's New Possession. Its Place in Bible History.* Mixing biblical myth and history, Davidson asserts that Cyprus's early occupants "can be traced as far back as to Noah," that the island was "one of the first places . . . where the Gospel was preached," and that it was "probably destined to be a spot of great importance in connection with the fulfilment of ancient prophesy, and the return of the Jews to their own land."[29] Similar references to the island's importance as a Christian site—as "a garden of the Lord and an isle of Saints"[30]—are found in several books and articles of the time. Linked to the widespread enthusiasm for the Empire's acquisition of a "holy land," was the moral satisfaction for what the British public essentially saw as the emancipation of the island's Christian population from a barbaric Muslim Empire.

For many Victorian Britons, then, the acquisition of the island was a verification of the Empire's might. It was a place full of economic opportunities and a colony towards which Britain had a moral obligation to protect fellow Christians from the Ottomans. Many of the educated Britons, whose writings often fueled the general frenzy, also saw Cyprus as part of the glorious ancient Greek world. If Cyprus was an exceptional case, in the British colonial imaginary, at least among the more educated classes, it was also because it posited itself—historically but also based on the claims of Greek-Cypriots—as part of the Hellenic world; a world that British universities taught and identified with since their inception. As Stathis Gourgouris writes, "If the story of India is the paradigmatic condition of the colonialist imaginary, then the story of Greece is the paradigmatic colonialist condition *in* the imaginary";[31] Modern Greece, Gourgouris continues, is "history's sole witness of the consequences of . . . the colonization of the ideal." The emergence of the "real" Modern Greek nation, in the early nineteenth century, became the catalyst against which the Hellenic ideal was measured. Apart from the Ionian Islands, which were part of the British Empire from 1814 to 1863, Cyprus was the only territory with a majority of a Greek population that was colonized by the British. Naturally, nineteenth-century travelers and correspondents to the island were often struggling with the same constructs as their fellow travelers to Greece. They were obsessed with the Cypriot blood-line, with whether Cypriots were the descendants of their glorious Greek ancestors, whether their physiognomy resembled that of the ancient Greeks, and whether their language, their customs, or their manners were Greek. As was the case with travelers to Greece, most are categorically against the theory of Hellenic descent and some are fervent supporters of it. It is against the background of this completive *claim to Greekness* by both the colonized and the colonizers—the colonial inheritors of the Hellenic Ideal and the nationalistic supplicants of Modern Hellenicity—that the British presence in Cyprus would be defined. Hence, many of the newspapers' early reports from Cyprus, and many of the books published in the first years of the occupation, address the issue of the island's Hellenic identity and the natives' relationship to it.

If there is something that distinguishes the "Cyprus frenzy" from other Victorian obsessions, such as Egyptomania or Philhellenism, it is precisely because the newly acquired colony of Cyprus could occupy, simultaneously, several contesting positions: it was Christian and Muslim, Ottoman and British, Oriental and Greek, sensual and corrupting. What the reasons I outlined above corroborate, and what this book will further establish, is that the Cyprus frenzy, which took Britain by storm in the second half of 1878 and through the early months of 1879, was largely due to the way in which Britain's newest acquisition could steer the colonial imaginary. The island, if we judge from the many volumes, articles, advertisements and literary works devoted to it, could seemingly satisfy practically everyone who looked to it for inspiration or gain (political or economic). For the entrepreneurs, it became a potential field for profit; for the politicians, a contested ground on which to push their respective agendas; for the ideologues, a great symbol of Imperial Power; for the religious, a moral justification of the Empire's civilizing mission and the emancipation of Christian populations; for inventors, an opportunity to test their inventions; for classical scholars, a piece of the ancient Greek world that they could potentially explore; and for military officers, a chance to become reformers and participate in the glory of the Empire's expansion.

SOURCES AND METHODOLOGY

In recent decades, several volumes have been published that have paved the way for a more substantial examination of the history and the impact of British colonial rule in Cyprus. The work of scholars such as Robert Holland, David French, Evanthis Hatzivassiliou, Petros Papapolyviou, Mary Roussou-Sinclair, Helen O'Shea, Tabitha Morgan, Gail Dallas Hook, Andrekos Varnava, Alexis Rappas, Hubert Faustmann, and William Mallinson, just to mention a few, has contributed enormously in firmly establishing the study of British colonialism in Cyprus, and has provided researchers with important findings on a variety of subjects: from the examination of travel literature and the study of colonial educational policies, to the Cypriots' reaction to the British occupation, the political and historical background of the island's colonization, its impact on the relationship between Greek-Cypriots and Turkish Cypriots, etc.[32] This book aims to contribute to this discussion by focusing on the early years of the British colonization of Cyprus and by closely examining the writings of the first British journalists who traveled to Cyprus to cover the occupation. As such, it is partly a study on the history of journalism in Britain as well as of the way in which the press participated in, or enabled, the dissemination of colonial discourse. Its heavy leaning on newspaper archives is founded on the understanding that these constitute the most popular tool to understand the circulation and internalization of ideology and its connection to several parallel projects unfolding in the drama of colonial history.

What can these archives tell us about the reaction of the more educated Victorians—correspondents, entrepreneurs, scholars, religious priests, military men, politicians, or poets—to the occupation of Cyprus? Apart from a close examination of newspapers, I consider travelogues, poems, theatrical performances, biographies, autobiographies, lectures, or historical studies of the same period, in order to examine the simultaneous push and pull in the colonialist imaginary: on the one hand, the exotic, sensual, or celebratory expressions regarding the acquisition of the island and, on the other, the scornful, derogatory or hegemonic descriptions that characterize many of the texts published in this period. By considering a wide variety of texts—from literature to editorials and advertisements—I argue that this ever-present splitting in colonialist discourse is intrinsically connected to the tension between fantasy and reality. Most importantly, it is connected to the personal relationships between the authors of these texts (their friends and their enemies), their aspirations, their ideological positions or, in short, the intimacy through which they filter their descriptions of the colony, the colonizers and the colonized.

The first chapter of this book considers the Cyprus frenzy in the context of intimate relationships. It approaches intimacy in two distinct ways. First, as an expression that characterizes the relationship between the two main groups of individuals involved in the colonialist project in Cyprus: Wolseley and his close circle of associates, and special correspondents. Here I find Benedict Anderson's memorable description of Creole Pioneers, in *Imagined Communities*, useful in our understanding of the comradery and the ideological connectedness both within and between these groups. Second, I approach intimacy as an inherent characteristic of this frenzy. Two parallel expressions can be traced in the early years of the island's occupation: on the one hand, the island is presented, primarily in cultural representations, as a paradise on earth and on the other as a sickly and worthless acquisition. To examine this splitting, I briefly consider cultural representations of Cyprus in poems, fictional narratives, musical compositions and theatrical performances, in the weeks that immediately followed the transition of power on the island.

The second chapter of the book delves further into the Cyprus frenzy in Britain by considering advertisements, which appeared in leading newspapers in 1878 and 1879. Apart from providing us with a remarkable glimpse into the depth of the public's fixation with the island, advertisements also allow us to examine the close links between the capitalist and the colonialist projects. The range that they cover is indeed astounding: from the promotion of books on Cyprus to the sale of medicine, bicycles, maps, fabrics, perfumes, furniture, insurance, etc. One particularly interesting story that we will pursue, in this chapter, is that of Thomas Cook, the famous travel agency, which announced the inclusion of Cyprus in their celebrated tours, even before the arrival of Wolseley.

The next six chapters comprise the main subject of this book and focus on the six British correspondents who arrived in Cyprus to cover the occupation. The research behind these chapters was immensely challenging. Part of the difficulty in dealing with Victorian journalism is the fact that correspondences were anonymous. In other words, since the correspondents' reports were unsigned, the identification of the author of each correspondence had to be verified through a number of other sources, which included dates of arrival and departure, autobiographies, other (signed) works by these authors that make reference to the same events, other journalists or scholars' more precise reference—by name—to the author of each correspondence, the writing style of these journalists, and the appearance of segments from their correspondences in their signed works. Out of the six correspondents that I consider in these chapters, only two are identified by the newspapers they represented: Hepworth Dixon, whose name is included in the heading of each correspondence, and Samuel Pasfield Oliver, who always signed his reports with the initials "S.P.O." Needless to say, these two cases constitute exceptions in the wider context of journalistic practices in Victorian Britain, where even the most famous of journalists did not sign their correspondences.

The third chapter focuses on St. Leger Algernon Herbert, who represented *The Times* and who was in the most peculiar position of all the journalists who visited the island. Apart from representing the most prestigious newspaper of the times, he was also Garnet Wolseley's private secretary in Cyprus. Herbert had graduated from Oxford in 1874 and worked briefly in Canada, as Lord Dufferin's private secretary, before he was invited by Wolseley to participate in the Cyprus expedition. The fact that such an inexperienced young man simultaneously represented *The Times* and served as Wolseley's private secretary, speaks volumes about the general's ability to surround himself with trusted people who served as liaisons between the press and the military.

Archibald Forbes, who is the focus of the fourth chapter, was the most famous special correspondent in Britain at the time. The Scottish-born journalist had attended the lectures of William Howard Russel, the forefather of journalism in Britain, at the University of Aberdeen, and, after a brief career in the army, landed a job as a correspondent for *The Daily News*. His unparalleled writing style resulted in a rapid increase of the newspaper's circulation and he soon became the most appealing correspondent in Britain. Praised by Mark Twain and loathed by Oscar Wilde, Forbes enjoyed an unequal status among journalists in Victorian Britain. His reports were discussed extensively by the public and his exploits were read aloud in the British Parliament. Consequently, his dramatic reports from Cyprus were eagerly anticipated and were, by far, the most extensively discussed commentaries on the occupation. One could argue that his article "The 'Fiasco' of Cyprus," published in October 1878, in *The Nineteenth Century*, once he returned from the island, was an important milestone in changing the perceptions of Cyprus in the minds of many Britons.

The Irish correspondent John Augustus O'Shea, the central figure in the fifth chapter, traveled to Cyprus on behalf of *The London Evening Standard*, and, like Forbes, he was one of the most prominent journalists of his time. O'Shea was a fervent supporter of the British Army and, in fact, his correspondences directly challenged and contradicted Forbes's reports from the island. Apart from his Cyprus correspondences, we will also consider two Cyprus-inspired short stories O'Shea published after his return from the island. As it will become clear, he was one of the most emblematic cases of the congenial relationship between the army and the press and one of the sternest defenders of British colonial ideology.

The sixth chapter focuses on Edward Henry Vizetelly, a rather fascinating figure as he was the only journalist who relocated to Cyprus and resided there from August 1878 to February 1882. He traveled to the island to represent *The Glasgow Herald*, but he also held several other jobs in Cyprus, including editor of a local newspaper, and secretary of some of the most prominent individuals in the island's first administrations: Dr. Frederick Heidenstam, Claude Delaval Cobham, Colonel White and Robert Fisher. Vizetelly was the least known member of a very well-known family of publishers and correspondents. But unlike Forbes, O'Shea and Herbert, he lacked military connections and he was rather critical of the government's work in Cyprus, of the British soldiers stationed on the island and of the English settlers. His reports, as well as his critical attitude, got him in trouble with both the locals and the British authorities in Cyprus, and he was forced to depart from the island.

The seventh chapter focuses on the representative of *The Illustrated London News*, Samuel Pasfield Oliver. Oliver, who was both an artist and a correspondent, was completely unknown among the British journalists in Cyprus. He had just retired from the army and he was better known among scholars for his work on Madagascar; his commission with *The Illustrated London News* was, in fact, his first serious venture into journalism. Yet, his reports from Cyprus provide us with some of the most detailed descriptions of the British military presence on the island and are quite unique in their combination of the visual (i.e., sketches) and the descriptive.

Chapter 8 examines the correspondences of one of the most popular and controversial figures in Victorian London, Hepworth Dixon. Dixon was a prolific writer of historical books and widely seen by the literary establishment as hyperbolic, pompous, and a falsifier of historical facts. His style led to the coinage of the adjective "Dixonian," which was mockingly used by some scholars as a reference to his flippant and flamboyant style. He was mocked by Wolseley and O'Shea and befriended by Alessandro Palma di Cesnola, whose brother, Luigi, was the first director of New York's Metropolitan Museum. Though his book *British Cyprus* is one of the best-known texts among researches of colonialism in Cyprus, little is known about his service as a special correspondent for several provincial British newspapers during the early months of the occupation. These "Letters from Cyprus" are indeed some of the most representative accounts of the intimacy that defined the attitudes towards both the colonizers and the colonized.

In the final chapter of this book, we will turn to the hundreds of letters to the editor about Cyprus, which appeared in leading newspapers, and particularly *The Times*. "Letters to the Editor" offers a unique tool in the examination of reader reception and response. Who were the authors of these letters and how did the dialogue unfold between them in the editorial space of British newspapers? What motivated them to participate in this frenzied discussion, and what particular issues did they deem important enough to raise regarding Cyprus? Though we consider several scholars who participated in this discussion and fueled the Cyprus frenzy—from explorers to doctors, politicians, classical scholars, archaeologists, etc.—the greatest part of this chapter examines the writings and the actions of two individuals: John Lawton Haddan and Verney Lovett Cameron. Haddan was an engineer and the inventor of the Pioneer Railway, a supposedly cheaper and more efficient railway system. Cameron became well-known as an explorer in Victorian Britain after the publication of his book *Across Africa*. He was also a close friend of Richard Francis Burton, one of the most celebrated explorers of his time, with whom he later co-authored *To the Gold Coast for Gold.* Haddan and Cameron collaborated, after the announcement of the occupation of Cyprus, and they aggressively promoted the use of the island as a midway point in the transfer of goods from the colony of India. Their scheme was not simply expressed in several letters to the editor of *The Times* but also led to Cameron's journey to Cyprus, to explore the possibility of realizing this ambitious plan.

This book is founded on the premise that colonialism functions, first and foremost, as an internalized psychic phenomenon which is projected on—it determines and it is determined by—intimate relationships: friendships, identifications, affiliations, sympathies and antipathies. Its powerful and destructive force becomes mingled, in this sense, with identity politics and perceptions of the self. In other words, the way these individuals perceive themselves, their self-worth, becomes intertwined with the grand ideological mechanisms that sustained the colonialist phenomenon. The examination of the British colonization of Cyprus, as it appeared in the pages of British newspapers, illustrates the intimate connections between the individuals involved in the project of colonialism and it reveals the closed networks that these individuals belonged to or aspired to belong to. This book makes the case that the history of colonialism and the mechanisms by which it functioned, must be reexamined by taking into account the interrelations between the individuals who kept the colonial mechanisms in motion.

NOTES

1. Hans Robert Jauss, *Towards an Aesthetic of Reception*, trans. Timothy Bahti (Minneapolis: University of Minnesota Press, 1982), 36.
2. Ibid.
3. Throughout the book, I try to use the term "Ottoman Empire" as opposed to "Turkey" (or "Ottoman" as opposed to "Turk") since the Republic of Turkey officially came into being in 1922, when the Sultanate was abolished. This, however, was not the practice in Victorian Britain, where the terms are used interchangeably (i.e., the terms "Turkey" and "Turkish Empire" are often used by journalists, politicians and scholars to indicate the Ottoman Empire). Hence, in discussing these sources, I maintain the use of the term "Turkey."
4. George Francis Hill, *A History of Cyprus* (Cambridge: Cambridge University Press, 1952), 300. In his *History of Cyprus,* Hill reproduces the entire text of the convention (see Hill 300–304). Also see Murat Metin Hakki, *The Cyprus Issue: A Documentary History, 1878–2007* (London: I.B. Tauris, 2007), 3–5.
5. Ibid., 300.
6. *Times*, July 4, 1878, p. 5.
7. Hill, *History of Cyprus*, 289.
8. *Daily Telegraph*, 8 July 1878, p. 5.
9. *Times*, July 8, 1878, p. 5.
10. Sir Garnet Wolseley, *Cyprus 1878: The Journal of Sir Garnet Wolseley*, 2nd ed. (Nicosia: Cultural Centre of the Cyprus Popular Bank, 1992), 1.
11. Ibid., 4.
12. *Times*, July 9, 1878, p. 6. Interestingly, in the House of Commons, William Gladstone noted the peculiar language of the announcement: "I desire to ask the right hon. gentleman a question as to one portion of the document the language of which did not appear to be quite clear. In the first part of the document I think it speaks of an engagement of the Sultan that Cyprus should be occupied and administered by England, these words not of necessity involving a transfer of sovereignty, while in the latter part of the document the word transfer is used. Perhaps the right hon. gentleman will explain, either now or to-morrow, whether the sovereignty of the island will remain in the Porte" (*Times*, July 9, 1878, p. 6). The subject of the legal status of the British occupation of Cyprus became one of the most contested political issues.
13. "Cyprus," *Chambers's Encyclopædia* (Edinburgh: W & R Chambers, 1874), 386.
14. HL Deb. 19 July 1878 vol. 241 cc1948. The entry for "Cyprus" in the 1878 edition of *Encyclopaedia Britannica* was considerably longer. It was written by Edward Herbert Bunbury, Earl Granville's fellow Liberal M.P. (in the House of Commons).
15. *Times*, July 9, 1878, p. 9.
16. "Cyprus," *Pall Mall Gazette*, July 10, 1878, p. 10.

17. *Times*, July 10, 1878, p. 5.
18. *Times*, July 10, 1878, p. 5.
19. *Times*, July 10, 1878, p. 5.
20. *Times*, July 10, 1878, p. 5.
21. *Times*, July 10, 1878, p. 9.
22. See Hill, *History of Cyprus*; Kyriakos Demetriou, "Victorian Cyprus: Society and Institutions in the Aftermath of the Anglo-Turkish Convention, 1878–1891," *Byzantine and Modern Greek Studies* 21, no. 1 (1997): 1–29; Heinz A. Richter, *Ιστορία της Κύπρου* (Athens: Vivliopolion tis Estias, 2007); Andrekos Varnava, *British Imperialism in Cyprus 1878–1915: The Inconsequential Possession* (Manchester: Manchester University Press, 2009); Gail Ruth Hook, *Protectorate Cyprus: British Imperial Power before World War I* (London: I.B. Tauris, 2015).
23. Florence Nightingale, *The Collected Works of Florence Nightingale*, vol. 5 (Ontario: Wilfrid Laurier University Press, 2003), 320–21.
24. Ibid., 321.
25. Ibid., 320–24.
26. Ibid., 321.
27. *Diss Express and Norfolk and Suffolk Journal*, August 16, 1878, p. 6.
28. *Durham County Advertiser*, August 16, 1878, p. 3.
29. John Thain Davidson, *Cyprus: England's New Possession. Its Place in Bible History* (London: Hodder and Stoughton, 1878), 6.
30. Ibid., 58.
31. Stathis Gourgouris, *Dream Nation* (Stanford: Stanford University Press, 1997), 6.
32. See Petros Papapolyviou, *Η Κύπρος και οι Βαλκανικοί πόλεμοι. Συμβολή στην ιστορία του κυπριακού εθελοντισμού* (Nicosia: Cyprus Research Centre, 1997); Evanthis Hatzivassiliou, *Britain and the International Status of Cyprus, 1955–1959* (Minneapolis: University of Minnesota Press, 1997); Robert F. Holland, *Britain and the Revolt in Cyprus: 1954–1959* (Oxford: Oxford University Press, 1998); Mary Roussou-Sinclair, *Victorian Travellers in Cyprus: A Garden of Their Own* (Nicosia: Cyprus Research Centre, 2002); Varnava, *British Imperialism*; Hubert Faustmann and Nicos Peristianis, eds., *Britain in Cyprus: Colonialism and Post-Colonialism 1878–2006* (Möhnesse: Bibliopolis, 2009); William Mallinson, *Britain and Cyprus: Key Themes and Documents since World War II* (London: I.B. Tauris, 2011); Alexis Rappas, *Cyprus in the 1930s: British Colonial Rule and the Roots of the Cyprus Conflict* (London: I.B. Tauris, 2014); Tabitha Morgan, *Sweet and Bitter Island: A History of the British in Cyprus* (London: I.B. Tauris, 2015); David French, *Fighting EOKA: The British Counter-Insurgency Campaign on Cyprus, 1955–1959* (Oxford: Oxford University Press, 2015); Helen O'Shea, *Ireland and the End of the British Empire: The Republic and Its Role in the Cyprus Emergency* (London: I.B. Tauris, 2015); Hook, *Protectorate Cyprus*.

Chapter One

Empire of Intimacy

Throughout the pages of this book, I treat the concept of intimacy as a foundational theme that informs the manifestations of the colonial imaginary, be it the descriptions of special correspondents, the advertisements, or the editorials that appeared in the British press in the first years of the occupation. Intimacy presumes a closeness and a familiarity. It unfolds in a setting that is often understood to be private, allows for the expression of liberties, and is always connected to acts that make people familiar with one another. In the context of colonialism, I approach intimacy as the backdrop against which colonial discourse unfolded.

The most famous expression of colonial intimacy, in the case of Cyprus, can be traced, perhaps, in Lawrence Durrell's *Bitters Lemons*, which was published in 1957, three years before the British left the island. The book is essentially a memoir of Durrell's residence on the island from 1953 to 1956, immediately before and during the turbulent years of the Cypriots' anti-colonial insurrection (1955–59). If there is one persistent theme in the book, it is, undoubtedly, the subject of the Anglo-Greek amity. Throughout the book, Durrell keeps reminding his reader of two important facts that underline his relationship to the Greek-Cypriot natives: first, that he knows "more about Greece than they do";[1] second, that the so-called Anglo-Greek amity would never permit the Cypriots to rebel against their British colonizers. "We love the British. How could we Greeks not?" a taxi driver tells him, as he drives him to the northern town of Kyrenia in the book's opening chapter.[2] Similar hyperbolic and emphatic declarations of the deep bonds of love between the Greeks and the British are scattered throughout the book. "We all love the English," another character tells him once he settles in a small village on the slopes of the Pentadaktylos range. "There is nothing anti-English in Enosis," he adds, referring to the demand of the Greek-Cypriots for a union with Greece.[3] This love affair between the British and the Greeks persists, in Durrell's descriptions, even as the violent anticolonial insurrection, and the British draconian response to it, rages on. When Durrell decides to permanently depart from the island, due to the Cypriots' uprising, another taxi driver, on the way to the airport, talked to him about the love of Georgios Grivas Dighenis, the leader of the anticolonial insurrection, towards the British:

> "Even Dighenis," he said thoughtfully, "they say he himself is very pro-British." It was one of those Greek conversations which carry with them a hallucinating surrealist flavour—in the last two years I had endured several hundred of them. "Yes," he continued in the slow assured tones of a village wiseacre, "yes, even Dighenis, though he fights the British, really loves them. But he will have to go on killing them—with regret, even with affection."[4]

These are in fact Durrell's concluding words in *Bitter Lemons.* His insistence on the existence of an intimate bond between the British and the Greeks goes as far as depicting the anti-colonial rebellion more as a senseless civil war between two brothers rather than the reaction of the colonized against their colonizers.[5]

This brief literary example of the love affair between the colonizer and the colonized in Cyprus, is of course linked to the British relationship with ancient Greece, epitomized in the much-discussed British philhellenic tradition. Virginia Woolf captures this intimate bond well when she sarcastically writes, around 1906, that in Greece, "Germans are tourists and Frenchmen are tourists but Englishmen are Greeks."[6] As we will see, the British claim to the ancient Greek inheritance was indeed an important filter through which the relationship between the colonizers and the colonized was defined since the early years of the island's occupation. In fact, such relations of intimacy can be traced back to the "Cyprus Frenzy" of 1878 to such an extent that they determined key colonial practices.

Contrary to the study of colonialism as a top-down hegemonic phenomenon, understanding colonial intimacy presupposes a closer consideration of the actors involved in the overarching system of colonial relations: their writings, their friendships, their relationships to each other, their backgrounds, their family ties, etc. It also presupposes an understanding of the settings which allowed for intimacy to unfold. For instance, while British newspapers and magazines provided an important public and collective forum for the expression of colonial perceptions, their careful examination reveals a private intimacy: through their pages, individuals who were often well-acquainted with one another, corresponded, argued, agreed and disagreed. They put forth plans connected to imperial projects, they described personal experiences and, most importantly, they kept themselves informed about familiar figures and their involvement in events unfolding hundreds of miles away from home. It was simultaneously a private, a collective and an ideologically loaded space. Naturally, as it will become clear in the chapters that follow, other institutions also functioned as spaces that allowed for intimacy to be expressed in the frame of colonialism. The Royal United Service Institute, for example, founded in 1831, served as an equally important space where many of the same actors met and discussed their opinions. Its magazine bears testimony to the events that it hosted and, most importantly, to the intimate discussions that followed each lecture. The Royal Geographical Society (founded in 1830), as well as its counterpart in Scotland, and the Royal Society of Arts (founded in 1754), provided similar meeting grounds.

In a more specific context, intimacy, in this book, can be understood in two distinct ways. First, it refers, rather literarily, to the relationships between the people involved in the colonial project in Cyprus. Understanding the way in which special correspondents reported on the occupation of the island, for example, is contingent on examining their relationship to the military establishment: their own military background, their friendships with soldiers and officers, their coverage of other historical events—battles, explorations, missions, etc.—alongside the same military men. Their access to information and their opinion regarding the occupation of Cyprus was often dependent upon these intimate relationships. Second, intimacy refers to the way in which the announcement for the occupation of Cyprus led, quite astonishingly, to a collective frenzy in Britain that manifested itself in multiple ways: the publication of hundreds of articles and books, the composition of poems and songs, the staging of several theatrical performances, and of course, the preoccupation of British newspapers with the occupation (in news reports, editorials, advertisements, etc.). This love affair with England's newest colony, brief as it may have been, pointed to a deep passion, a desire to understand, or possess, the colony, to make it part of the British cultural, political and historical imaginary. These two points deserve further elucidation, as they set up the ideological background in which the chapters of this book unfold.

PERSONAL INTIMACY

At the very core of the colonial project there exists a conundrum. On the one hand, one of its most astounding characteristics is undoubtedly its sheer magnitude. As Robert Young informs us, "by the time of the First World War, imperial powers occupied, or by various means controlled, nine-tenths of the surface territory of the globe."[7] The British Empire alone "governed one-fifth of the area of the world and a quarter of its population." On the other hand, this vastness of the British Empire, both in terms of geography and population control, is countered by the equally astounding fact that the

Colonial office in London employed a staff of 113 civil servants in 1913 and "remained comparatively small" through the 1930s with a staff of around 400 people.[8] In other words, the vast British Empire was in fact managed by a very small number of bureaucrats. During the first decade of the twentieth century, this small department had the herculean task of sorting through about 40,000 to 50,000 incoming communications per year.[9] Apart from the obvious necessity of establishing bureaucratic mechanisms to control the colonies, these numbers point to a certain cohesiveness in the management of the Empire. Nowhere is this discrepancy between the vastness of the Empire and its management more pronounced than in the post of the high commissioner or governor of the colonies. As Stephanie Williams writes, in a period of 55 years (1857–1912), at the height of the Empire's rule, "there were over 300 governors, or lieutenant governors, administrators, high commissioners and presidents, as they were called, depending on where they served."[10] Most of the Empire's administrators were educated, even if briefly so, at Oxford or Cambridge Universities, and they were, as expected, white males.[11]

Even a cursory consideration of the early years of colonialism in the island of Cyprus points to an undisputable fact: if theory was drafted and discussed in London by a relatively small number of politicians and bureaucrats, the actual practice of colonial policy and ideology was put to the test by men who were well-acquainted with one another and who, in many cases, were intimately and closely connected. It also points to the peculiar state colonial administrators found themselves in during their careers. These administrators were obliged to travel around the world to serve an Empire that possessed a fifth of the world's geographical territories. Most of the high commissioners or governors who served in Cyprus, from the beginning of the British occupation until the country's independence in 1960, served in the colonies of the African continent. Many of them served in the Caribbean and in Asia. They traveled between the colonies—from Jamaica to Ceylon, British Guinea or Gambia—with frequent stops to London and with many titles bestowed upon them for their service to the Empire. They inherited each other's triumphs, as well as their blunders, they documented their positions and their actions, and their endeavors were frequently discussed by the bureaucrats of the Colonial Office in London or the Empire's political elites. The newspapers in London reported their achievements, or their slipups, in frequent correspondences and telegrams. In this sense, the journeys of these administrators may be paralleled with that of the "creole pioneers" in the eighteenth and nineteenth centuries, that Benedict Anderson so memorably describes in *Imagined Communities.* In recounting the journey of a young recruit who was called upon to assist in the administration of the Empire (a kind of "homo novus"), Anderson parallels his course to that of a religious pilgrim:

> Talent, not death, charts his course. He sees before him a summit rather than a centre. He travels up its corniches in a series of looping arcs which, he hopes, will become smaller and tighter as he nears the top. Sent out to township A at rank V, he may return to the capital at rank W; proceed to province B at rank X; continue to vice-royalty C at rank Y; and end his pilgrimage in the capital at rank Z. On this journey there is no assured resting-place; every pause is provisional. . . . And this: on his upward-spiralling road he encounters as eager fellow-pilgrims his functionary colleagues, from places and families he has scarcely heard of and surely hopes never to have to see. But in experiencing them as traveling-companions, a consciousness of connectedness ("Why are *we . . . here . . . together?*") emerges, above all when all share a single language-of-state.[12]

Unlike Anderson's Creoles, the British "fellow travelers" who were called upon to serve in the Empire's administrative positions around the globe, possessed a "consciousness of connectedness" even before the onset of their "pilgrimage." But the bonds that brought them together, as we will see, go far beyond the consciousness of belonging to the "greatest Empire in the world." If we can imagine the Empire's administrators as a family of pilgrims, which includes diplomats, military officers, soldiers, and special correspondents, in the late nineteenth century, one man functioned as a kind of archpriest who played a central role in this feeling of connectedness: Sir Garnet Wolseley. The fact that he had fought in every significant battle the Empire had launched against its enemies, earned him the title of "Britain's only General," a characterization that was extensively used by the British press at the time.

Wolseley's Circle

On July 8, 1878, Wolseley met with the Secretary of State for War, Colonel Frederick Stanley, who informed him that Her Majesty's government had appointed him "High Commissioner and Commander in Chief of Cyprus."[13] Wolseley accepted the new position but pointed out that "in carrying out a difficult job, [he] should be assisted by men in whom [he] placed the fullest confidence."[14] In his many years of service in the British army, Wolseley had formed a close circle of devoted friends, confidants and supporters who followed him around the globe. In military circles this exclusive "clique" was known as the "Wolseley Ring." As Halik Kochanski writes, the Ring originates in the Red River expedition of 1870 and "can be defined as a select group of officers personally chosen by Wolseley for their abilities and loyalty to serve on his staff on the various campaigns he commanded."[15] For his Cyprus appointment he brought with him his close friend Colonel Greaves as his chief of staff, Lt. Colonel Baker Russell as his assistant military secretary, Captains Hugh McCalmont and Lord Gifford as his aides de camp, Lt. Colonel Henry Brackenbury as his quartermaster general as well as Colonel Robert Biddulph and Captain J. F. Maurice. These were men who shared the battlefield with Wolseley and who appear often in his journals and his private correspondence. Greaves, Brackenbury and Russell had served under him in the Anglo-Ashanti wars of 1873–74, and McCalmont knew Wolseley from their service during the American Civil War.[16] Colonel Greaves, Wolseley writes of his chief of staff in his autobiography, is a "clever and determined man, of iron will and tireless energy. . . . Indeed no general could have had a better man at his side, and no one was ever better or more ably served than I was by him."[17] In his own memoir, Greaves describes Wolseley as a "lifelong friend."[18] In an 1879 letter to his wife, from the Transvaal, Wolseley describes Baker Russell as a "splendid fellow" and praises his achievements in the battlefield.[19] John Frederick Maurice is similarly characterized as "very hard working and abundantly clever";[20] "Lord Wolseley," reported the *Navy and Army Illustrated* in 1901, "became his warm supporter and best friend. . . . [W]henever Wolseley was called to active service Maurice was summoned to go with him."[21] Similar praise is generously given by Wolseley to most of his close associates.

One of the most interesting friendships in relation to the administration of Cyprus is that between Wolseley and Robert Biddulph. The two men exchanged many letters over the years sharing their views on some of the most important military campaigns of their times (such as the American Civil War and the Egyptian Campaign of 1882),[22] and they were both close to the Secretary of War, Edward Cardwell, during the latter's attempt to restructure the British Army.[23] In fact, in 1904, Biddulph would publish a book on the history of the Cardwell administration in which he praises his friend, Wolseley, as a brilliant general, deserving of his position and as the main reason behind the successful Ashanti Expedition (1873–74) and the Egyptian campaign of 1882.[24] Likewise, Wolseley, in his autobiography, describes Biddulph as one of the most able men he met during his career:

> Mr. Cardwell's private secretary was an old and highly esteemed comrade of mine, then Major, now General, Sir Robert Biddulph. A very able man, well read upon all military subjects, who had seen much active service in the Crimean, during the Indian Mutiny and in China, he was a man who thought, and was certainly one of the best soldiers all round I ever knew. He understood our Army thoroughly, and was fully alive to its backwardness in all that goes to make up military efficiency. He was of the outmost use to Mr. Cardwell at a time when that great War Minister had determined to abolish the Purchase System, to reform the Army and bring it up to a level with modern requirements. The Secretary of State for War who has a soldier of such ability and experience as his private secretary is indeed fortunate.[25]

Figure 1.1. "Cyprus: Sir Garnet Wolseley holding a reception in the Konak, Nicosia, at the Turkish festival of Bairam." ***Source: The Illustrated London News*, November 2, 1878.**

On July 22, at 7am, the HMS *Himalaya* arrived in Larnaca, Cyprus, with General Wolseley on board. Wolseley would take over the administration of the island from acting-governor Admiral John Hay, who had arrived a few days earlier with an impressive armada of British ships.[26] Also present in Cyprus was Walter Baring, who was sent from Egypt to assist Wolseley in the early days of the island's occupation; Baring was the younger brother of the famous governor of Egypt, Lord Cromer, whose administration and description of Egypt are classic examples of Orientalist thought and Victorian imperial attitudes.[27] Biddulph, who was given the task of commanding the Royal Artillery, was appointed civil commissioner of the island's capital, Nicosia.

About a year after his arrival in Cyprus, General Wolseley was summoned back to London in preparation of his command of the troops in the Anglo-Zulu War which was raging on; in 1879 he was proclaimed high commissioner for Natal, the Transvaal, and the neighbouring countries. Biddulph stayed behind to replace Wolseley as the island's second high commissioner. His tenure lasted for about seven years, until 1886. During his commandership of Cyprus, Charles Anthony King-Harman was appointed as his private secretary. In 1888, King-Harman married Biddulph's second daughter, Constance. After several colonial appointments that brought him to the Barbados, Mauritius and Saint Lucia, King-Harman eventually became governor of Sierra Leone, in 1900, and returned to Cyprus, in 1904, with Constance, to take over as the colony's sixth high commissioner.

Once again, Biddulph was one of Wolseley's closest friends and King Harman was Biddulph's son-in-law. That three of Cyprus's first high commissioners were so intimately acquainted should not be a surprise. These men were members of a select few who administered British colonies across the globe. Wolseley and Biddulph fought together, under the Queen's flag, in the most important battles of their times. They commanded officers that they knew well, who had also fought by their side and who faithfully followed them as they ascended to higher posts in the colonial hierarchy. Their families knew each other and spent time together. In 1903, in a letter to his wife, General Wolseley describes a meeting between himself, Biddulph and General Edward Bulwer:

> Edward Bulwer and one of his daughters . . . and Biddulph and a new young daughter dined here last night—what a dreadfully dull evening it must have been for the two girls to sit and listen . . . to four aged gentlemen tell old stories and laugh at events that took place long before the poor girls were even thought of.[28]

General Bulwer had served with Wolseley and Biddulph in the British Army during the Crimean War (1853–1856) and during the Indian Rebellion of 1857. His brother, Henry Ernest Gascoyne Bulwer, was also appointed, after Wolseley and Biddulph, to the post of high commissioner of Cyprus (1886–1892). Prior to his appointment to the highest post in Cyprus, Bulwer's powerful family connections allowed him to serve at several prestigious posts in the Empire. He served as secretary to his uncle, Henry Lytton Bulwer (Lord Dalling), the British Ambassador to the Ottoman Empire in Constantinople,[29] and moved on to posts in Trinidad and Dominica before becoming governor of Labuan, lieutenant governor of Natal (1875–80) and, eventually, governor of Natal (1882–85). Interestingly, the lieutenant governor whom Bulwer succeeded in Natal, in 1875, was none other than General Wolseley. The two men met each other at Durban on August 27, 1875,[30] and four years later, in 1879, they would meet again when Wolseley "was rushed from [Cyprus] to Natal where, during Bulwer's term in office, one bungle after another threatened the British army with defeat at the hand of the Zulus."[31] Consequently, Bulwer was placed under the orders of Wolseley[32] and in 1881, another administrator, Sir Walter Sendall, was initially appointed to the post of lieutenant governor of Natal as Bulwer's replacement. Due to political pressures, however, Sendall's appointment was canceled and Bulwer was appointed governor of Natal in 1882.[33] Ten years later the paths of the two men would cross again, when Sendall was called upon to replace Bulwer as governor of Cyprus. After the appointments of Wolseley, Biddulph and Bulwer, Sendall became the fourth governor of Cyprus in 1892 and kept the post until 1898.

If this brief description of the relationships between the high commissioners of Cyprus is somewhat confusing and latent with repetitions of names and places, it is precisely because British colonial administrators were part of a relatively small and intimate network and because their paths often crossed in their respective journeys from one colony to the next. The bonds that sustained the intimacy between these men were not merely expressed in their empathies or antipathies, their joint military expeditions, or their close family ties. In the case of Wolseley's circle, they are also documented in the dozens of books that Wolseley and his men published during their lifetime. Henry Brackenbury, George Greaves, Hugh McCalmont, John Frederick Maurice, to mention just a few of the military officers who were close to Wolseley, wrote several memoirs and autobiographies, or books on historical and military affairs. Their reputation was dependent on bearing testimony to each other's achievements, their greatness in battle, their strategic thinking, etc. In this sense, personal intimacy shaped both colonial practices (i.e., the treatment of natives or the implementation of laws) and colonial perceptions. The description of Cyprus and its people was, to a large extent, defined by the common perceptions of Wolseley and his men as well as by their friendships with newspaper correspondents.

Special Correspondents

"The 'news' in its modern sense," Roger Stearn writes, "was a nineteenth-century creation and the Victorian war correspondents were, with few arguable exceptions, the first."[34] The public's thirst for descriptions of the Empire's "exotic" dominions, for the obstacles that the British army encountered in the process of "civilizing the barbarians," for heroic battles and for the deeds of the Empire's heroes, created and sustained a culture of traveling journalists who were entrusted with the important task of entertaining and enlightening the British public, in brief telegrams, extensive reports, and sketches. As one of Rudyard Kipling's characters puts it in his 1890 novel *The Light that Failed*, correspondents were like gladiators, sent out to satisfy "the blind, brutal, British public's bestial thirst for blood."[35] Cyprus, of course, was not a war zone, yet public imagination was as intense and demanding.

The practical details in the life of a "special correspondent" are important in both understanding and researching colonial attitudes as propagated in the press of Victorian England. First and foremost, special correspondents had to travel to the field of action. To achieve this, they often depended on their military connections who secured safe and timely passages to the desired destinations around the globe. Military connections were important since they also were, as expected, the source of military information. Correspondents submitted their reports to newspapers in two ways: by telegram and by mail. The revolutionary invention of telegraphy in the nineteenth century radically modified the perceptions and the expectations of news reporting. Events were now being transmitted in incredible speed through telegrams sent from all corners of the earth. In the case of Cyprus, information sent by telegrams would be published in newspapers one to three days after the correspondents' transmission. The latter mode of communication was more complicated. Correspondents often mailed multiple letters, describing events in a certain number of days, which the newspapers published in serialized form. Hence, correspondences would often appear in consecutive editions of the newspapers, and they often included relatively "old" information, in the sense that the situations or opinions described in the letters might have significantly changed by the time the parcels reached England. The mail left with particular steamers and took the long journey to England, traveling from port to port and often collecting additional parcels of letters along the way. It was not unusual to see correspondents' letters dated two weeks prior to publication, or longer, depending on the journalists' location. Correspondents, wherever they were, had to be informed of the steamers' departures. They often had to rush to complete a report before the steamer sailed port. They were also careful about the kind of information they included in the letters sent via mail as opposed to telegrams. The former usually included impressions, descriptions, or objective opinions that could endure the test of time. The latter usually included hard facts.

Letters and telegrams were published anonymously, making the identification of the particular correspondent behind the report, in most cases, very difficult. Thankfully, there are multiple sources that could safely lead researchers to a rather confident identification of these correspondents. Their fellow journalists often reported their names and the newspaper they represented in their columns, particularly if they were established correspondents. They reported, for example, that a particular correspondent had departed for a certain location and he would soon be in a position to describe events from there. In other occasions, special correspondents published eponymous articles, stories, or books referring to the time they spent in a certain location. Apart from helping researchers identify the names of correspondents and the time they spent in a particular location, these works are often indicative of the correspondent's writing style and, in some instances, they include passages from the correspondences themselves (making identification much easier). Finally, the most important piece of information enabling the identification of correspondents is the indication included in the beginning of their report: letters or telegrams could have been submitted by "special correspondents," "occasional correspondents," "our correspondent," "a correspondent," etc. All the reports submitted by the journalists who were assigned with the particular task of covering the Cyprus occupation on behalf of *The Daily News* or *The Standard*, for example, included the sub-heading "from our special correspondent." *The Times*' reports were submitted by "our own correspondents." These are all reports that are cohesive and continuous: correspondents remind the readers, for example, of previous submissions, or they continue from where they left readers in their previous correspondences.

The response of the leading British newspapers, following the announcement of the occupation of Cyprus, was the immediate dispatch of special correspondents who would provide the English readers with firsthand accounts of the state of the island and its imminent transformation. Several newspapers, such as *The Times*, *The Daily News*, *The Daily Telegraph*, *The Standard*, *The Illustrated London News* and *The Glasgow Herald*, sent special correspondents to the island. The importance of their work in the forging of attitudes and opinions vis-à-vis the acquisition of Cyprus was such that when *The Times* decided to send one of their most senior correspondents to the island, Antonio Gallenga, who was at the time stationed in Constantinople, "Sir Austen Layard protested by wire against the selection of so dangerous a writer" and managed to cancel his appointment.[36] In the early days of the occupation, *The Times*' correspondent was St. Leger Algernon Herbert, who was also entrusted with the duty of serving Garnet Wolseley as his private secretary. Evaluating the significance of the new acquisition, *The Daily News* sent out Archibald Forbes, the most famous correspondent of his times,[37] whom Mark Twain would later describe as both "a soldier and war correspondent."[38] Edward Vizetelly, who would later publish one of the most detailed accounts of his experiences in Cyprus in the early days of the occupation,[39] was a special correspondent for *The Glasgow Herald*. John Augustus O'Shea, another established journalist, was the Cyprus correspondent for *The Standard*, and Samuel Pasfield Oliver worked for *The Illustrated London News*. As was the practice at the time, their reports from Cyprus were submitted anonymously.

The reports and telegrams of these correspondents, along with those of their colleagues stationed in other countries, provided a picture of astounding detail. They submitted reports from Alexandria, Constantinople, Brindisi, Malta, Larnaca and elsewhere, describing every minute detail that surrounded the occupation. Following adventurers, entrepreneurs, soldiers and administrators, they described the movement of troops and individuals, the status of their health, the names of people on each ship in the fleet bound for Cyprus, the landscapes and the people they met along the way. Once again, the level of detail in these correspondences is impressive. On July 13, 1878, *The Times* informed its readers that, since July 11, Walter Baring had the Sultan's firman announcing the British takeover of Cyprus, in his possession.[40] In its July 15 edition, it reported news concerning the occupation from three different locations, following the movements of three main characters in the Cyprus story (Wolseley, Baring, and Hay): from Larnaca, on July 12, it reported that the firman was read by Samih Pasha at the presence of Vice-Admiral Lord John Hay and that the "ceremony for hoisting the British flag" was scheduled for the very next day; from Constantinople, on July 13, it reported that Walter Baring was "instructed to remain in Cyprus until the arrival of Sir Garnet Wolseley and to engage interpreters for the service of the army"; and from Malta, on July 14, it reported that the British troops were expected to depart for the island the following Thursday, as soon as Wolseley arrived from England.[41] On July 16, from Brindisi, it reported that Wolseley and his staff departed for Malta at midnight on board the transport *Madura*.[42] On the 18th, from Malta, it reported that the ships *Himalaya*, *Tamar*, *Orontes* and sixteen other transports were scheduled to sail for Cyprus at 7.00 and that "forty-eight men of the 9th Bengal Calvary are sick through poisoning by carbolic acid, served instead of lime-juice from mislabelled boxes."[43]

These details, often insignificant, or even irrelevant, to the larger story of the acquisition, are indicative of the excitement the occupation had generated among the press and the public. The vast number of reports, articles, and editorials submitted to the press is indeed overwhelming if one considers that, prior to the occupation, the island was relatively unknown to the British public. Just a few days after the announcement of the acquisition of Cyprus in the Parliament, the editors of *The Graphic* described the public's fixation with Cyprus in the following way:

> A week ago most of our countrymen knew no more of Cyprus than that it was a large island somewhere in the Mediterranean Sea, and even persons with a taste for geography would have been puzzled—unless they were fresh from school—to decide offhand whether Crete or Cyprus lay most to the eastward. The promulgation of the Anglo-Turkish Treaty has in a moment raised the island from obscurity to celebrity. Able editors have been busily hunting up gazetteers and all over available sources of information, and so it comes to pass that at the present time the majority of what may be styled "the well-informed classes" know rather more about Cyprus than they know about Bedfordshire.[44]

In a similar tone, John Augustus O'Shea, *The Standard*'s correspondent, wrote from Bari, in Italy, on his way to Cyprus, that "a week ago and not one in a hundred of what we term in England the educated classes knew anything of Cyprus . . . except that it was a large island in the Levant, or eastern part of the Mediterranean. But what a change has come over us since!"[45] The "available sources," however, may have been reprinted and proliferated in incredible speed, but the information they provided was both limited and, in most cases, outdated. Hence, there was much room for the British imagination to construct a view of the island through the abundant rumors. When he arrived in Malta, the same correspondent wrote that "there are thickets of oak and firm and clumps of cherry, carob, and walnut there. But if it be but a legend! The truth is nobody knows anything about Cyprus. . . . The consequence of this universal ignorance about Cyprus is that there is a splendid field for the exercise of the imagination."[46] By the end of July, and particularly after the arrival of journalists on the island, details of its history, its geography, its demographics, the character of the natives, etc., were extensively presented to British readers, who were now becoming familiar, most of them for the first time, with the names of new cities, small villages, mountains, and rivers. Apart from reporting on the movements of Wolseley, events organized on the island, or important meetings, and apart from historical, geographical and anthropological descriptions, the newspapers were largely concerned with two main subjects: the restoration of Law (i.e., the transition from the Ottoman to the British legal system) and the healthiness of the troops in Cyprus. As we will see, the correspondents' reports, and particularly their position on the main issues that surrounded the occupation, were filtered through their personal allegiances and intimate relationships.

Like the military officers, correspondents too may be compared to Anderson's creoles: they were, in many ways, fellow travelers who followed the Empire's protagonists (most of all, the military officers), as they charted the events that shaped the present and future of British history. As Roger Stearn writes, the professional journalists "knew each other, formed friendships and rivalries and, sharing experiences, needs and values, enjoyed [a] robust yet sometimes sentimental camaraderie."[47] They also "aspired to the same social class as the [military] officers," "mixed up with them socially" during campaigns, and "enjoyed an "ill-defined quasi-officer status."[48] They usually identified with the military and "often eulogized senior officers, especially successful commanders."[49] This synergy between the army and the press, was largely a result of their common experiences during campaigns. Consider, for example, that, Archibald Forbes, John Augustus O'Shea, and three members of the Vizetelly family (Edward Henry, Ernest-Alfred and Henry-Richard) had all covered the Franco-Prussian War of 1870–71. O'Shea and Forbes were also together in the Siege of Paris and the Carlist Wars in Spain as was at least one member of the Vizetelly family.[50] St. Leger Algernon Herbert followed Wolseley during the Anglo-Egyptian War and Forbes was with him during the Anglo-Zulu War. In fact, apart from his high admiration for Wolseley, Forbes, in his books, often praises several of the officers who belonged to Wolseley's Ring: Evelyn Wood, Redvers Buller, George Colley, Herbert Stewart and others. As we shall see in the forthcoming chapters, when Wolseley's forces landed in the marina of Larnaca, in the southeast coast of Cyprus, along with the journalists who joined them to cover the occupation, many of the main actors in the unfolding drama of the island's colonization were already familiar with one another.

CULTURAL INTIMACY

The story of the British acquisition of Cyprus, in 1878, is nothing short of an astounding example of the Empire's collective frenzy over, and fixation with, its colonies. Beginning on July 8, when *The Daily Telegraph* leaked the news of the forthcoming occupation and forced the Disraeli government into an official confirmation of the island's acquisition, the largely unknown island of Cyprus became a household name for politicians, entrepreneurs, explorers, travelers, writers, publishers, scholars, university professors, and religious leaders. In the weeks that followed, hundreds of articles and editorials discussing the small and previously little known Mediterranean island made their appearance in British newspapers and magazines. Advertisements began to appear announcing the sale of authentic Cypriot products, confirming the plan of several businesses to open branches in Cyprus, or merely expressing an entrepreneur's desire to relocate to Cyprus. Capitalists saw what was akin to a gold rush in Cyprus, explorers assembled their gear, scholars began to compile whatever information they could find in consular reports and in encyclopedia entries.

A cursory look of the books published in England within the first three years of the British occupation of Cyprus would suffice to understand the magnitude of this fixation. Before the end of 1878, within weeks of the acquisition of the island, a significant number of books on Cyprus made their appearance, including: A. R. Saville's *Cyprus*, Frederic Henry Fisher's *Cyprus, our new Colony*, Phil Robinson's *Cyprus: its Physical, Economical, Historical, Commercial and Social Aspects*, Benjamin Harris Cowper's *Cyprus: its Past, Present and Future*, John Joseph Lake's *Ceded Cyprus: Its History, Condition, Products and Prospects*, E. Clarke's *Britain's New Colony: Cyprus, Past and Present*, Hamilton Lang's *Cyprus: its History, its Present Resources, and Future Prospects*, Rev. John Thain Davidson's *Cyprus: Its Place in Bible History*, Ernst Georg Ravenstein's *Cyprus: Its Resources and Capabilities with Hints for Tourists*, as well as several anonymous compilations including *Cyprus: its Value and Importance to England* and *Cyprus and Asiatic Turkey: a Handy General Description of our New Eastern Protectorate.*[51] These books essentially prepared the ground for the eventual descent of travelers, visitors or administrators to Cyprus, and primarily drew their information from consular reports, encyclopedia entries and from the few travelogues, historical, and archaeological books available in English. Some of the most quoted pre-occupation texts that these authors consulted were Giovanni Mariti's *Travels through Cyprus, Syria and Pales-*

tine (1792) and Ali Bey's *Travels in Morocco, Tripoli, Cyprus, Egypt, Arabia, Syria and Turkey* (1816).[52] Franz von Löher's *Cyprus, Historical and Descriptive*, was swiftly translated into English, in 1878, to satisfy the public's curiosity over the new colony.[53] As Löher's translator, Mrs. A. Batson Joyner, noted in her introduction,

> the sudden interest created by recent political events in everything relating to Cyprus, an island which, from its geographical position, seems destined to play no unimportant part in modern history, has rendered the appearance of Herr von Löher's narrative of his recent journeying through the length and breadth of that country extremely welcome.[54]

Another important source was Luigi Palma di Cesnola's *Cyprus: its ancient Cities, Tombs and Temples* which, as luck would have it, was published in London the previous year (1877) and which would have probably remained largely unnoticed had it not been for the British takeover of the island.[55] By 1880, the number of monographs and articles devoted to the island grew considerably. In 1879, the first two important travelogues made their appearance: Hepworth Dixon's *British Cyprus* and Samuel Baker's *Cyprus as I saw it in 1879.*[56] John Thompson's impressive collection of photographs from the island was also published in 1879 under the title *Through Cyprus with the Camera in the autumn of 1878*.[57] In 1880 two more travelogues, both written by female authors, were published in England: Lady Annie Brassey's *Sunshine and Storm in the East* and Esmé Scott-Stevenson's *Our Home in Cyprus*.[58]

Meanwhile, hundreds of lectures by travelers, historians, archaeologists, classicists, politicians, diplomats, military men, journalists and even priests, around Britain, were devoted to Cyprus. Some of these lectures were even accompanied by representations of Cypriot culture: a lecture on "Life in Cyprus and Syria," presented in Liverpool, in August of 1878, by the American Consul John B. Hay, for example, was accompanied by "Persons in Native Costume representing the Cypriot Boatmen, Judge, Effendi, Merchant, Moslem and Christian Woman of Bethlehem."[59] Indeed, one of the most fascinating manifestations of this interest in Cyprus was the speed with which it penetrated the British cultural sphere. Within the first few months of the occupation, several musical, and mostly comical, compositions on Cyprus began to circulate and were performed in venues across Britain. Though many of these were anonymous or were written by relatively unknown composers, such as the "Cyprus Galop" composed by a certain H. de Vaux, several of them were written by popular composers of the Victorian era. G. W. Hunt, who specialized in music-hall songs, and the famous Jolly John Nash, wrote songs on Cyprus.[60] Another Cyprus-inspired popular tune was Vincent Davies and Edwin V. Page's "What shall we do with Cyprus?," which was advertised under the heading, "a great questione solved in a humorous manner."[61]

The main medium through which the fascination with the island was expressed was, as expected, literature. Hundreds of poems—both sarcastic and patriotic—were published in British newspapers and magazines in the months following the occupation. Mrs. Joseph Fearn, author of a book of Christian poems titled *Plain Rhymes for Plain People or Verses on the Five Books of Moses* (1866),[62] composed an enthusiastic poem titled "Cyprus."[63] Fearn's poem bears the subtitle "A song for a (sigh-p'r-us)," which encapsulates the author's lament for the "poor" island ("There soundeth from Cyprus/a *sigh* for a song") as well as her view of the Empire as the protector and the savior of the wretched Christians from the Ottoman heathens ("Britannia! a nestling / Comes under thy shield / Where foes cease their wrestling— / Thy flag on the field"). The poem concludes with the following exalting stanza, describing the acquisition of the island and praising the Empire's colonial might:

> A gem of rich lustre
> Is added, I ween,
> To all the bright cluster
> Of England's fair Queen.[64]

Richard Henry Horne, best known for his epic composition *Orion* (1843), published the poem "Unknown Graves in Cyprus," in *Macmillan's Magazine*, which is basically a reminder of the island's connection with the story of Othello. Horne presents the transition from Ottoman to British rule as an opportunity to lament the death of the two lovers, Othello and Desdemona, and remember the villainy of Iago. The lovers' tomb might forever be lost, Horne suggests, but their story remains famous because someone wrote it down:

> While evening draws her funeral veil's soft pall
> Over this little isle of old renown,
> Till 'neath the sunrise gleams a snow-bright Swan
> Symbol of one who wrote your history.[65]

The evening's funeral veil—a reference to the ousting of the Ottomans from the island—is here contrasted to the symbol of the swan gleaming under the new sunrise. The hopeful symbol of the swan, of course, refers to Shakespeare ("one who wrote your history") and implicitly connects the story of the wretched lovers, which, in this allegorical reading, is also the story of the wretched isle, with the promising transition to British rule.[66] Britain's most famous literary export, Shakespeare, is presented here as saving the lovers' true story from oblivion as, by association, Britain's takeover signals the rewriting of the island's "true" history.

Other Cyprus-inspired works in the period 1878–1880, all written by relatively minor poets, were Eric Mackay's long poem "Pygmalion in Cyprus," John Conroy Hutcheson's "Ianthe, or, The Maiden of Cyprus," published in the *Family Novelist* in serialized form, and R. M. Hayley's "Berengaria: a Talk of Cyprus," also published in serialized form in *The Sheffield Daily Telegraph*. As one would expect, most of these poems and stories centered on mythological, literary and historical figures that were intimately familiar to British readers, such as Richard the Lionheart and Berengaria, Othello and Desdemona, Aphrodite and Pygmalion. But apart from the serious patriotic or applausive responses to the acquisition of Cyprus there were also several satirical or critical responses to the Beaconsfield government's plans in occupying the island. As Andrekos Varnava has argued, the satirical magazine *Punch* published several poems and cartoons ridiculing the conservative government's political positions on Cyprus.[67]

One of the most amusing episodes surrounding the Cyprus-related literary production appeared, in poetic form, in the July 26 edition of *The Morning Post*. An anonymous correspondent, writing under the heading "Rhyme and Reason," offered the British Poet Laureate, Lord Alfred Tennyson, a full cask of the island's wine if he could meet the challenge of finding a rhyme for "Cyprus."[68] Though Tennyson did not respond to the challenge, over the next few editions of *The Morning Post*, several readers rushed to the Laureate's rescue, submitting their own solutions to what the newspaper described as a "rhythmical puzzle." The Earl of Winchelsea and Nottingham wrote that the anonymous correspondent ought to send him "a dozen champagne (which, by the way, is the produce of the Cyprus grape transplanted)" since the Muse furnished *him* with the inspiration to compose the following couplet:

> Decidedly weak, but undoubtedly vip'rous
> Are the Peacemongers' sneers at the cession of Cyprus[69]

Apart from the word "vip'rous," other attempted rhymes to Cyprus included "Russ" (referring to Russia), "fuss," "nitrous," and "Pruss" (referring to Prussia). Apparently, the significance of these playful exchanges is founded on the premise that Cyprus has now become a household name and, as such, it deserves a rhyme in the English language. As *The Morning Post's* anonymous correspondent put it: "If held till a rhyme be found out that will fit, / We shall ne'er of our new acquisition be quit."[70]

In September 1878, the new ballet "Cyprus" was staged at the South London Palace. It was produced by the proprietor of the theater, John Joshua Poole, and it had a very successful run. According to the advertisements of the ballet, "200 beautiful ladies" and "13 principals and pantomimes" took part in it.[71] The stage design, accredited to Grieve and Son, included a large picture depicting a "Cyprian sea-port town, with [Mount] Olympus in the distance."[72] It also included a "peep" into the Ottoman Harem, in accordance to the Empire's orientalist and voyeuristic view of the East. The *Era*'s review of this depiction is exemplary of this treatment:

> Directly the curtain goes up, and we find ourselves given a peep into the Eastern harem, where beauties recline and other beauties waft them cool breezes with ostrich feather fans, we know that there is a treat in store. We do not care much for the savage-looking and dusky-skinned Pasha who owns all these beauties without deserving half a one; but our attention is very quickly arrested by the dancers, who use their veils, not to hide their loveliness, but to assist in forming with banners borne by other beauties a bower for the gyrations of other dancers, and for the marches of gorgeously clad Amazons. The eye is fairly dazzled by so much beauty, and we are sure that many in gazing upon it if they could persuade themselves that it was a truthful picture would be off to Cyprus to-morrow.[73]

The ballet afforded the opportunity to the British public to celebrate the occupation of Cyprus, which was understood by many to be a monumental achievement of the Empire, and at the same time to reenact the popular orientalist themes of the time. Apart from the savage Pasha and the harem, the production included a depiction of a scene where English sailors were taken prisoners and subsequently freed, black slaves (described as "masters of the acrobatic art"), Cypriot natives (who were "pleasant enough to look upon"), British marines, and the island's first High commissioner, Sir Garnet Wolseley.[74]

In October 1878, another Cyprus-inspired ballet, entitled *Aphrodite*, was produced by Charles Merion at the Metropolitan. The public's curiosity was such that, according to newspaper reports, the theater was so full that "sitting room was occupied in every part of the large Hall from the opening of the doors, and soon there was not even standing room."[75] The casting of the famous actor and dancer John D'Auban in the role of Prime-minister Beaconsfield, probably helped to boost ticket sales. The rather ambiguous plot of the story seems to be loosely based on *Faust*. The ballet opens in the Prime minister's study, who has fallen asleep on his chair and dreams of Cyprus. A character representing Mischief appears onstage and, as the scenery changes, the Premier follows her to Cyprus. There, Mischief informs the natives that the "Premier is coming to see England's new acquisition."[76] Beaconsfield appears riding on an elephant—despite the fact that elephants are not endemic to Cyprus—and is greeted enthusiastically by the natives and a single soldier representing the British Indian Army. Like the South London Palace's *Cyprus Ballet*, *Aphrodite* simply provided an excuse to showcase Victorian fantasies regarding the exotic and sensual colonial subject. As Michael Given has argued, for the British colonizers, the Greek goddess Aphrodite "was the key to hidden fantasies of lust and power, and the symbol of open perversion and degeneracy."[77] Indeed, apart from showcasing "the neat and prettily dressed girls of Cyprus," *Aphrodite* even featured the exotic Madame D'Auban holding "an apparently live snake in her hands."[78]

The theatrical companies' participation in the Cyprus frenzy was not limited to the production of exotic ballets. In several occasions, and particularly during the Christmas season of 1878, the island was used as a background in productions that had no historical or thematic connection to Cyprus. A pantomime of "Robin Hood: or, Harlequin, the Merry Men of Sherwood Forest," at the National Standard Theatre, presented "the spectacles of the Trysting Tree, Sherwood Forest, ballet of foresters and their maidens, a representation of the Isle of Cyprus, a pageant, illustrating the conquest of Cyprus by Richard Coeur de Lion, in 1195, and the marriage of Richard and Queen Berengaria."[79] The play included a "dioramic view of Famagusta Bay" and depicted "the Crusaders, in gorgeous costumes and brilliant accoutrements . . . descending the rocks by a rough circuitous passage, driving the wild inhabitants before them."[80] Interestingly, a few years later, in 1892, this conflation of the stories of Richard the Lionheart and Robin Hood would appear in Alfred Tennyson's play *The Foresters: Robin Hood and Maid Marian*, in which Friar Tuck, Robin's companion, suggests that "Richard is the lion of Cyprus" as "Robin is the lion of Sherwood."[81] But if this conflation had some vague historical foundation, other productions were simply capitalizing on the Cyprus frenzy of 1878. At Glasgow's Gaiety Theatre, many of the scenes in the staging of *Cinderella* took place in Cyprus.[82] The production of *Robinson Crusoe, or Friday and his Family Friends*, at the Royal Alexandra Theatre, in Liverpool, featured Crusoe heading to Cyprus "to keep out both Turks and Russians/And introduce our British institutions."[83] At Staffordshire's Hanley Theatre, a production of *Beauty and the Beast* featured Cyprus as the abode of the Beast,[84] and the staging of "Sinbad the Sailor" at the Hull Theatre Royal presented Sinbad going to a certain "Diamond Valley" in Cyprus to discover "heaps of treasure, amongst which is the diamond talisman, which enables its possessor to have every wish gratified."[85] The New Theatre Royal, in Leeds, presented the play *Turko the Terrible, or Harlequin Bluebeard the Great*, featuring a scene in Cyprus where an army of amazons was depicted alongside "Grenadiers, Highlanders, Ghoorkas, and Jack Tars" and Sir Garnet Wolseley unfurling the Standard.[86] Cyprus was also the "principal subject" in the production of *Harlequin Robinson Crusoe, or the Captain, the Cabinet, the King of the Cannibal Islands, and the Good Fairy Prosperity* at Cardiff's Theatre Royal.[87]

Once again, the occupation of Cyprus penetrated the British cultural sphere through an amalgamation between the exotic and the familiar; Britain's newest colony was featured, in other words, alongside historical, folk and literary heroes, who were familiar to the British public: Richard the Lionhearted, Robin Hood, Cinderella, Beauty and the Beast, Robinson Crusoe, and others. Myth, legend, literature and history were thus conflated in a rather burlesque representation of the island and its people. The extent to which these performances, poems, or compositions were willing to go in modifying British historical, literary or cultural paradigms to appropriate Cyprus in the Imperial imagination, points to the very intimacy—a kind of frenzied love affair—between the British popular imagination and the Empire's colonies. Naturally, as we will see in the next chapter, the reality in Cyprus was much harsher than what public imagination in Britain allowed. Though it took a little longer for this love affair to deflate in cultural representations, the realization that Cyprus was not a gold mine would eventually gain the day. Not surprisingly, it was entrepreneurs and capitalists who first had to come to terms with the vast distance that separated British fantasy from the harsh reality in Cyprus.

NOTES

1. Lawrence Durrell, *Bitter Lemons* (London: Faber and Faber, 1957), 114.
2. Ibid., 26.
3. Ibid., 105.
4. Ibid., 251.
5. Ibid., 141.
6. Virginia Woolf, *The Complete Shorter Fiction of Virginia Woolf*, ed. Susan Dick (San Diego: Harcourt Brace Jovanovich, 1989), 63.
7. Robert J. C. Young, *Postcolonialism: An Historical Introduction* (Oxford: Blackwell Publishing, 2001), 2.
8. Ronald Hyam, *Understanding the British Empire* (Cambridge: Cambridge University Press, 2010), 212.
9. Ibid., 212.
10. Stephanie Williams, *Running the Show: Governors of the British Empire* (London: Viking, 2011), 11.
11. For a more substantial consideration of the profiles of British administrators, in the period 1858–1966, see Anthony Kirk-Greene, *Britain's Imperial Administrators, 1858–1966* (New York: Palgrave, 2000).
12. Benedict Anderson, *Imagined Communities*, rev. edition (New York: Verso, 2006), 55–56.
13. Wolseley, *Cyprus 1878*, 4.
14. Ibid.
15. Halik Kochanski, *Sir Garnet Wolseley: Victorian Hero* (London: The Hambledon Press, 1999), 51.
16. Charles Rathbone Low, *General Lord Wolseley of Cairo: A Memoir* (London: Richard Bentley and Son, 1883), 341.
17. Garnet Wolseley, *The Story of a Soldier's Life* (Westminster: Archibald Constable and Co., 1903), 280.
18. George Richards Greaves, *Memoirs of General Sir George Richard Greaves* (London: John Murray, 1924), 121.
19. George Arthur, ed., *The Letters of Lord and Lady Wolseley 1870–1911* (London: William Heinemann, 1922), 45.
20. Ibid., 42.
21. "Major-General Sir Frederick Maurice," *Navy and Army Illustrated*, no. 236 (August 10, 1901): 513.

22. See H. Biddulph, ed., "The American Civil War: Contemporary Letters from Lt. Col. G.J. Wolseley," *Journal of the Society from Army Historical Research* 18, no. 69 (1939): 38–40; H. Biddulph, ed., "Egyptian Campaign of 1882. Contemporary Letters from Lt. Gen. Sir Garnet Wolseley," *Journal of the Society from Army Historical Research* 18, no. 70 (1939): 77–79; H. Biddulph, ed., "Canada and the American Civil War: More Wolseley Letters," *Journal of the Society from Army Historical Research* 19, no. 74 (1940): 112–17.

23. These are the famous "Cardwell Reforms" that took place between 1868 and 1874.

24. Robert Biddulph, *Lord Cardwell at the War Office: History of his Administration 1868–1874* (London: John Murray, 1904), 220–224, 247.

25. Wolseley, *A Soldier's Life*, 252–53.

26. Wolseley considered Admiral Hay one of the most incompetent, ignorant and egotistical men he encountered during his career. See Wolseley, *Cyprus 1878*, 9.

27. In *Orientalism*, Edward Said discusses extensively Lord Cromer's orientalist writings, as well as his tenure as British consul in Egypt. In fact, he considers Cromer as one of the most emblematic inheritors of "modern Western Orientalism: knowledge about and knowledge of Orientals, their race, character, culture, history, traditions, society, and possibilities." Edward Said, *Orientalism* (New York: Vintage Books, 1979), 38.

28. Arthur, *Letters of Lord and Lady Wolseley*, 410.

29. Lord Dalling was a fervent supporter of the Greek Revolution of 1821 and visited Greece in the Autumn of 1824. His book *An Autumn in Greece* documents his experiences there. See Henry Lytton Bulwer, *An Autumn in Greece* (London: John Ebers, 1826).

30. Kochanski, *Sir Garnet Wolseley,* 82.

31. Diane Weston Makrides, *Sendall in Cyprus, 1892–1898: A Governor in Bondage* (Nicosia: Moufflon Publications, 2014), 17.

32. Low, *Lord Wolseley of Cairo*, 362.

33. For details on the matter of Sendall's appointment and cancellation see Makrides, *Sendall in Cyprus*, 17, and for the firsthand account of Francis Reginald Statham, the controversial newspaper editor, see Francis Reginald Statham, *My Life's Record: A Fight for Justice* (London: Gibbings and Co., 1901), 88–93.

34. Roger T. Stearn, "War Correspondents and Colonial War, c. 1870–1900," in *Popular Imperialism and the Military: 1850–1950*, ed. John M. MacKenzie (Manchester: Manchester University Press, 1992), 139.

35. Rudyard Kipling, *Selected Works of Rudyard Kipling: The Light that Failed; Plain Tales from the Hills* (New York: Peter Fenelon Collier and Son, 1900), 50.

36. *Cornishman*, August 15, 1878, p. 3. Antonio Gallenga was very critical of the administration in his correspondences to *The Times*. On July 8, 1878, newspapers were reporting that "Savfet Pasha has requested Sir Austin Layard to consent to the expulsion of Mr. Gallenga from Constantinople, and the British Ambassador has referred the matter to the Consular Judge" (*Scotsman*, July 9, 1878, p. 5). Apparently, *The Times* decided that Gallenga's Cyprus appointment would solve the problem but, as it turned out, their correspondent was equally disliked by both the British and the Turkish governments.

37. Stearn, "War Correspondents," 141.

38. *Hartford Daily Courant*, November 18, 1881, p. 2.

39. Edward Henry Vizetelly, *From Cyprus to Zanzibar by the Egyptian Delta* (London: C. Arthur Pearson, 1901).

40. *Times*, July 13, 1878, p. 7.

41. *Times*, July 15, 1878, p. 5.

42. *Times*, July 16, 1878, p. 5.

43. *Times*, July 19, 1878, p. 5.

44. *Graphic*, July 13, 1878, p. 26.

45. *Standard*, July 18, 1878, p. 2.

46. *Standard*, July 23, 1878, p. 5.

47. Stearn, "War Correspondents," 142.

48. Ibid., 147.

49. Ibid.

50. For more information on the coverage of these correspondents see Mitchel P. Roth, *The Encyclopaedia of War Journalism, 1807–2010* (Amenia, NY: Grey House Publishing, 2010).

51. See A.R. Saville, *Cyprus* (London: Her Majesty's Stationery Office, 1878); Frederic Henry Fisher, *Cyprus, Our New Colony and what We Know about it* (London: George Routledge and Sons, 1878); Philip Stewart Robinson, *Cyprus: Its Physical, Economical, Historical, Commercial and Social Aspects* (London: William Clowes and Sons, 1878); Benjamin Harris Cowper, *Cyprus: Its Past, Present, and Future* (London: Book Society, 1878); John Joseph Lake, *Ceded Cyprus: Its History, Condition, Products, and Prospects* (London: Effingham Wilson, 1878); E. Clarke, *Britain's New Colony: Cyprus, Past and Present* (London: A.H. Moxon, 1878); Robert Hamilton Lang, *Cyprus: Its History, Its Present Resources, and Future Prospects* (London: Macmillan and Co., 1878); Davidson, *Cyprus*; Ernst Georg Ravenstein, *Cyprus: Its Resources and Capabilities, with Hints for Tourists* (London: George Philip and Son, 1878); The English Cyclopaedia. *Cyprus and Asiatic Turkey: A Handy General Description of our Eastern Protectorate* (London: Bradbury, Agnew and Co, 1878).

52. See Giovanni Mariti, *Travels Through Cyprus, Syria, and Palestine: With a General History of the Levant* (Dublin: P. Byrne, 1792) and Ali Bey, *Travels of Ali Bey: In Morocco, Tripoli, Cyprus, Egypt, Arabia* (London: Longman, Hurst, Rees, Orme, and Brown, 1816).

53. Franz von Löher, *Cyprus: Historical and Descriptive*, trans. A. Batson Joyner (London: W.H. Allen and Co, 1878).

54. Löher, *Cyprus*, v.

55. See Luigi Palma di Cesnola, *Cyprus: Its Ancient Cities, Tombs, and Temples* (London: John Murray, 1877).

56. See William Hepworth Dixon, *British Cyprus* (London: Chapman and Hall, 1879), and Samuel White Baker, *Cyprus as I Saw it in 1879* (London: Macmillan and Co, 1879).

57. Thomson, John. *Through Cyprus with the Camera in the Autumn of 1878* (London: S. Low, Marston, Searle and Rivington, 1879).

58. Annie Brassey, *Sunshine and Storm in the East: Or Cruises to Cyprus and Constantinople* (London: Longmans, Green, and Co., 1880), and Esmé Scott-Stevenson, *Our Home in Cyprus* (London: Chapman and Hall, 1880).

59. *Liverpool Mercury*, August 19, 1878, p. 1.

60. Hunt's song was advertised as "a comical-tropical-political-topical song upon Britain's new acquisition" (*The Era*, July 21, 1878, p. 13). Nash's composition was described as a "topical song" which found "plenty of admirers" (*The Entr'acte*, August 31, 1878, p. 5).

61. *The Standard*, December 26, 1878, p. 8. The song began with the following sarcastic lines: "Here's another little baby Queen Victoria has got,./ Another little Colony, although she has got a lot. / Another little Island, very wet and very hot,./ Whatever will she do with little Cyprus?" (in Varnava, *British Imperialism*, 285). As we will see, by 1879, when Page wrote these lyrics, the promising new colony had turned out to be hotter, poorer and unhealthier that the British had anticipated.

62. Mrs Joseph Fearn, *Plain Rhymes for Plain People or Verses on the Five Books of Moses* (London: William Macintosh, 1866).

63. *The Kent and Sussex Courier and Southern Counties Herald*, August 23, 1878, p. 7.

64. *The Kent and Sussex Courier and Southern Counties Herald*, August 23, 1878, p. 7.

65. Richard Henry Horne, "Unknown Graves in Cyprus," *Macmillan's Magazine* 38 (1878): 404.

66. In Shakespeare's *Othello*, Emilia, Iago's wife and Desdemona's attendant, is stabbed by Othello. As she is about to die, she says: "I will play the swan. / And die in music." She then proceeds to sing a song right before she dies. Apparently, Horne is playing with the idea that art overcomes death since the swan is presented here as singing at the tragic moment of death. The symbol of the swan underlines the notion that Shakespeare rescued the lovers' story from oblivion.

67. Andrekos Varnava, "Punch and the British Occupation of Cyprus in 1878," *Byzantine and Modern Greek Studies* 29, no. 2 (2005):167–86.

68. *Morning Post*, July 26, 1878, p. 6.

69. *Morning Post*, July 27, 1878, p. 5.

70. *Morning Post*, July 27, 1878, p. 5.

71. *Entr'acte*, October 5, 1878, p. 2.
72. *Entr'acte*, September 21, 1878, p. 5.
73. *Era*, September 29, 1878, p. 4.
74. *Era*, September 29, 1878, p. 4.
75. *Era*, October 6, 1878, p. 4.
76. *Era*, October 6, 1878, p. 4.
77. Michael Given, "Corrupting Aphrodite, colonialist interpretations of the Cyprian goddess," in *Engendering Aphrodite: Women and Society in Ancient Cyprus*, eds. Diane R. Bolger and Nancy J. Serwint (Boston: American Schools of Oriental Research, 2002), 426. Also see Yiannis Papadakis, "Aphrodite delights," *Postcolonial Studies* 9, no. 3 (2006): 237–50.
78. *Entr'acte*, October 5, 1878, p. 5
79. *Illustrated London News*, Vol. 73, December 21, 1878, p. 591.
80. *Illustrated London News*, Vol. 73, December 28, 1878, p. 610.
81. Lord Alfred Tennyson, *The Foresters: Robin Hood and Maid Marian* (London: Macmillan and Co, 1892), 125.
82. *Glasgow Herald*, December 16, 1878, p. 4.
83. *Liverpool Mercury*, December 21, 1878, p. 3.
84. *Staffordshire Daily Sentinel*, December 27, 1878, p. 3.
85. *Hull Packet and East Riding Times*, December 27, 1878, p. 5.
86. *Leeds Times*, December 28, 1878, p. 5.
87. *Cardiff Times and South Wales Weekly News*, December 28, 1878, p. 2

Chapter Two

Advertisements

"Cyprus! Cyprus! Cyprus!"

Nowhere does the excitement over the acquisition of Cyprus become more apparent than in the hundreds of advertisements, which appeared in the daily press. In fact, the widespread enthusiasm and the increase of advertisements concerning Cyprus were noted by the editors of *The Times* just a few days after the official announcement in the Parliament. In a description that is latent with a kind of romantic fantasy, which conflates capitalist ventures with archaeological and literary references, they noted:

> Already our advertisement columns show how far popular curiosity is aroused. Excursions contractors are announcing tours, bankers are opening agencies. Archaeologists will follow up the clue detected by General Cesnola. Maltese and Italians will establish hotels in cities where, General Cesnola declares, "no hotels of any description exist." Larnaca and Paphos and Famagosta will have their winter season to surpass Palermo and vie with Madeira; and Shakespeare's unfortunate reticence will be atoned for by diligence drivers and ciceroni, who will have discovered entirely to their own satisfaction where sojourned the famous Moor, and where it was Desdemona gasped out her innocent life.[1]

Indeed, as soon as the acquisition of the island was announced, and more than a week before Garnet Wolseley set foot on the island, entrepreneurs and fortune seekers rushed to jump on the Cyprus wagon. A retired military officer who had "recently conducted a business in London," writing to *The Times* as early as July 12, announced that he was "now desirous of connecting himself, with a Wholesale Firm, for the purpose of developing the same in the Island of Cyprus."[2] Similarly, an English engineer, who presented himself as a "good linguist and with business experience," announced, under the heading "Cyprus and Asia Minor," that he "would be glad to inaugurate or carry out any new understanding in these parts."[3] "A Gentleman of active habits," read another ad in *The Standard*, "with same capital, would be glad to meet with a partner to go out at once to see what facilities there may be for future business, commercial or otherwise."[4] Dozens of similar advertisements were submitted by individuals looking for any opportunity to invest in the new colony. Excitement was such, at the prospect of making one's fortune in Cyprus, that oftentimes, the reference to the island in these ads was completely irrelevant to the content of the announcement. A "Splendid Opportunity," wrote an advertiser desirous to let his space to a prospective renter: "a Shop, with Fittings complete, in a first class position in Hereford; must be Let, present occupier going to Cyprus. Rent low."[5] Wine merchants announced their intention to sell their wines in Cyprus and were looking for "any one of responsibility leaving for that island" to accompany their products.[6] A London-based mercantile firm, apparently perplexed about the most profitable opportunities in the island, announced that it was "now establishing itself in Cyprus" and that it was "prepared to treat for Steam-Ship, Insurance, Coal, and Wine Agencies and General Consignments."[7]

From Cyprus, Colonel White, whom Wolseley had appointed as civil commissioner of Larnaca, announced that he was looking for water and gas engineers to supply water from elevated grounds to "public fountains and to private houses" and to install public gaslights. Larnaca's population, the ad noted, was "expected to increase . . . rapidly," apparently as a result of the British occupation.[8] About a month into the occupation, the press was reporting that "within the past fortnight six companies, with an aggregate capital of four million one hundred and forty five thousand pounds have been registered for the purposes of carrying operations in connection with Cyprus."[9] Reporting on the West Midlands' iron coal and hardware trades, the *South Wales Daily News* similarly wrote that "the hardware trades of the town and district maintain the improvement lately reported. Energy is being directed towards the trade with Cyprus. Several merchants are sending out representatives, who take with them samples."[10] Some of the best-known British companies opened branches in Cyprus in an effort to supply administrators, soldiers, travelers, merchants and the local population with products and services that one would expect to find in the "civilised west."[11] One of the largest British firms to establish a branch in Cyprus was Henry S. King and Co. which "arrived with a great flourish of trumpets, representing a number of good manufacturing houses, and consigners of general merchandise."[12] In an ad published in *The Times*, a mere ten days after the announcement of the acquisition of the island, Henry S. King and Co. reported that "they have opened a branch house in Cyprus, under experienced management, and are prepared to offer facilities there in all departments of their banking, agency, supply and forwarding business."[13] Their Cyprus branch, they further added, "will undertake the disposal of consignments, the agency of merchants and manufacturers, and negotiations regarding the purchase and transfer of land, produce & c."[14]

The most exemplary advertisements in connection with the Cyprus frenzy of 1878, were, without a doubt, the dozens of items that were marketed as authentically Cypriot, or as indispensable sources in understanding the Empire's newest possession. Naturally, some of the most popular items were maps of Cyprus, since the British readers were largely unfamiliar with its location. In the first few weeks, newspapers advertised the publication of enlarged maps of Cyprus in their forthcoming issues, and publishers rushed to design new maps to accompany visitors or to satisfy the curiosity of the British public. The curiosity for the maps of the island was such that Lewis' Department Store, on Ranelagh Street, Liverpool, ran the following eye-catching ad in *The Liverpool Mercury*, in order to attract customers at its store:

> CYPRUS! CYPRUS!
> CYPRUS! CYPRUS! CYPRUS!
> CYPRUS! CYPRUS! CYPRUS!
>
> ——
>
> A BEAUTIFUL MAP
> GIVEN AWAY
> AT LEWIS'S, RANELAGH-STREET.
>
> ——
>
> CYPRUS! CYPRUS! CYPRUS! CYPRUS!
> CYPRUS! CYPRUS! CYPRUS![15]

W. H. Smith and Son, which was owned by the First Lord of Admiralty, William Henry Smith, one of the first English politicians to visit Cyprus during Wolseley's governorship, announced the publication of a new map "of Eastern Europe and Asia Minor, showing the changes effected by the Berlin Congress, and giving an enlarged map of Cyprus. On the back of the map is the full text of the [Anglo-Turkish] Treaty with an article descriptive of Cyprus."[16] Edward Stanford, who had designed one of the most accurate maps of London a few years earlier, announced, in August 1878, the publication of a new map of Cyprus "showing the present Administrative Divisions, the Roads and Ruins; the Names of Ancient Sites; Enlarged Plans of Famagusta, Larnaca, Limasol [*sic*], Kerynia, and the Ruins of Salamis."[17] In its July 11 issue, *The Daily News* published another map by Stanford "in order that [its] readers may realise the position of the island Cyprus, which has been conditionally added to England."[18] James Wyld, the distinguished cartographer and former member of the Parliament, also designed a map of Cyprus, the press announced.[19] Several newspaper articles referred to an earlier map of Cyprus designed by the well-known German cartographer Dr. Heinrich Kiepert, which was made popular from its inclusion in Cesnola's book on Cyprus.[20]

Before the end of the year, publishers rushed to announce the publication of new books on the subject of Cyprus, looking to capitalize on the general enthusiasm over the acquisition of the island. A number of books—including Frederic Henry Fisher's *Cyprus: our New Colony and What we Know about it*; Rev. John Thain Davidson's *Cyprus: England's New Possession. Its Place in Bible History*; Phil Robinson's *Cyprus and Sokotra: the New Colony and the New Field for Missionary Enterprise*; John Joseph Lake's *Ceded Cyprus: Its History, Condition, Products and Prospects*; the English Cyclopaedia's *Cyprus and Asiatic Turkey: A Handy General Description of our New Eastern Protectorate*; and Franz von Löher's *Cyprus, Historical and Descriptive*, translated by Mrs. A. Batson Joyner—appeared, in astounding speed, before the end of the year. Apart from introducing the unaware public to the new and hitherto unknown colony, these publications also aimed to serve as guides to the many travelers and tourists who were projected to visit the island, as well as for the soldiers and administrators who were expected to serve in Cyprus.

A number of companies began to advertise their products as indispensable for any traveler to Cyprus. Oetzmann and Co., a furniture company founded in 1848 that "catered to smaller budgets,"[21] accompanied their ad with a line from *The Daily News*: "Advices from Cyprus state that everything is enormously dear there."[22] Oetzmann and Co. also named one of their furniture "The Cyprus"; a stand which, as they explained, could be used for books, newspapers and music sheets.[23] Mapping and Webb, one of the best known firms specializing in silverware and other household items, suspecting that a vibrant hotel industry would now flourish in Cyprus, announced that they were prepared to "supply instantly any quantity of Table Cutlery, Spoons, Forks and other Plated Ware, Bedsteads, Bedding & c. suitable for hotels, at the lowest wholesale prices."[24] For the convenience of travelers to Cyprus, iron bath chairs were advertised, "specially adapted for tropical climates" at the price of 15 pounds (about 1,665 British pounds by today's standards).[25]

A few days into the occupation of Cyprus, correspondents, editors and other scholars began an intense discussion over the infectious diseases on the island, in response to what seemed like an outbreak of fever in Cyprus; some claimed that the fever was a result of malaria and others, such as the former British Consul to Cyprus, Hamilton Lang, that it was merely heatstroke. Capitalizing on the dangers of infectious diseases and the first reports of unhealthiness on the island, several companies promoted their products with direct references to Cyprus. The popular Morrison's Vegetable Universal Medicine, whose pills promised to purify the blood and cure every kind of disease, announced that a depot would soon be established on the island, and Keating's insect powder was marketed as imperative "before you go to Cyprus."[26] Another ad read that "no one should think of visiting this island without providing himself with a stock of Kaye's Worsdell's Pills which, by strengthening the system, will enable him to defy fevers and all complaints likely to attack him."[27] James Crossely Eno, the inventor of the famous "Eno's fruit salt," submitted an ad which exaggerated the unhealthiness of Cyprus:

> THE TOPIC of the DAY
> THE OCCUPATION of CYPRUS
> INCREASE OF FEVER at NICOSIA
> THE fever here is increasing. Captain Rawson, the acting commandant is down with it, and also Captain Hill of the Goorkas, and about a dozen of his company. Unquestionably Nicosia is extremely unhealthy.[28]

"To Europeans residing in Cyprus," the ad continued, Eno's Fruit Salt is "an indispensable necessary [*sic*]." Apart from the obvious triggering of paranoia to sell their product, Eno's ad attempted to convince potential travelers of the unhealthiness of the island, by referring to particular and, by then, well-known individuals in the Cyprus saga: Captain Harry Rawson, the commander of the HMS *Minotaur* and Captain Hill of the Goorkas, the Nepalese soldiers serving in the British-Indian army. Most importantly, these ads underline the intimate connection between capitalist enterprises and the colonial economy: there was an entire industry in Britain whose economic survival was dependent upon the designation of colonies as dirty, unhealthy and undeveloped. Any contact with these colonies was bound to infect European blood but, luckily for them, scientific advances provided several antidotes to these poisonous settings.

Fabrics were perhaps the most aggressively advertised Cyprus products in British newspapers. By 1879, dozens of clothiers around Britain presented their fabrics as authentically Cypriot or merely gave the name of "Cyprus" to specific pieces of clothing. J.P. Smith and Sons, in Dundee, offered "Summer overcoats in all the newest materials and shades" and presented "the new Cyprus mixture."[29] Dublin's Todd, Burns and Co. offered "Cyprus Herringbone Calico," "especially made for [them] and not to be had elsewhere."[30] The Cole Brothers, in Sheffield, similarly offered "Wool beiges, Foule Cachemires [*sic*], and Cyprus Clothes."[31] S. Prowse, in Gloucester, announced the arrival of its autumn ties "of the latest fashion: Cyprus, Sefton, Advance, Whitehall, & c."[32] The Carter Brothers of Stockton on Tees, advertised their "Cyprus and Madras muslin curtains,"[33] Samuel Wright, a hosier and shirt maker in Ipswich, announced "The New Patent Collars: The 'Cyprus' and 'Allies,'"[34] and London's Aker and Crisp offered "Cyprus cloth, Cashmeres, and other Materials for Autumn wear."[35]

Apparently, the name of Cyprus was used in order to evoke a certain exoticism that was now accessible to English consumers. But if the use of the island's name for marketing purposes had a certain basis for the clothing industry, since Cyprus exported cotton and wool even before the British occupation, in several other cases, it was simply used in a purely opportunistic way. The long list of items that appeared in 1878, immediately following the occupation, incudes cigarettes, advertised by the manufacturer Joseph Grunebaum, who claimed that "Cyprus grows the finest tobacco" and that "Cyprus cigarettes surpass all others in delicacy of aroma."[36] Willway Bicycles in Bristol named their new model "The Cyprus" and described it as "a thorough good roaster."[37] Similarly, W. Wells Stationery, advertising in *The Salisbury Times*, offered their new "Cyprus Note" paper-design along with the accompanying Cyprus envelopes. Two weeks after the official announcement of the occupation, Piesse and Lubin, whose scents were infamously used by the Cambridge Anthropological Expedition of 1901 to test the sense of smell in the natives of Torres Straits,[38] presented their new perfume under the name "Eau de Chypre":

> This is an ancient perfume from Cyprus. During the national career of Egypt, Persia, Greece, and Rome, the island of Cyprus was the resort of the elite, learned, and refined. It was at the time of the Crusades, when Richard I of England assumed the title of King of Cyprus and that the famed Eau de Chypre was introduced into Europe, the composition of which is yet preserved in the archives of the laboratory of Piesse and Lubin. Those who are curious in ancient perfumes can be gratified at 2 New Bond-street, London.[39]

"Eau de Chypre" was, of course, a much older concoction, made in France; in fact, George William Septimus Piesse, who had partnered with the famous French perfumer Pierre Francois Lubin to form Piesse and Lubin, includes the chemicals necessary to make "Eau de Chypre" in his 1857 book, *The Art of Perfumery and Method of Obtaining the Odors of Plants* (almost two decades before the occupation of Cyprus). In this book, the description of the scent is not nearly as historically loaded as his 1878 promotion. "This is an old fashioned French perfume," he simply writes, which is "presumed to be derived from the *Cyperus esculentus* by some, and by others to be so named after the Island of Cyprus."[40] His 1878 advertisement of the perfume succinctly captures the colonial narrative connected with the occupation of Cyprus: the repossession of the island is at the end of a lineage that connects ancient wisdom with the contemporary European civilization, *through* the mediation of Richard the Lionheart. Hence, the perfume's secret recipe is passed on from the ancients, to Richard I, and, in modern times, "is preserved, in archives of the laboratory of Piesse and Lubin." Piesse and Lubin were not the only perfumery that attempted to capitalize on the excitement caused by the occupation. One of the most celebrated perfumers of London,

Eugene Rimmel—who had previously published his well-known *Book of Perfumes*[41] and his *Recollections of the Paris Exhibition of 1867*[42]—announced, in August 1878, the creation of a new perfume, "Cyprus Flowers," which was "culled in Paphian bowers" and was "sweet and durable."[43] Rimmel, whose other exotic fragrances, available in 1878, included "Star of India," "Ihlang-Ihlang" and "Vanda," alluded, of course, to the connection of the new colony to the ancient Greek goddess Aphrodite and her birthplace of Paphos.

One particularly interesting story that emerges through the pages of the British press, and captures both the initial frenzy over the Empire's new acquisition, as well as the subsequent disappointment, is that of Thomas Cook, the most popular travel agent of Victorian England. Since the 1840s, Cook and his son, John, organized "managed, controlled and relatively cheap" excursions to the exotic lands of the Empire.[44] When the news of the Cyprus acquisition broke out, Thomas Cook and Son issued an announcement, on July 17, under the title "Cyprus Under British Rule," in which they stated that they were "preparing programmes for their Autumnal Tours to Greece, Turkey, the Levant, Palestine, Egypt & c., and will combine with their usual arrangements the best possible facilities for visiting Cyprus."[45] The following day they issued yet another announcement, under the same title, explaining that they were "dispatching one of their chief representatives to Cyprus, for the special purpose of sending home reliable information as to the points of interest to Tourists, Merchants, and others, and as to the facilities for traveling through the Island."[46] They also explained that the representative's report was expected around mid-August but, in the meantime, they were "prepared to book passengers through to Cyprus" for an October tour that would be led by John M. Cook himself. They continued to run the same reassuring ad in major newspapers until mid-August, when they corrected the expectation for the representative's report, indicating that "his report may be expected shortly."[47] The report was eventually submitted in late August and, in early September, Cook announced that it was "not advisable to conduct a party of Tourists before the spring. Two medical gentlemen who went to report upon the health of the island are seriously ill."[48] Soon afterwards, the Thomas Cook representatives' report was published and it was quite damning. The man who was sent to investigate the conditions in Cyprus, on behalf of Thomas Cook, was Alexander Rostovitz, a resident of Cairo and John Cook's "right hand man on the Nile";[49] he was accompanied by Dr. M'Lean, who was responsible for ascertaining the healthiness of Cyprus. The investigation took place from August 6 to August 20 and the final report was widely circulated in the British press in September. From June to October, Rostovitz and Ma'Lean noted, "fevers and diarrhoea abound" on the island, due to "the excessive heat and great humidity, the bad quality of the water, and the storms."[50] The Cypriots "live upon vegetables and fruits, rarely eating meat," they drink plenty of raki and "sleep in the open air." Only eight doctors are to be found on the island and five of them are located in Larnaca. There are no roads, no regular postal communication, and the saddles the locals use on their mules are "impracticable for Europeans." There are also no respectable hotels to be found though there are plenty of reptiles and insects. Referring to the Europeans who rushed to Cyprus, believing that they would make a fortune, Rostovitz writes:

> But I fear that many people will repent of their haste, and have their illusions dispelled by suffering great losses. Thus also will suffer the hosts of speculators who flock from all parts, thinking to find a new California, and, after a time, lack even the means to go back. The country is poor, and, there being no roads, industrial enterprise and agriculture are very difficult, if not impossible, and the necessary improvements cannot be made all at once.[51]

The report caused quite a stir both in political and journalistic circles. *The Freeman's Journal* opined that "all controversy respecting the merits or demerits of Cyprus as a happy hunting ground for the irrepressible tourist has been closed by the admirable pamphlet of Messrs. Thomas Cook and Son."[52] Paraphrasing much of the information already reported in *The Times*', the journal praises Rostovitz and M'Lean for "disregarding all devices of the special correspondent for elaborating an expected narrative."[53] Though the question of Cyprus's unhealthiness was raised in the British Parliament as early as July 15,[54] Cook and Son's commissioned report added much fuel to the critics of the Disraeli government over the treaty with Turkey. As the Scottish journalist William Fraser Rae wrote in 1891, "this pamphlet attracted the attention of the public, and it received special notice from members of the House of Commons. . . . It also served as a work of reference to persons in high official position who afterwards paid a visit to the island."[55] Many years later, Basil Stewart, a travel writer who worked as an assistant engineer in the Cyprus Government's Railway in the 1900s, wrote that he read a copy of the report in the Guildhall Library, in London. Though he misattributes the author of the report as Thomas Cook himself, he recalled its contents quite vividly: it spoke of the island "as anything but a health resort, with the result that Cook has not since ventured to exploit the island for the benefit of the tourist. It is, without doubt, the most unhealthy place in the Mediterranean."[56] Indeed, Thomas Cook and Son did not get to realize any grand tourist projects in Cyprus, but they did use the island as a stop-over in their tours of the eastern Mediterranean.

NOTES

1. *Times*, July 22, 1878, p. 9.
2. *Times*, July 16, 1878, p. 3.

3. *Times*, July 16, 1878, p. 3.
4. *Standard*, July 18, 1878, p. 8.
5. *South Wales Daily News*, August 9, 1878, p. 3, and *Gloucester Citizen*, July 26, 1878, p. 3.
6. *Times*, July 16, 1878, p. 3.
7. *Times*, July 16, 1878, p. 3.
8. *Times*, September 14, 1878, p. 1.
9. *Evening News*, August 13, 1878, p. 3.
10. *South Wales Daily News*, August 9, 1878, p. 4.
11. As Edward Vizetelly writes, in Larnaca, which was, at the time of the occupation, considered the center of political and economic activity, a number of "principal English firms . . . rushed off to Cyprus to make their fortunes—Henry S. King and Co., F.O Harvey and Co., Truefitt from Bond Street, Williams from Constantinople, Janion from Liverpool, and Zealous Zachariah Williamson, a smart up-to-date Constantinopolitan Jew" (Vizetelly, *From Cyprus to Zanzibar*, 8).
12. Ibid., 9.
13. *Times*, July 18, 1878, p. 1.
14. *Times*, July 18, 1878, p. 1. Soon after it established its Cyprus branch, Henry S. King and Co. would be involved in a legal dispute with the editor of the first Cypriot newspaper. *Kypros-Cyprus* was printed in both Greek and English at the printing house of Henry S. King and Co. and it had two editors: Theodoulos Constantinides, a Cypriot teacher who returned to Cyprus from Alexandria in the first days of the British occupation, and Archdale Stuart Palmer, a Cambridge graduate and one of the many Englishmen who looked to make their fortune in Cyprus. Palmer's daughter, Eva Mary Palmer, would later marry Anthony King Harman's and Constance Biddulph's son, Captain Robert Douglas King-Harman. When Constantinides and Palmer encountered financial difficulties with their newspaper business, the latter mortgaged it with Henry S. King and Co., apparently without Constantinides's knowledge. Eventually, Henry S. King and Co. confiscated the premises of the newspaper and continued to print the English edition with its own editorial staff. Wolseley describes Palmer in his journal as "a double-distilled English vagabond" (Wolseley, *Cyprus 1878*, 111). For a more thorough historical account of the first newspaper in Cyprus, see Andreas Sophocleous, *Συμβολή στην Ιστορία του Κυπριακού Τύπου, Τόμος Α' (1878–1890)* (Nicosia: Ekdotikos Oikos Nicolis, 2008).
15. *Liverpool Mercury*, August 29, 1878, p. 1.
16. *Bath Chronicle and Weekly Gazette*, July 25, 1878, p. 6.
17. *Times*, August 14, 1878, p. 15.
18. *Daily News*, July 11, 1878, p. 3.
19. *Daily Express*, August 30, 1878, p. 7.
20. Due to the territorial readjustments decided during the Berlin Congress, delegates asked Heinrich Kiepert to "assist in drawing the maps which are to form an appendix to the [Berlin] protocol." (*Western Daily Press*, July 10, 1878, p. 8).
21. Deborah Cohen, *Household Gods: The British and Their Possessions* (New Haven: Yale University Press, 2006), 52.
22. *Times*, August 14, 1878, p. 15.
23. *Graphic*, September 28, 1878, p. 28.
24. *Times*, August 14, 1878, p. 15.
25. *Times*, September 6, 1878, p. 1.
26. *Times*, August 14, 1878, p. 15.
27. *Times*, August 14, 1878, p. 15.
28. *Times*, September 25, 1878, p. 12.
29. *Evening Telegraph*, April 2, 1879, p. 1.
30. *Daily Express*, December 10, 1879, p. 4.
31. *Derbyshire Times*, September 17, 1879, p. 1.
32. *Citizen*, September 9, 1878, p. 4.
33. *Northern Evening Mail*, May 31, 1879, p. 4.
34. *Ipswich Journal*, November 23, 1878, p. 2.
35. *Graphic*, October 19, 1878, p. 2.

36. *Times*, September 25, 1878, p. 12.

37. *Western Daily Press*, September 18, 1878, p. 1.

38. See Alfred Cort Haddon, *Reports of the Cambridge Anthropological Expedition to Torres Straits: Physiology and Psychology* (Cambridge: Cambridge University Press, 1901), 182–85. Also see Martin N. Nakata, *Disciplining the Savages, Savaging the Disciplines* (Canberra: Aboriginal Studies Press, 2007).

39. *Times*, July 23, 1878, p. 14.

40. George William Septimus Piesse, *The Art of Perfumery and Method of Obtaining the Odors of Plants* (Philadelphia: Lindsay and Blakiston, 1857), 137. In subsequent editions of his book, Piesse incorporated the historical narrative that first appeared in 1878 under the description of "Eau de Chypre."

41. Eugene Rimmel, *The Book of Perfumes* (London: Chapman & Hall, 1865).

42. Eugene Rimmel, *Recollections of the Paris Exhibition of 1867* (London: Chapman and Hall, 1868).

43. *Times*, August 14, 1878, p. 15.

44. Michael Colin Hall and Hazel Tucker, *Tourism and Postcolonialism: Contested Discourses, Identities and Representations* (London: Routledge, 2004), 173.

45. *Times*, July 17, 1878, p. 8.

46. *Times*, July 18, 1878, p. 1.

47. *Times*, August 10, 1878, p. 8.

48. *Sunderland Daily Echo and Shipping Gazette*, September 5, 1878, p. 3.

49. Andrew Humphrey, *On the Nile in the Golden Age of Travel* (Cairo: The American University in Cairo Press, 2015), 124.

50. *Times*, September 14, 1878, p. 7.

51. *Times*, September 14, 1878, p. 7.

52. *Freeman's Journal and Daily Commercial Advertiser*, September 24, 1878, p. 5.

53. *Freeman's Journal and Daily Commercial Advertiser*, September 24, 1878, p. 5.

54. HL Deb 15 July 1878 vol. 241, cols. 1433–6.

55. William Fraser Rae, *The Business of Travel: A Fifty Years' Record of Progress* (Leipzig: Bernhard Tauchnetz, 1892), 158.

56. Basil Stewart, *My Experiences of the Island of Cyprus* (London: Skeffington and Son, 1906), 37.

Chapter Three

St. Leger Algernon Herbert and *The Times* of London

The Times' correspondent, St. Leger Algernon Herbert, was the son of a Royal Navy commander, Frederick Charles Herbert. After graduating from Oxford, in 1874, he traveled to Canada and worked as private secretary to Lord Dufferin, the governor-general, who recommended him to Garnet Wolseley. As several newspapers announced, in July 1878, "Sir Garnet Wolseley has taken as his private secretary to Cyprus Mr. St Leger Herbert, . . . a very smart young gentleman indeed, as well as an Oxford first-class man, and thoroughly up to his business."[1] Out of the men the general selected, Herbert was the only "new appointment."[2] His performance, however, impressed Wolseley and, the following year, he kept him as his private secretary when he was appointed high commissioner of South Africa. While accompanying Wolseley's close friend, General Herbert Stewart, in the Khartoum expedition, as a special correspondent for *The Morning Post*, he was shot dead in the Sudan, on January 19, 1885, at the age of thirty-five.[3]

In Cyprus, Herbert was Wolseley's right-hand man, his errand boy, and served as clerk in the newly formed Legislative Council.[4] He was sent to inquire about every kind of affair and report back to the high commissioner. He also followed Wolseley in his daily excursions and entertained important guests, like the Brasseys, when they arrived on the island. Wolseley describes him as "an admirable secretary" who has bad handwriting but "is very clear-headed and has a rough but good knowledge of the principles of English law."[5] Indeed, his *Times*' correspondences from Cyprus testify to his good knowledge of the Law and the problems that emerged in the transition from Ottoman to English Law. Archibald Forbes, his fellow correspondent, remembers his dispatches from Cyprus, in an article published a month after his death in the Sudan, "as faultless in style as they were brilliant in scholarship."[6] Most importantly, he also recalls that, though Herbert was "rather a sybarite" when he arrived in Cyprus, his association with soldiers in Wolseley's camp gave him the "fighting fever, and thenceforward there was no more ardent aspirant to participate in the joys of war."[7] In fact, a few years later, Forbes continues, Herbert volunteered as a private in the Mounted Infantry, during the Egyptian campaign of 1882, which was led by Wolseley. His claim is corroborated by Wolseley himself who, in a letter to his wife, on September 11, 1882, a day before the Battle of Tel el-Kebir, writes that Herbert asked to be part of the action:

> St. Leger Herbert has arrived, and I told him the only thing I could do for him was to attach him as a private to the mounted infantry, where he should have every opportunity of being shot afforded to him. The last time I saw him he had managed to find a private soldier's red jacket and was then starting to join the Corps. He is a very plucky fellow; I wish I had a thousand like him. [8]

Considering Wolseley's well-known despise for newspaper correspondents, it may seem peculiar that he would hire St. Leger Herbert as his private secretary for the Cyprus expedition. Just a few years before his Cyprus appointment, Wolseley had published *The Soldier's Pocket Book*—a kind of panacea for all practical questions military men might have in the field—where he famously describes newspaper correspondents as "newly-invented curses to armies,"[9] a "race of drones," and an "encumbrance to an army; they eat the rations of fighting men, and do no work at all." "Their numbers," he suggests, "should be restricted as much as possible."[10] But in a quite revealing passage in the same manual, he also suggests the following:

> An English general of the present day is in the most unfortunate position in this respect, being surrounded by newspaper correspondents, who, pandering to the public's craze for "news," render concealment most difficult. However, the post and telegraph will always be in the general's hands, so he can lay an embargo on the mails whenever he wishes it, without its being known for a long time; or he can, by spreading false news among the gentlemen of the press, use them as a medium by which to deceive an enemy. [11]

Wolseley's suggestion points to his much-discussed desire to assume full control of the projects he was entrusted with; at the same time, it sheds light on the cunning strategy—which is also rather contemporary—to use the press as "a medium" to achieve military objectives. This suggestion eventually developed into standard practice for Wolseley, who did not only use the media to deceive an enemy, but he essentially conceived what, more than a century later, the American Department of Defense would promote under the label of "embedded journalism." As some of Wolseley's contemporaries had noted, the general often worked behind the scenes in order to secure that members of his immediate circle would become correspondents for major newspapers. In May 1879, *The Worcestershire Chronicle* wrote that "no [other] man is so sensible of the value of retaining the services of journalists" as Wolseley:

> In the Ashantee War, his own private secretary, Captain Maurice, was the special correspondent of a leading journal; when he went to Natal, in 1875, he subsidized the local press to a large extent; when he was ordered to Cyprus, he begged that Mr. St. Leger Herbert, his private secretary, might be made *Times* correspondent, and now certain members of his staff will *sub rosa* undertake similar duties.[12]

Similarly, the famous explorer of Africa, Henry Morton Stanley, who periodically worked as a newspaper correspondent for *The New York Herald* and *The Daily Telegraph*, described Wolseley's strategy of controlling the press by using members of his own staff as journalists. In the following passage, as Stanley is on board the steamship *Benin*, in 1873, traveling from England to Africa, he happens upon Wolseley's *Soldier's Pocket Book*. Irritated by the general's demeaning criticism of journalists, Stanley inquires further into the matter:

> I ask a gentleman on board who are on Sir Garnet Wolseley's staff? I am answered—
>
> "Captain Brackenbury for one."
>
> "Ah! yes Brackenbury, of course, the 'Times' man. A military correspondent, nothing would ever stop him from writing to the 'Times.' Strange that Sir Garnet, with his unconcealed hatred to newspaper people, should choose such an indefatigable caterer for the Press as Captain Brackenbury. Who else, pray?"
>
> "Lieutenant Maurice."
>
> "What, Maurice the author of the 'Wellington Prize Essay.' He is another Press writer. I would bet anything he writes for one if not two newspapers. You need not name the others; I will take it for granted that they are mostly all newspaper writers in military clothes."[13]

Even though Stanley seems to confuse Henry Brackenbury with his brother, Charles, who was indeed a *Times'* correspondent and a military officer—Henry worked occasionally as a correspondent for *The Standard* instead[14]—his central point, that Wolseley employed members of his immediate circle as journalists, is certainly accurate. That at least three of Wolseley's closest acquaintances occupied the dual position of military men and journalists should not be surprising, particularly in the context of his position vis-à-vis newspaper correspondents.[15] The general "conciliated and manipulated correspondents to his own advantage,"[16] and, as we will see, this strategy served Wolseley well during his governorship of Cyprus.

Archibald Forbes's suggestion that St. Leger Herbert associated mostly with soldiers in Cyprus, and that he caught "the fighting fever" during his time there, is corroborated by Wolseley's own admission that he secured a position for him, as a "private volunteer," immediately before the Battle of Tel el-Kebir. Henry Brackenbury, one of Wolseley's most entrusted associates—who was assistant adjunct general and later chief of police and prosecutor in Cyprus—writes of his friendship with Herbert and describes him as a "keen soldier"; "if ever a man loved fighting," he notes, "it was St. Leger Herbert."[17] He further describes Herbert "as handsome as a young Greek god" and as "a civilian with all a soldier's instincts and love of adventure."[18]

Herbert's identification with the troops and his allegiance to Wolseley extended beyond his dual role as the general's private secretary and as a newspaper correspondent. As Stearn writes, most correspondents "were from or aspired to the same social class as the officers. On campaign they usually mixed with them socially and enjoyed an ill-defined quasi-officer status"; they were "proud of their relationship with officers, . . . identified with them," and they "often eulogized senior officers, especially successful commanders."[19] They also "largely shared officers' attitudes to war."[20] Herbert's reporting from Cyprus is exemplary of this identification with the army and it verifies his unequivocal support of Wolseley. The portrait of the general, as it emerges from these reports, is one of grandeur and wisdom. The Greeks, he writes in one of his early dispatches from the island, regard him as their "Deliverer" who was sent by God to save them.[21] A rather characteristic description of Wolseley's splendor is recorded on the occasion of the second Bayram, when a spectacular and highly symbolic celebration was arranged by the high commissioner. Herbert vividly described the procession of officials to the *konak* (the official residence) in Nicosia, on Thursday, December 5, 1878, where they were to meet with His Excellency for a State reception. Wolseley and his staff "appeared in full dress, in the complete glory of scarlet tunics and waving plumes" and led the procession.[22] "A little way outside the gate of the town," he notes, "some of the notable men and leading officials, on horseback, had ranged themselves in a line."[23] The readers are offered detailed descriptions of each Turkish official: the dress and shoes they wore; the horse, mule or pony they rode; their official capacity in Cyprus; etc. "Thus escorted," Herbert continues, "in the midst of a crowd of horsemen and footmen who had no very clear conception of the orderly marshalling of processions, his Excellency reached the konak":

> In the konak the notable people of Nicosia presented themselves to his Excellency, in accordance with immemorial custom, in four separate classes. First came the religious class; secondly the great men of the place; thirdly, the officials, and, fourthly and lastly, the merchants.[24]

Herbert proceeds to describe each member of the "four classes" and concludes by conveying their satisfaction with the change of government. Such accounts apparently solidified Wolseley's image as a great leader in the minds of the British public, and represented, in highly symbolic fashion, the subordination of the natives to Her Majesty's representatives.

At every opportunity, Herbert underlines the excellent work taking place in Cyprus under Wolseley's leadership, as well as his certainty of the island's future prospects. With many journalists and members of the parliament already doubting the usefulness of the acquisition, he repeatedly asserts his conviction that "the country, under honest and wise management, will increase rapidly in wealth"[25] and that "wealth by vast strides will be added to the island."[26] In a quasi-romantic assessment of the island's future prospects, three months into the occupation, Herbert attempts to counter any claims that the British were tricked by the Turks into administrating a useless possession:

> After a consideration of the circumstances of the island which I have shortly described in this letter, I do not see how any one can find room to doubt that Cyprus, if it can now in these present conditions pay the cost of its own administration, as it can be carefully calculated that it can do, will in the very early future become a thriving and rich possession. We have not, I have tried to show, been beggared by the Turk of our State lands; we shall own, cultivate, and enrich the forests; and the trampling of busy feet about the neglected soil and around the ruinous gatherings of its fruits will shake off the old shackles from the earth, and bring overflowing wealth where before there was but bare subsistence. For, those, then, who care to busy themselves thus early in the day with speculations of profit and loss and ways and means, it may be assumed that in taking over Cyprus we have not brought a burden, but we have rather entered upon a harvest.[27]

Herbert repeatedly juxtaposes what he perceives as the dark ages of the Ottoman Period with the imminent and assured enlightenment of the British era, which was just beginning to dawn.

On January 22, 1879, *The Times* reported that a European journal published a very dismal description of the Prisons of Cyprus, which, in turn, was translated and published by an American newspaper. These publications seemingly described inmates in Cypriot prisons as "heavily chained and kept in iron cages in dark champers."[28] In the case of one prisoner, it was reported that he had "for many years been obliged to wear a chain of a hundred pounds weight."[29] The publications reached the office of William Tallack, the prison reformer and secretary of the Howard Association, responsible for penal reform in Britain, who informed Lord Salisbury and Wolseley of these allegations. Herbert rushed to write a response to Tallack, which was also published by *The Times*, in which he admits that, "though somewhat exaggerated," the reports of brutality were indeed true during the Ottoman administration but that the British acquisition of the island has remedied the problem.[30] Progress, he continues, was painfully slow, but that was due to the corrupt system of the past, inadequate laws, old customs, etc.; the British government in Cyprus was never criticized or blamed by the locals for any of these problems. In fact, when Herbert reported, in October 1878, that the great advances in Cyprus had been halted, he explained that this was because Wolseley could not constitute the laws he desired, due to legal complexities surrounding the acquisition of Cyprus. He suggested that the British government gives the high commissioner more power to constitute laws, to use the Queen's seal and, in cases of emergency, "to make laws, to have an effect for six months, without the advice of the Legislative Council."[31]

Herbert's reports from Cyprus present a picture of the island as desolate and poor but put a lot of faith in the administration's capability to modernize it, civilize it, and usher it out of the backwardness of Ottoman times. Relevant to his suggestion of giving the high commissioner more power to constitute new Laws, he informed *The Times'* readers that in order to deal with the outdatedness of certain Ottoman laws, Wolseley gave the civil commissioner of each district a manual of instructions, which notified them of their right to overturn any court sentence that was not to their liking ("to punish or acquit a prisoner at their own discretion").[32] His position towards one of the most contested issues in Cyprus, the health of the troops, was repeatedly dismissive of the general panic the reports of fever had created upon the arrival of the British. In one of his first extensive reports from Larnaca, he writes that the camp where the troops disembarked "has been found, as it promised, to be most healthy," and that that the only casualties were "one or two men" who died of sunstroke.[33] He gives the same assurances in subsequent reports. On August 15, he writes: "The people of England, to judge from the newspapers we have received, have been beset by a panic in regard to the unhealthiness of the island, which is certainly without good grounds. . . . All the troops on shore have enjoyed excellent health."[34] A few days later, in an attempt to reconcile the fact that an overwhelming number of reports, in other newspapers, indicated that troops were severely sick, *The Times* attributed their sickness to "sun-fever of a slight kind, which in many cases turned into ague."[35]

Soon, however, and with the Thomas Cook representatives' damning report already circulating in the British press, *The Times* was forced to adjust its position on the healthiness of the island; the September 14 issue marks a turning point in its reporting from Cyprus. Interestingly, this is the same issue where Rostovitz's damning report was published in *The Times* adding fuel to an already contested affair. "Now that we have entered on the possession of Cyprus," the editors noted, "the difficulties of our position, as might have been expected, are beginning to make themselves felt"; they added that the health of the troops is "far from good" and that "the [Anglo-Turkish] convention was a little hurried."[36] In a similarly apologetic tone, Herbert rushed to clarify his previous remarks that sun-fever was the cause of sickness in Cyprus.[37] But he remained emphatically supportive of the administration and continued to firmly believe in its civilizing mission.

Another subject that elicited much attention in regard to the occupation of Cyprus, and which is extensively mentioned in Herbert's reports, was the state of slavery on the island. The "Abolition of the Slave Trade Act," of 1807, and the "Slavery Abolition Act," of 1833, made both maintaining and selling slaves illegal in England and its colonies (with some notable exceptions). In the case of Cyprus, the information we have on the attitude of British consuls regarding slaves and slave-trafficking, during the Ottoman Period, appears to be somewhat conflicting. The existence of slave-trade in Cyprus was noted, for example, by Consul Robert Hamilton Lang in a dispatch to Ambassador Henry Elliot, in 1872, a few years before the British occupation of the island. Lang notes that "for some time past, in this Island, an increase has been observable in the trafficking in slaves."[38] He also describes an incident where, upon receiving information on the trafficking of slaves from the coast of Barbary, he informed Aziz Pasha, the Ottoman governor general, who arranged for the arrest and prosecution of the captain involved in the slave-trafficking.[39] As early as 1852, British consular offices, including the British consulate in Cyprus, were informed that any slaves in the possession of British subjects in the Levant must be set free.[40] At the same time, when several slaves fled to the British vice-consulate of Cyprus, in 1857, and Vice-Consul Antonio Palma took the authority to set them free, Britain's secretary of state for foreign affairs, the Earl of Clarendon, reprimanded him for this intervention. Mr. Vice-Consul Palma "had no authority to liberate these slaves," he wrote to Robert Campbell, the British consul in Rhodes, asking him to caution the British vice-consul in Cyprus, "to be careful in future not to allow the sympathy he naturally must feel in favour of negro slaves, to carry his interference on their behalf beyond proper bounds."[41] Earl Clarendon's objection related to the impropriety of interfering with foreign Law and, two decades later, the confusing language of the 1878 Anglo-Turkish convention did not help to clarify which Law would take precedent in the British administration of Cyprus.

The parliamentary debate around the issue started just three days after the official announcement for the acquisition of the island, and it was repeatedly discussed in sessions, until July 1879. The debate was, as expected, split along party lines, with the Liberals arguing that the ruling Disraeli's Conservative government was essentially administrating a territory where slavery was allowed due to its inability to change the existing Ottoman Law. In the July 11, 1878, session of the House of Lords, Anthony Ashley Cooper, the 7th Earl of Shaftesbury, asked the president of the council "whether it is the intention of Her Majesty's Government, on assuming the occupation and administration of Cyprus, to maintain or suppress, as has been done in Her Majesty's Dominions in India, the system of slavery now existing in the Island?"[42] The question apparently took the Conservatives by surprise. The president of the council, Charles Henry Gordon Lennox, the Duke of Richmond and Gordon, replied that the government would be in a position to respond when Sir Garnet arrives in Cyprus: "it will be his duty to make full inquiry and investigation into all the institutions of the Island and everything connected with them."[43] When the Earl of Kimberly expressed his dismay over the response—expecting instead a more definitive statement regarding the government's position—the Duke of Richmond and Gordon responded again that Her Majesty's government was "as much opposed to slavery as the noble Earl, or any other Member" in the House of Lords.[44] The same scenario was repeated in the July 19 and July 23 sessions, with heated exchanges between Earl Granville, the Marquess of Salisbury (the Secretary of State for Foreign Affairs), Viscount Cardwell, the Lord Chancellor (Hugh McCalmont Cairns) and Lord Selborne. But it was the comments of Charles W. Dilke, a few months later, that created quite a sensation and forced Wolseley to defend his administration's work in Cyprus.

The Cypriot poet and intellectual Onoufrios Jassonides, an Oxford graduate who, among other endeavors, had translated Shakespeare and Byron into Modern Greek,[45] intervened on behalf of the Greek-Cypriots and what he perceived as their unjust treatment by the Wolseley administration. In early March of 1879, through his English connections—the Rev. N. Tozer and William Edward Forster, the Liberal M.P. in the House of Commons—Jassonides submitted reports to the Parliament, written by himself, the Bishop of Citium (Kyprianos Economides), and Aristotelis Palaiologos (president of the Cypriot Fraternity in Limassol), accusing the British administration of a number of oppressive policies and laws, which included the following: the Christian natives, who constituted the majority of the island's inhabitants were a minority in the Legislative Council; any application or petition written in Greek was rejected by the Administration whereas documents written in Turkish were accepted; the legal system still functioned under Ottoman procedures; the British interfered with the jurisdiction of the Church (a jurisdiction that the Turks had respected); the natives were engaged in forced labor, by Law, for which they were never paid.[46] Following these accusations, in the March 24, 1879, session of the House of Commons, Charles Dilke launched a caustic critique against Wolseley, accusing him of inducing forced labor, flogging, censoring and excluding Greek newspapers, refusing to allow barristers to plead, and not recognizing "the mother tongue of the Cypriotes."[47] The most sensitive of these subjects was, of course, the issue of slavery, which Dilke paralleled to slavery sanctioned by the State;[48] "besides forced labour," he told his colleagues in the Parliament, "there was Negro domestic slavery still existing on the Island, in the Turkish families under the shadow of our Flag."[49] Robert Bourke struggled to respond to these accusations, stating that if slavery existed on the island he was certain it would soon be abolished. William Edward Forster vouched for the credibility of Jassonides's character, accused Bourke of ignorance, and inquired as to why the British administration in Cyprus hadn't conducted a proper study on the status of slavery and why hadn't Wolseley issued a proclamation prohibiting slavery. William Harcourt also made statements to the same effect.[50]

Naturally, the debate rekindled the press's interest in Cyprus; the newspapers reported extensively on Dilke's allegations and took a particular interest in the issue of forced labor. From the beginning of the occupation, the issue of slavery featured prominently as one of the subjects linked to the administration of the island. Much of the debate was fueled by the administration's evident obliviousness about slavery in Cyprus and the complete absence of any relevant information. Some newspapers, particularly those akin to the Liberals, protested the administration's inability to provide any clear answers when questioned on the issue, and some, particularly those that endorsed the ruling Conservatives, were reporting that the issue was simply one of investigating, ascertaining and eventually dealing with slavery, if it was found to exist. The confusion was such that, though the administration repeatedly reported that they did not see any indications of the existence of slavery in Cyprus, in September of 1878, newspapers announced that the mayor of Larnaca, Frederick Charles Heidenstam, had "emancipated the persons formerly held in slavery."[51] The conflicted reports on slavery in Cyprus forced Humphrey Sandwith, secretary of the British and Foreign Slavery Society, to submit an editorial in several newspapers, stating that he had no doubt that, since Britain acquired Cyprus "there are now many slaves . . . living under our flag."[52] Although he admits he had not investigated the issue thoroughly, he expresses his certainty that "there must be slaves there, as all Turkish householders have slaves."[53]

St. Leger Herbert took note of the early debates on the subject of slavery in Cyprus, and responded with the following confident remark:

> As questions have been asked in England in regard to the sale of slaves in Cyprus, you will be glad to learn that, according to the unanimous testimony of the most reliable authorities, no slave has been sold publicly in Cyprus for many years. A report spread among the English in the town last Friday, the weekly market-day, that a slave had been sold in the market, but the story turned out to be ridiculous.[54]

His reference that the rumor "spread among the English in the town" was an indirect reference to the journalists covering the occupation of Cyprus. In fact, Wolseley provides us with more specific information in his journal. According to his account, it was Archdale Stuart Palmer who started the rumor, "stating that he had seen women slaves offered for sale in the public market."[55] Wolseley did not find the allegation convincing but, nevertheless, sent Walter Baring "to make every possible inquiry."[56] He also sent Herbert to the archbishop "to find out from him if he had heard of this sale and to ask him to inquire into it."[57] The archbishop told Herbert that he "did not believe a word of it as no slave had been sold openly in Cyprus for many years."[58] According to Wolseley, Archibald Forbes of *The Daily News* also knew of the incident and Palmer's culpability in spreading the false rumor. His own correspondence from the island, composed on August 3, just like Wolseley's journal entry, suggests that the slavery that exists in Cyprus is "domestic servitude of the generic Eastern characteristic" rather than proper slavery.[59]

A few days later, however, and despite Herbert's assurances, a woman came forward "averring herself to be a slave, complaining of ill-treatment at the hands of her master, and demanding liberation."[60] Herbert's report explained that the civil commissioner of Nicosia was instructed to fully investigate the issue and should her statements proved to be true, "to take steps for her liberation, and for the punishment of the master who has illused her."[61] A few weeks later, he updated *The Times*' readers on the particular case:

> I mentioned to you in one of my former letters that a case of enforced slavery had been reported to the Civil Commissioner of Nicosia, who had ordered an inquiry to be made in the matter. Some delay occurred in the investigation owing to a difficulty in securing the presence of the alleged slave, a woman who had left the town and run away to a village in the neighbourhood. The woman, a negress, finally came before the Court, the principal Court of Nicosia, and stated that she had been in slavery in the house of a professor in the Government school of the town and formally demanded her liberty. The court declared the woman free, citing a decree of the Sultan's to the effect that all slaves appealing for liberation should be freed. The charge of assault against the master was not proved. I hear that there are now and then, but very rarely, cases of this nature of slaves demanding their freedom, and that in every instance the Court declares their detention to be illegal and sets them at liberty.[62]

Here, again, Herbert aims to appease the rumors concerning the existence of slavery in Cyprus; he stresses the fact that, even when such rare cases emerge, "in every instance" the Court sets the slaves "at liberty." His explanation, however, points clearly to the ambiguity concerning the legal system, which was in place in the island. Whatever the legal status of slavery was in the U.K., in Cyprus it was the sultan's *firman* that legally set the slaves free and not the benevolence of the British administration.[63] The question of which law had precedence in the island was repeatedly raised in the British Parliament, and in one of the earliest attempts to resolve the Gordian knot of the treaty's ambiguity, the attorney general, Sir John Holker, had clarified that that British subjects in Cyprus adhered to British law whereas natives traveling outside the island would be treated as Turkish subjects. While he acknowledged England's right to make laws and ordinances when necessary, he did underline the fact that "Cyprus will not become a part of Her Majesty's possessions in any other sense than as an island which is to be occupied and administered by Her Majesty, according to the terms of the Convention."[64] If the issue of slavery became a contested topic in the Parliament and in newspaper columns, it was less a result of an actual problem and more a symptom of the vague terms of the Anglo-Turkish Convention and of the British reluctance to unilaterally establish British Law in Cyprus. In fact, according to Wolseley, the Marquis of Salisbury's instructions were "not so much to reform Turkish Law and institutions as to *purify* them."[65] Echoing Wolseley's conviction that the Turkish Law was "a sound and good system," Herbert stressed, in his reports from Cyprus, the fairness of the Turkish legal system and attempted to dispel any misperceptions British readers might have had:

> And if there is any one who imagines that the indolent Turk has no provision for these wants, or has only, as it were, the barest, tattered, disorderly, ill-fitting provision for them, he is far in error. It is not the want of laws that is the disease of Turkish government, but the disregard of laws; not bad laws do the most injury, but the bad administration of good laws.[66]

In this context, the task of the first British administration of Cyprus, according to their own justifications and proclamations, was not to replicate English Law but to purify and enforce the good Turkish laws that the Turks themselves had failed to implement.

As expected, Herbert's correspondences for *The Times* represent an homage to Wolseley and his competent administration of Cyprus. Herbert was merely twenty-eight years old when he accepted Wolseley's offer to join him in Cyprus as his private secretary and this was only his second job in the Colonial office. Eventually, his experiences in Canada, Cyprus, Egypt, and South Africa would solidify his firm belief in the civilizing mission of the British Empire. In 1884, he published the article "Our Colonial Policy," an extensive apologia of colonialism, in *The Fortnightly Review*, one of the most popular and influential magazines of the times. Launching a scathing critique against certain Radicals' emotional call for the freedom or self-government of colonies, Herbert blasts these proposals as unpractical and as indicative of the conflict of interest that might arise, if the principle of self-determination is allowed, between Imperial policy and colonial governments. "That colonies are entitled to manage their own affairs subject to the saving of Imperial interests," he emphatically writes, is a proposition in which there is "neither value nor meaning."[67] He attacks radical liberals such as Thorold

Rogers and Goldwin Smith for painting an ideal picture of the colonies in Canada and elsewhere, and suggests that these "hollow and dangerous illusions" had rendered mass opinion in England "perverted and intractable."[68] Arguing against giving the colonies more power to determine their own affairs, in the usual paternalistic tone through which colonial power was often justified, he writes:

> The English nation, with its intense philanthropy, its generous care for weaker races, its sensitiveness to the bonds of family feeling, is the last power than can pretend, unless with ludicrous insincerity, absolutely to abdicate all concern in any part of the doings and sufferings of its dependent communities.[69]

Though he acknowledges that, to a large extent, the dissatisfaction in the colonies stems from the fact that they are not represented in the British Parliament, he suggests that the way to remedy this problem is to form a bipartisan committee which would advise the secretary of state for the colonies on colonial matters.[70]

Undoubtedly influenced by his mentor, Wolseley, Herbert developed into a staunch supporter of the colonial project and a firm believer of Britain's duty to control, manage and govern what he describes as the "weaker races" of the world. His untimely death in the Sudan, in 1885, did not leave his fellow correspondents, or the army he adored so much, indifferent. On June 16, 1888, ten years after St. Leger Algernon Herbert's service in Cyprus, Lord Wolseley unveiled a memorial in St. Paul's Cathedral, dedicated to war correspondents who lost their lives in the Sudan Campaign. The memorial was designed by the artist Herbert Johnson, it was financed by the Press, and it bore the names of seven journalists: Edmund O'Donovan of *The Daily News*, Frank Vizetelly of *The Illustrated London News* (Edward Vizetelly's more famous uncle), Frank Power of *The Times*, John A. Cameron of *The Standard*, William H. Gordon of *The Manchester Guardian,* Frank J. L. Roberts of *Reuters* and, of course, St. Leger Algernon Herbert who was, at the time of his death, working for *The Morning Post*. Bearing testimony to the intimate relationship between military men and correspondents, *The Graphic* hailed the unveiling of the memorial as "a noteworthy event in the history of the Newspaper Press in England. It associated the Army and the Press in a way they have never been associated before, for it acknowledged that the soldier and the war-correspondent share equal dangers, if they do not win equal rewards."[71] This was a momentous event indeed, as it was emblematic of the intimate relationship between the army, the press and the political establishment. Apart from Wolseley, the ceremony was attended by several distinguished officers and politicians, including Lord C. Beresford, M.P., Major General Evelyn Wood, Major General William Butler, Colonel Reginald Talbot and Colonel J. H. Sandwith.[72] After the unveiling, the attendees gathered at the London Press Club, where James Walker, president of the Club, Henry H. S. Pearse, correspondent for *The Daily News*, Wolseley and Beresford gave intimate speeches that celebrated what amounted to an official consecration of the sacred bond between the press and the army. James Walker "expressed the satisfaction all journalists felt at the presence of Lord Wolseley and his distinguished colleagues."[73] In an almost parodic reference to Wolseley's relationship with journalists (and in total denial of the contested passage in *The Soldier's Pocket Book*), Pearse said that the General "had always shown his interest in war correspondents by affording them every facility. No word of their messages had ever been suppressed by his lordship that was not indiscreet and likely to jeopardise the success of military operations."[74] Lord Beresford talked about his personal friendship with Leger Herbert and John Cameron and expressed his happiness that "Lord Wolseley endeavoured to afford [war correspondents] every facility by putting them in a position to ascertain and tell the public the truth."[75] But the most interesting speech was by Garnet Wolseley himself, who put great effort in expressing his gratitude and his intimate connection with correspondents. *The York Herald* paraphrased his speech as follows:

> Mr. O'Donovan and Mr. Power were countrymen of his own; Mr. Roberts fell a victim to the climate of Suakim and the very day he (Lord Wolseley) arrived there; Mr. Vizetelly, a man of genial and kind nature, and an artist of a high order, he had known longest; with Mr. Cameron he had been in more than one campaign, and well remembered his galloping across the desert with his messages; Captain Gordon he had known for a long time as of high character, and reliable wherever and on whatever duty employed; and St. Leger Herbert was a personal friend of his own—a man of great daring, high education, and very great ability. (Cheers.) He hoped the example of those whose names they had so justly commemorated would be an incentive to others to follow in the same course of devotion to duty.[76]

In what is probably a remarkable symbolic coincidence that exemplifies the intimate, even symbiotic relationship between the army and the press, in 1902, Wolseley would unveil yet another memorial in St. Paul's Cathedral, for Archibald Forbes, another one of the Cyprus correspondents. Apart from the graves of some of the Empire's most important military men, including Field Marshal Frederick Sleigh Roberts and Horatio Nelson, the Cathedral hosts plaques commemorating the fifteen correspondents who perished during the Boer War of 1899 and, as we have discussed, the seven correspondents who died during the Sudan Campaigns of 1883–1885. Britain's "First and Greatest of War Correspondents,"[77] Sir William Howard Russell, the celebrated correspondent whose lectures Forbes had attended at the University of Aberdeen, was also buried in the Cathedral. On March 31, 1913, after an impressive funeral procession and cheered by a large crowd of spectators, General Wolseley himself was interred at St. Paul's Cathedral.

NOTES

1. *Evening Telegraph*, July 17, 1878, p. 3.
2. Kochanski, *Sir Garnet Wolseley*, 91.
3. James Williams, "St. Leger Algernon Herbert," in *Dictionary of National Biography*, eds. Leslie Stephen and Sidney Lee, vol. 9 (London: Smith, Elder & Co, 1908), 663.
4. *Pall Mall Gazette*, May 29, 1879, p. 8.
5. Wolseley, *Cyprus 1878*, 43, and Arthur, *Letters of Lord and Lady Wolseley*, 32. Wolseley's only problem with Herbert, as well as with his friend, General Herbert Stewart, was that both "were unbelievers in revealed religion, which to [Wolseley was] always terrible to contemplate " (Arthur, *Letters of Lord and Lady Wolseley*, 171).
6. *Daily News*, February 19, 1885, p. 3.
7. *Daily News*, February 19, 1885, p. 3.
8. Arthur, *Letters of Lord and Lady Wolseley*, 78.
9. Garnet Wolseley, *The Soldier's Pocket Book* (London: Macmillan and Co., 1871), 82.
10. Ibid., 86.
11. Ibid., 225.
12. *Worcestershire Chronicle*, May 31, 1879, p. 3.
13. Henry Morton Stanley, *Coomassie and Magdala: The Story of Two British Campaigns in Africa* (London: Sampson Low, Marston, Low, and Searle, 1874), 3.
14. Henry Brackenbury, *Some Memories of my Spare Time* (London: William Blackwood and Sons, 1909), 57–58.
15. Interestingly, this strategy of embedding journalists with the troops, or using military men as correspondents, was widely discussed in England, particularly in the aftermath of the *Soldier's Pocket Book*'s publication. The debate is astoundingly similar to the one that followed the U.S. Department of Defense's strategy of embedding journalists during the Iraq War. The Anglo-Indian author George Birdwood suggested, for example, that the use of journalists in this fashion is beneficial to both "the Government and the public" since they provide "the fairest and best interpretation of policy" and the description of military incidents are provided by "military experts." He further suggested that this practice should be made official and regulated and that correspondents should sign their letters. See George Birdwood, "The Story of the Ashantee Campaign, by Winwood Reade and Coomassie and Magdala by Henry M. Stanley," *The Academy: A Weekly Review of Literature, Science, and Art* 6 (August 1874): 118. For a comparable view on embedded journalism during the Iraq War see Shahira Fahmy and Thomas J. Johnson, "'How we performed': Embedded journalists' attitudes and perceptions towards covering the Iraq War," *Journalism and Mass Communication Quarterly* 82, no. 2 (2005), 301–17.
16. Edward M. Spiers, *The Late Victorian Army, 1868–1902* (Manchester: Manchester University Press, 199), 196.
17. Henry Brackenbury, *The River Column: A Narrative of the Advance of the River Column of the Nile Expeditionary Force, and Its Return Down the Rapids* (London: William Blackwood and Sons, 1885), 8–9.
18. Brackenbury, *Some Memories*, 337–338. Herbert is also mentioned fondly by Hugh McCalmont, Wolseley's aide de camp in Cyprus. See Hugh McCalmont, *The Memoirs of Major-General Sir Hugh McCalmont* (London: Hutchinson & Co., 1924).
19. Stearn, "War Correspondents," 147.
20. Ibid.
21. *Times*, August 15, 1878, p. 8.
22. *Times*, December 24, 1878, p. 4.
23. *Times*, December 24, 1878, p. 4.
24. *Times*, December 24, 1878, p. 4.

25. *Times*, October 23, 1878, p. 10.
26. *Times*, October 29, 1878, p. 8.
27. *Times*, October 24, 1878, p. 4.
28. *Times*, January 22, 1879, p. 6.
29. *Times*, January 22, 1879, p. 6.
30. *Times*, January 22, 1879, p. 6.
31. *Times*, October 23, 1878, p. 10.
32. *Times*, August 8, 1878, p. 8.
33. *Times*, August 8, 1878, p. 8.
34. *Times*, August 15, 1878, p. 8.
35. *Times*, August 20, 1878, p. 7.
36. *Times*, September 14, 1878, p. 9.
37. *Times*, September 14, 1878, p. 6.
38. Harry Charles Luke, *Cyprus Under the Turks 1571–1878* (Oxford: Oxford University Press), 245.
39. Ibid.
40. Ibid., 194–195. For more information on the existence of slavery in Cyprus during the Ottoman period see Mete Hatay, "Servants, Slaves and Concubines," in *Ottoman Cyprus: A Collection of Studies on History and Culture*, eds. Michalis N. Michael, Matthias Kappler, Eftihios Gavriel (Wiesbaden: Harrassowitz Verlag, 2009).
41. "The Earl of Clarendon to Consul R. Campbell, December 19, 1857," in *Correspondence with British Ministers and Agents in Foreign Countries and with Foreign Ministers in England Relating to the Slave Trade. From April 1, 1857, to March 31, 1858* (London: Harrison and Sons, 1859).
42. HL Deb, 11 July 1878, vol. 241, cc1224.
43. HL Deb, 11 July 1878, vol. 241, cc1225.
44. HL Deb, 11 July 1878, vol. 241, cc1226.
45. Despite his leading the campaign against the British administration in Cyprus, Jassonides was subsequently employed, in 1884, as a translator for the Legislative Council. Interestingly, one of his complaints against Wolseley was that the Greek language was excluded from official documents because British and Turkish officials could not read it. For more information on Jassonides see Aristides Koudounaris, "Ιασονίδης Ονούφριος του Ιωάννου," in *Βιογραφικό Λεξικό Κυπρίων 1800–1920*, 6th ed. (Nicosia: n.p., 2010), 186–87.
46. For a full account of the complaints and Wolseley's responses see UK. Parliament, "Correspondence Respecting Complaints, Made Against the Government of Cyprus (C. 2324)," in *Parliamentary Papers*, vol. 54 (London: Her Majesty's Stationery Office, 1879).
47. HC Deb, 24 March 1879, vol. 244, cc1510.
48. Mindful of how Wolseley's "forced-labour" ordinances in Cyprus might be misperceived as a promotion of slavery, the Marquis of Salisbury sent a telegram to Wolseley, on October 25, 1878, warning him that punishment "should be a fine on village, and not fall on individuals; otherwise we shall be charged with setting up slavery." In a subsequent letter to Wolseley, the marquis insisted that Wolseley's ordinance on forced labor should be removed since it could be misrepresented as slavery and it would compromise England's position on abolition. See U.K. Parliament, "Correspondence Respecting an Ordinance Enacted in Cyprus, Providing for the Execution of Public Works, C. 2326," in *Parliamentary Papers*, vol. 54 (London: Her Majesty's Stationery Office, 1879).
49. HC Deb, 24 March 1879, vol. 244, cc1512.
50. For the full debate see HC Deb, 24 March 1879, vol. 244, cc1509–93. Wolseley was asked by the Marquis of Salisbury to respond to these allegations and he submitted extensive responses, alongside a barrage of responses by his administrators in Cyprus: Colonel Warren, the commissioner of Limassol; Colonel Greaves, the chief secretary; Delaval Cobham, the Larnaca commissioner; A. G. Wauchope, the Paphos commissioner; James Inglis, the Famagusta commissioner; Walter Holbech, the Kyrenia commissioner; H. G. White, the Nicosia commissioner; and M. B. Seager, the assistant commissioner of Nicosia. They all protested and refuted all the accusations made against their administration. In one of his letters to the Marquis of Salisbury, Wolseley writes: "In replying to these charges, which I am sure would never have

been made by any member of our Parliament had their authors been as well known in England as they are here, I have had to ring the changes upon the words 'not true' through every possible variation; but I trust that in refuting them I have not expressed myself too bluntly or in too forcible language. When writing in defence of carefully-selected English officers who have devoted themselves, as those under my command have done, with zeal and energy to the task of governing a mixed population under no ordinary difficulties, it is not easy to write calmly regarding reckless charges wherein truth has been intentionally suppressed, and cruelty and wrongdoing designedly imputed to others by those who originated them." For the full exchange and the ensuing investigation see: U.K. Parliament, *Correspondence Respecting Complaints* and U.K. Parliament, "Further Correspondence Respecting Complaints made against the Government of Cyprus (C. 2355)," in *Parliamentary Papers*, vol. 54 (London: Her Majesty's Stationery Office, 1879).

51. *Standard*, September 21, 1878, p. 5.
52. *York Herald,* September 4, 1878, p. 6. Also published in several other newspapers.
53. *York Herald,* September 4, 1878, p. 6.
54. *Times*, August 15, 1878, p. 8.
55. Wolseley, *Cyprus 1878*, 39.
56. Ibid.
57. Ibid.
58. Ibid.
59. *Daily News*, August 15, 1878, p. 6. The condition of the konak prison in Nicosia, however, he further reported, "puts the slavery of Louisiana into the shade" and "puts humanity to the blush. Yet the Turks seem to accept it as a simple matter of course."
60. *Times*, September 7, 1878, p. 10.
61. *Times*, September 7, 1878, p. 10.
62. *Times*, October 12, 1878, p. 4.
63. In a letter to the Marquis of Salisbury, on April 10, 1879, Wolseley verified the fact that in Cyprus, the Administration was following the Ottoman code of Law: "As to the procedure in the Courts of Law, it is of a very simple nature, suited to the habits and customs of the simple people concerned. In all criminal cases, and whenever any civil case of importance is tried, an English officer is present to see that impartial justice is administered, and the High Native Court (the Temijez of Nicosia) is presided over by Mr. Justice Phillips, a most able Judge, of about twenty years' experience on the Bench. The law existing in Cyprus, and by which all Cypriots are tried, is the Nizam, and not the Sheri or Sacred Law. The Nizam law is a modern code of Turkish laws, based upon the Code Napoleon, and is a sound and good system, an opinion which is entertained both by Mr. Cookson, my late legal adviser, and by Mr. Justice Phillips, who now occupies that position here. The only Court where the law of the Koran—known as the Sheri or Sacred Law—prevails, is that known as the Sheri Court, the jurisdiction of which is exclusively confined to religious and domestic questions." See Sir G. Wolseley to the Marquis of Salisbury, April 10, 1879, in U.K. Parliament, *Correspondence Respecting Complaints.*
64. HC Deb, 23 July 1878, vol. 242, cc41.
65. Wolseley, *Cyprus 1878*, 51. Emphasis added.
66. *Times*, August 15, 1878, p. 8.
67. St. Leger Algernon Herbert, "Our Colonial Policy," *The Fortnightly Review* 35, no. 206 (1884): 244.
68. Ibid., 245–46.
69. Ibid., 249.
70. Ibid., 254–55.
71. *Graphic*, June 23, 1888, p. 15.
72. Both Wood and Butler belonged to Wolseley's Ring.
73. *York Herald*, June 18, 1888, p. 6.
74. *York Herald*, June 18, 1888, p. 6.
75. *York Herald*, June 18, 1888, p. 6.
76. *York Herald*, June 18, 1888, p. 6.

77. The plaque on Russell's grave in St. Paul's Cathedral reads: "The First and Greatest of War Correspondents" (see Roth, *Encyclopedia of War Journalism*, 316).

Chapter Four

Archibald Forbes and *The Daily News*

By the time he went to Cyprus to cover the occupation on behalf of *The Daily News*, Archibald Forbes was already considered a veteran war correspondent. The forty-year-old journalist, described as "the prince of war correspondents" by his peers,[1] was nothing short of a celebrity, and his journey to Cyprus confirms the great importance with which the press approached the acquisition of the island, as well as the unparalleled excitement that the occupation elicited among journalists. In what testifies, perhaps, to his unmatched fame among journalists and his great gift of narration, Lord Wolseley himself mailed a letter to his wife, the day after his arrival in Cyprus, with the following instructions: "Whilst I think of it, remember to take in the *Daily News*, for Mr. Forbes of that paper is here and will send home letters describing our doings."[2]

Forbes, who was born in Scotland, had studied at the University of Aberdeen and later attended "a course of lectures by (Sir) William Howard Russell," the forefather of war corresponding in Britain.[3] Like many other correspondents of his times, he was trained in the army, having spent several years in the Royal Dragoons. While still serving in the army, he launched his journalistic career with articles in the *Morning Star* and *Cornhill* magazine. His collaboration with *The Daily News* started in 1870. "The ability of one man," writes J. S. R. Phillips, "to give popularity to a newspaper was never exhibited more clearly."[4] His reports on the Franco-Prussian War skyrocketed the newspaper's sales, increasing its circulation "from 50,000 to 150,000 a day."[5] Before he came to Cyprus he had covered, with unparalleled success, the establishment of the Paris Commune (1871), the Carlist Wars in Spain (1872–76), the Serbian-Turkish War (1876–78) and the Russo-Turkish War (1877–78).[6] His popularity, among the public and his peers, was unsurpassed. His lectures—be they in Britain, America, or Australia—

drew large and enthusiastic audiences. He was often controversial, irritable and rather proud of his success in reporting from war zones. He often boasted of his achievements and "much as you might wonder and admire" them, "he, like Ulysses, wondered and admired more."[7] A sign of his disciplined, soldier-like character was the following announcement that accompanied some of his lectures: "Mr. Forbes particularly requests his audience to be Punctual, as he has been much annoyed lately by late arrivals."[8] During his American tour of 1881–82, he was highly praised by Mark Twain[9] and, at the same time, got into a widely reported feud with Oscar Wilde.[10] In 1881, the celebrated Victorian artist Hubert von Herkomer painted his portrait, "which created a sensation when it was exhibited at the Royal Academy that year."[11]

Forbes was a remarkably gifted craftsman of language. In recognition of his captivating narrative style, his description of the battle of Ulundi, during the Zulu War, "was read out in both houses of Parliament amid loud applause."[12] His writing was indeed incomparable; as one of his contemporaries put it: "No man living can pen such brilliantly vivid pictures of what he has seen on the battlefield as Archibald Forbes."[13] The member of Parliament, Sir Henry Havelock, the son of General Henry Havelock, whom Forbes would memorialize in a biography in 1890, requested that the Parliament extend a mark of favor to the great war correspondent "in recognition of the public services performed by him in being the bearer of the despatches of the successful action at Ulundi, under circumstances of considerable personal hazard, fatigue, and endurance."[14] As late as 1915, Members of the Parliament remembered "the brilliant, stirring, and dashing descriptive accounts we had from Mr. Archibald Forbes of the Battle of Tel el Kebir," and the M.P. William Byles, anxious about recruiting during the First World War, bemoaned that "if we had only such articles now, England would be ablaze with national feeling, and we should have no anxiety about recruiting."[15]

At the request of *The Daily News,* Forbes undertook the Cyprus assignment "for the purpose of narrating the circumstances of the occupation of it by the British officials and soldiers, and of describing the characteristics which the island presented in its various aspects."[16] Like most of his compatriots, he was clueless about the island, and his first reaction was "to grope for the position of Cyprus on the map."[17] And, like the British authorities, Forbes later wrote, he searched for information in John Murray's *Handbook for Travellers in Turkey in Asia*. Naturally, the 1878 edition of the handbook was significantly updated due to the thirst of the British public for information on the island and due to its potential usefulness as a tourist guide. Apart from more extensive information on Cyprus, much of it borrowed from Luigi Palma Di Cesnola's 1877 book *Cyprus: Its Ancient Cities, Tombs, and Temples*, the revised handbook included commentary that reflected the new status of the island as a British colony and connected the British past (i.e., Coeur de

Lion's capture of Cyprus) with the present. "And now after an interval of 687 years," the editors proudly noted in the revised edition, "the island has again come under the sway of an English sovereign and Queen Victoria may adopt the title borne by Richard Coeur de Lion" (i.e., Queen of Cyprus).[18] Previous editions of the handbook, however, including the one Forbes had consulted before his journey to the island, were not as enlightening and, in his own words, the handbook was "better intentioned than resulting in practical benefit."[19]

Like Leger Herbert, Forbes accompanied Wolseley and his staff in the journey from England to Cyprus. On July 17 he was on board the *Madura*, off the coast of Sicily, on his way to Malta and reported in detail on the War Office's instructions to Wolseley.[20] They reached Malta on the following day and, from there, he reported that the Indian troops were behaving exceptionally well and that several soldiers had mistakenly been served carbolic acid instead of lime-juice and were consequently semi-poisoned. He also informed his readers that Wolseley "received a telegram from Cyprus giving good tidings of this new land of promise."[21] By the morning of July 22, the fleet reached Larnaca, and Forbes, who, like Wolseley, was on board the *Himalaya*, caught his first glimpse of the island. His vivid and thorough description of the landscape, included in his first extensive letter from Cyprus, was published in segments by *The Daily News* and it is exemplary of the reason why Forbes became so popular among British readers:

> There was little beauty in the scene, and yet less aspect of fertility. Where were the groves which some of the more sanguine of us had been picturing to ourselves; where the interlocking foliage drooped over marble fountains, whence pellucid water trickled away to irrigate velvet sward? Instead, a dull grim grey everywhere, relieved only by streaks of dingy white where the winter torrents on the slopes had laid bare the rock.[22]

Forbes's disappointment is rescued by the faint view of Larnaca, the patches of greenery and the view of some villages in the distance. "As we gaze on," he writes, "we realise that after all there may be some beauty in Cyprus."[23] After disembarking from the *Himalaya*, Forbes proceeds to the Strand, in Larnaca, in order to send his first telegram from Cyprus to *The Daily News.* His first letter proceeds to describe, in colorful detail, his initial impression of the Marina of Larnaca; he sees "Watermen and fishermen, with bare legs and fez on head," "brown limped fellows driving donkeys," "dark-faced, keen looking men of every nationality of Eastern Europe," a few women who do not inspire any comparison with Aphrodite, "a few negroes, shining in their blackness," "a few English sailors," a butchery so close to the water that "the waves are tinged with blood," "a dilapidated market-place," consular offices and "miscellaneous gentlemen desirous of acting as your dragoman or indeed of performing any service for you."[24] He confesses to his readers that his first letter from Cyprus is somewhat scattered and it includes information that he gathers along the way. He informs them, for example, that the intention of the Administration is to keep white troops in the same camp (near clean water) but to distribute colored troops throughout the island.[25] This distinction between colored and white troops is maintained throughout most correspondents' reports from the island, particularly in relation to the soldiers inflicted by fever. He also informs his readers that he just met Captain Rawson, who told him that the Turks of the island are thoroughly pleased with the occupation but that the Greeks are not satisfied since they hope that "the island will be annexed to Greece." "We may trust to time," Forbes comments, "to concert them from a delusion so Quixotic."[26] His account of the "installation of sir Garnet Wolseley as Lord High Commissioner" is, once again, a fine specimen of Forbes's unmistakable style:

> As a spectacle, the affair was a bagatelle, but it was pregnant with a deep interest of its own. It was an embodied allegory. Here the battered konak, with crumbled carving that the Turk had never wrought, broken oil lamp above the archway, a gate that would not shut, a symbol, in fine, of shiftless apathy; here the Turkish infantrymen, obsolete in equipment, slovenly in dress. There the British war ships, the latest triumphs of marine architecture, the huge riffed cannon, one shell from which would bring the konak rattling about the ears of the kaimakan; there the British soldiers, smart, armed with the newest weapons, trained to the strictest discipline. Here the kaimakan, sluggish, apathetic, unimprovable, there the Queen's Commissioner, fertile in schemes for regenerating the island, with liberty, justice, progress on his lips. It seemed that the Turks stood here recording the tacit admission the *quood* Cyprus at least they had failed, and were content in their sense of failure to shamble away, and let the men of energy and progress come in their room.[27]

His allegorical description is latent with all those elements in colonial discourse, that juxtapose the western civilization with the barbarity of the East: energy vs apathy, technology vs. primitiveness, destruction vs construction, the old vs. the new, the past vs. the future. This was a position shared among correspondents, politicians and the public alike, especially in the early weeks of the occupation: the advent of the British in Cyprus, after many years of Ottoman mismanagement, would restore the island to its ancient glory.

As the days waned by, Forbes became disappointed with practically everything that he saw in Cyprus. Despite his sensational reporting and the initial excitement over Britain's new acquisition, he grew bored rather quickly. For a correspondent who had covered some of the most glorious military battles of his times, the thrifty management of a new colony, which seemed to be slumbering, forgotten in time, and the monotony of life in this backward island was unbearable to him. His first days in Cyprus are rather unexciting and the events he describes are quite trivial. In his July 27 report—

published in the August 7 edition of *The Daily News*—he informs his readers, as Herbert did, on Wolseley's appointment of district commissioners, and outlines in detail the instructions they received.[28] From the 22nd to the 29th of July, Forbes was residing aboard the *Himalaya*. On the 29th he departs from the ship and arranges for a mule and a muleteer to take him to Nicosia in order to witness Wolseley's first entry into the capital of the island. Indeed, on the afternoon of July 30, he reported on the enthusiastic reception of the high commissioner, by both Greeks and Turks, in Nicosia. In a more balanced description, he reports that Nicosia is beautiful and picturesque from the outside—with its Venetian walls, its minarets and its domes—but "inside it is ruinous and squalid."[29] One of the most emblematic moments, indicative of both his style and his effort to find some excitement in the monotony of Cyprus, is the description of his journey from Larnaca to Nicosia. Resuscitating one of the most common orientalist sexual stereotypes in Western travel writing, Forbes writes:

> The dreary monotonous road from Larnaca to Nicosia has left with me but one pleasant memory, the memory of the beautiful foot belonging to one of these Turkish ladies, or rather in strict legality belonging to the pluffy gentleman on the dun mule, who was her owner. I wonder whether he appreciates his good fortune as the possessor of this charming foot. I fear not; he himself rode in slippers and drove his women in front of him as if they had been sheep.[30]

Beyond the apparent sexualization of the veiled Muslim female and the fetishization of her foot, in Forbes's description, the Muslim man is simultaneously presented as the all-powerful owner of his women and is symbolically castrated, as he is unable to appreciate the "charming foot" in his possession.

Even such "pleasant" details, however, did not help to enliven the monotony of life on the island. On August 3, Forbes wrote that "our life here since Sir Garnet came and took possession has been uneventful, and threatens already to become monotonous."[31] He complains that he "should like to see it an actual occupation of some sort, with a certain robust vigour in the carrying of it out."[32] Even the treatment of the natives seems too lenient to him; the Cypriots, he writes, "seem rather disappointed that they are not occasionally kicked" and are treated so generously by the British.[33] By August 4, less than two weeks after his arrival, he noted in his letter to *The Daily News* that "the Cypriot swan had turned out so unmistakably goose."[34] He spends his droning days visiting the dilapidated monuments of Nicosia and the Turkish prison, where he sees inmates held in horrid conditions, he joins a small crowd of spectators attending the British army's first parade in Cyprus, and he finds some solace in the beauty of Kyrenia, in the northern part of the island, which he visits with Colonel Baker Russell.

Despite all the monotony and the boredom, Forbes's gift of narration could indeed transform the most banal or peripheral subject into a dramatic and sensational event. As Captain N. L. Walford, one of his harshest critics, puts it, even "marches, which to those engaged in them have appeared dull and wearisome, are by his magic pen made interesting and exciting."[35] In fact, most of his reporting from Cyprus bears the unmistakable mark of sensationalism. Here is how he describes, for example, the death of a sergeant of the 42nd regiment from sunstroke, on Monday July 22:

> He was one of a mixed detachment of 42nd and 101st [regiments] who started from the beach early on Monday afternoon to march to camp, under the command of Mr. Druitt, of the latter regiment. The party was misdirected by a Turk near Larnaca, and took the Nittoria [*sic*] road. Mile after mile was traversed, till at length, from the distance covered, it was clear that the road had been mistaken. Druitt halted his little party for a rest under the shadow of a rock, and here poor M'Gaw, staggering a few paces, fell back into the arms of the officer. He never regained consciousness and was dead in an hour. Druitt left three men with their dead comrade, and having got some information as to the direction of the camp, resumed his march. Night fell, and the party bivouacked on the road finally reaching the camp at seven the following morning. A doolie was sent out, and M'Gaw's body brought into the camp; it was buried on the Tuesday afternoon; and it may be said that a good and staunch soldier had handselled the little burial plot under the locust tree.[36]

Sergeant M'Gaw, who had been decorated with the Victoria Cross for "his gallant exploits during the Ashantee war,"[37] was the first British casualty in Cyprus, and his death was widely reported by the British press. Naturally, the unhealthiness of the climate of Cyprus was one of the most discussed topics in Forbes's letters from Cyprus. In his first telegram, sent from Larnaca upon his arrival, he reluctantly reported that "fever is somewhat prevalent" in the island[38] and, in the next four days, despite Sergeant M'Gaw's death, he reported that "everything is going on favourably"[39] and that "the heat is intense, but the troops are healthy."[40] On August 3, Forbes expressed his first concerns about the healthiness of Cyprus. "Fever is extremely prevalent here," begins his report to *The Daily News*, published on August 5, 1878.[41] "Yesterday two officers and ten men were sent down invalidated," he continues. "Today seven more men on the sick list, a serious percentage on a detachment one hundred and twenty strong." Four days later he elaborated further, stating that "sickness is increasing at a portentous rate among the troops, and unquestionably at this season Cyprus is exceptionally unhealthy."[42] He reports that he counted about sixty-eight soldiers and officers who were affected with fever. By August 12, he reports that "the health of the troops is not improving. Typhoid fever appears more serious."[43] His subsequent reporting for the month of August is ever more dramatic, as he finds, upon visiting the island's capital, that "Nicosia, at this season of the year, is a fecund fever bed."[44] On August 15, *The Daily News* published Forbes's most intense reporting on the unhealthiness of Cyprus:

> Fever continues to paralyse the efficiency of the white troops. The 42nd regiment has 170 men on the sick list. The 101st has 130. Six officers in the battery of artillery, or one-third of its strength, are down. Of 136 sailors and marines who were sent inland to Nicosia, 84 are fever-stricken. . . . In all about twenty-five per cent of the white troops are fever stricken. About two-thirds of the medical force are also down. . . . The fever is everywhere. It is not deadly; only some five fatal cases have occurred; but its victims never quite recover while they remain on the island, but are liable to periodic relapses with chronically diminished vigour.[45]

Coming from the pen of Britain's most celebrated correspondent, these reports caused alarm in London. Forbes had already reported that "there is a vagueness in the language of the Convention which can hardly fail to give occasion to complication,"[46] and his reports on the unhealthiness of Cyprus further stained the image of the government, which appeared as completely incapable of dealing with the situation and as having rushed into acquiring a colony without fully investigating its condition. Following Forbes's revelations, on the very next day, the Liberal M.P. Morgan Lloyd raised the subject in the House of Commons:

> I take this opportunity of asking, Whether the statement in the "Daily News" this morning with regard to the health of the troops at Cyprus is correct or not, because, according to that account, the state of the troops is very alarming? The fever seems to be very extensive indeed, and it would seem that the troops are cantoned in places which must necessarily be unhealthy. . . . I wish to know, whether there is any foundation for the very alarming statement of the "Daily News"?[47]

The Secretary of State for War, Colonel Frederick Stanley, responded that according to a recent telegram he had received from Wolseley, "the sickness was about 6 per cent of the men in hospital, mostly for fever of a mild type."[48] He also added, in an apparent derogatory tone, that he is puzzled with "the discrepancy between the official and the private accounts" which he received "and the accounts which appear in some organs of the daily Press."[49] When Forbes arrived in Malta, on his return trip from Cyprus, he saw a copy of a newspaper which included Stanley's reply and he was infuriated. The statement, he would later write in an article, "was literally true, since the hospitals could hold no more, and, being literally true, was quite smart, although utterly misleading. Of course, the minister inculcated belief in the official version; and equally of course, he had his airy little gibe at the non-official person."[50] His fuming response, sent from Malta on August 26, was published in *The Daily News* on the very next day:

> Observing that a discussion has been arisen regarding the accuracy of the statements made by me respecting the state of health of the troops in Cyprus in the telegram printed in the *Daily News* on the 16th, I consider it due to myself to make the following remarks:
>
> I am no malcontent, and take no concern with political complications. My business is to transmit facts, in full knowledge of the responsibility for the truth or error of my statements. My authorities for the details given in the telegram in question are as follows:
>
> Respecting the 42nd, the commanding officer of the regiment, who had just signed the returns the data of which I transmitted.
>
> Respecting the 101st, the commanding officer.
>
> Respecting the Artillery, the medical officer of the battery.
>
> Respecting the belated detachment of Engineers, Surgeon-Major Beattie, in chief medical charge of the Indian expeditionary force.
>
> On the 14th inst. I went round the hospital marquees at the Pacha Chiflik cap with Surgeon-Major Menzies, the officer in charge there. I saw tent-full after tent-full of sick men in utter prostration; many with their heads or temples shaved, and blisters applied; some delirious.
>
> My statement that on the 14th 25 per cent. of the total European force on the island were unfit for duty from illness was rather under than over the precise figures.
>
> Assertion and counter-assertion are childish in a case when the returns furnish exact and detailed information. Colonel Stanley will find that the official returns sent in to Sir Anthony Home, the principal medical officer of the expedition, amply bear out the statements made in my telegram.
>
> To these I refer him.[51]

Forbes rebuttal fell on deaf ears. As he himself recalls, "officialism had the best of it after all. Parliament had risen before the telegram . . . reached England, and so no Parliamentary friend had the opportunity of enforcing the minister's admission of the accuracy of my statement by moving for the production of the returns."[52] The incident, however, underlines the complicated intimacy that described the relationship between administrators, correspondents and British politicians; this intimacy largely defined the public's reception of Britain's colonial policies. It reveals, for example, the importance of correspondents' reports, particularly Forbes', in guiding the positions taken by both the ruling government and the opposition. Herbert's reports, as we have seen, constantly underemphasized the unhealthiness of Cyprus, whereas Forbes's reports underlined the prevalence of fever; their statements were used as evidence to support each party's positions. The incident also reveals the strained, albeit interdependent, relationship between the British official narrative and that of the press.[53] It also points to the fact that political debates in Victorian England were largely based on information drawn from newspapers and magazines.

One incident that demonstrates the intimate connections between the main actors involved in the colonial affairs of Victorian England is Forbes's encounter with Walter Baring and Frederick Guarracino. The days after his arrival, losing no time at all, Forbes asked for permission to accompany Guarracino, one of Wolseley's interpreters, to the town of Famagusta, in order to deliver a message from the high commissioner to the Kaimakan. Guarracino's peculiar role in Cyprus is emblematic of the rampant nepotism that guided many of the appointments in the first weeks of the British administration. Guarracino was not a mere interpreter, nor was he in Cyprus by chance. Walter Baring, Lord Cromer's brother and the influential lawyer who had practically handled all the legal complexities of the island's transfer to Britain, was married to Guarracino's daughter. He had served in various posts in the British consular services, and Baring often used his powerful connections to secure positions for his father-in-law. Two years before their Cyprus adventure, Baring and Guarracino found themselves amid controversy. In 1876, Baring was sent to Bulgaria on behalf of the British government, to investigate news reports of Turkish atrocities against the Bulgarian population. As in the case of Cyprus, he requested that his father-in-law accompany him, as an interpreter, in the investigation. *The Daily Mail*, whose reports from Constantinople played a key role in the uncovering of the atrocities, conducted its own independent investigation and published the results in September 1876. Forbes's close friend, the American journalist Januarius Aloysius MacGahan, led the newspaper's investigation and submitted a damning report of the way Guarracino handled the official investigation on behalf of the government, accusing him of being a philoturk and biased against the Bulgarian people. More specifically, Guarracino was accused of falsifying evidence regarding the slaughter of the Bulgarian population at Perustitza. According to MacGahan, Guarracino

> tried to get the [Bulgarian] people to say that Aziz Pacha [*sic*] had sent them a summons to surrender; that they had fired on the bearer of the summons, and continued the fight; and when they refused to admit this, he bullied and browbeat them, called them insurgents, and told them they had brought it on themselves.[54]

Apparently, both Baring and Guarracino tried to tone down the reports of atrocities by the Turkish government, to prevent the rise of anti-Turkish sentiment in Britain. MacGahan's findings, however, caused quite an outrage in Britain and put the pro-Turkish Disraeli government into a very difficult position. Though Forbes's newspaper was behind the revelations, he makes no reference to the incident in his reports from Cyprus, when he meets Baring's controversial father-in-law.[55] Wolseley, however, does refer to the incident in his Cyprus journals. Commenting on Baring's weak character ("rather oriental in disposition"), he writes:

> He has made a mess of his career in marrying much beneath him, the daughter of a Mr. Guarracino who was in our Consular Service and whose character is not supposed to be of the best. Guarracino accompanied Baring on his trip into Bulgaria when drawing up his report on atrocities, and I believe the report was mostly drawn up upon Guarracino's information which was very unreliable.[56]

Wolseley disliked both Baring and Guarracino and felt that the latter's presence in Cyprus was highly suspicious. He suspected that Baring knew in advance of the potential acquisition of Cyprus by Britain, due to his previous position in the British Embassy in Constantinople, and told his wife, who subsequently informed her father, Guarracino, of the imminent transfer. Wolseley further suspected that the rumors for the acquisition of Cyprus most likely started with Guarracino, who came to the island looking to profit from the eventual transfer of power. Indeed, Wolseley writes, Admiral John Hay, Guarracino's "old acquaintance," "named him Assistant Secretary to the Govt. at a salary of £60 a month" as soon as he took over the island on behalf of the Queen.[57] Verifying the prominent position of both Baring and his father-in-law in the early days of the occupation, *The Standard*'s correspondent, John Augustus O'Shea, wrote, on August 22, that "when we first came [to Cyprus] we had to be entirely dependent on Mr. Baring and his father-in-law in our intercourse with the inhabitants."[58] *The Illustrated London News'* correspondent, Samuel Pasfield Oliver, went a step further, considering Guarracino's service indispensable: "Mr. Baring's father-in-law, who has been many years in our Consular service, is well fitted for the highest Government employ here; but the terms offered him are such as he could not possibly accept."[59]

The story, however, as recorded in Wolseley's Cyprus journals is somewhat different, as Guarracino was not even offered a permanent position. When Baring suggested that his father-in-law becomes Wolseley's dragoman, the general was forced to admit that, based on the rumors that were circulating, he didn't quite trust Guarracino for such an important position. Baring insisted, claiming that the rumors were unfair, and Wolseley assured him that he would request further information on Guarracino's character before deciding. Eventually, Wolseley was informed by Austen Layard, the British ambassador in Constantinople, that "he could not recommend [Guarracino] for any position of trust" and told Baring that his father-in-law could not be trusted and, since he was also stricken with fever, he should be asked to resign his post as interpreter.

Once again, it is unclear whether Archibald Forbes knew who Guarracino was when he accompanied him in Cyprus. However, he was intimately familiar with MacGahan and his report of Turkish atrocities in Bulgaria. "My most prominent colleague in the Russo-Turkish war," he wrote in "A War Correspondent's Reminiscences," "was Mr. Januarius Aloysius MacGahan. . . . Of all the men who have earned reputation in this profession of ours, I regard MacGahan as the most brilliant. . . . He it was who stirred Europe to its inmost heart by the terrible, and not less truthful than terrible, pictures of what have passed into history as the 'Bulgarian Atrocities.'"[60] In his 1885 *Souvenirs of Some Continents*, one of his best-known works, Forbes devotes an entire chapter on MacGahan, whom he met in the spring of 1877, about a year before his Cyprus journey. There he also writes that Baring was sent to Bulgaria "with intent to disparage" MacGahan's testimony. However, always according to Forbes, Baring was "an honest man with eyes and a heart" who eventually verified the MacGahan's findings.[61] He repeats the same allegation—that Baring eventually came to accept MacGahan's report—in his 1891 collection of essays, *Barracks, Bivouacs, and Battles*.[62]

If Forbes paints a rather attractive portrait of Baring's work in Cyprus, his description of Wolseley is less flattering. Unlike Herbert, who presented the high commissioner in all his military glory, his descriptions were far more objective, despite their dramatic tone. In describing Wolseley's first entry into Nicosia, for example, Forbes writes that the general decided to "enter the capital of Cyprus in an unostentatious manner rather than harass soldiers by futile marching in the hot weather."[63] He further describes an incident where Wolseley's horse fell sideways to the ground, "carrying his rider down with him."[64] Such descriptions, pragmatic as they might have been, undermined the official construction of the grand and heroic image that accompanied Britain's most celebrated general. Forbes's ambivalence towards Wolseley most likely stemmed from the general's disdain for war correspondents and from his call for the censorship of the news in the *Soldier's Pocket Book*. In fact, in several books and essays, Forbes repeatedly expressed his emphatic objection to Wolseley's position.[65] The two men—who were the most famous representatives in their respective professions—briefly met, for the first time in August 1871, during a military exercise in Surrey, England; the Cyprus expedition, however, was the first time Forbes had the opportunity to watch Wolseley "in action," albeit as an administrator and not as a combatant. A few years later, in 1885, Forbes published an extensive and largely flattering article on Wolseley, which appeared in the May issue of *The English Illustrated Magazine*, under the title "Wolseley: a character sketch."[66] In Cyprus, he writes in this article, he was given the opportunity "of watching [Wolseley's] methods as well as a commander as a civil organiser and administrator."[67] His main characteristic during the administration of the island, he observes, was "equanimity": the general never lost his temper despite the "characteristic obstructiveness of the Turkish authority."[68] He was energetic, worked hard and never fussed. The secret for his great success was the careful selection of a group of men who followed his orders to perfection. This, Forbes writes, is what outsiders have described as "the Wolseley Gang."[69] The general hand-picked every man who worked for him and each has his place in the Wolseley war engine;[70] seen in action, they were "a weapon of extraordinary and diverse force" and Wolseley was the mastermind who controlled everything.[71]

Though Forbes's reports from Cyprus shy away from laying the blame for the inaccurate portrayal of the occupation on Wolseley himself, he is clearly both disappointed with his experience of the island and frustrated with the political establishment's positive spin of what he perceived as a dreadful situation. His final letter from Cyprus was published on August 17, 1878, and it includes his most damning report of the occupation up to that point. He begins by admitting that in the first few weeks of the British occupation, they were only able to gain a "partial and cursory knowledge" of the population.[72] "What I long for," he writes, "is that I should be conversant with the debased Greek patois [i.e., the Greek-Cypriot dialect] which is the language of the people, and that I should put on a fez and a baggy pair of breeches and go among them as one of themselves, and find out all about them, from their songs to their prayers, from their cradles to their graves."[73] This fantasy of dressing like the natives, or of "going native" even for a brief period of time, fascinated many orientalists and famously enabled Richard Burton to adorn a Muslim attire in order to "infiltrate" Mecca. Unable to do so, Forbes informs his readers, in this final letter, he will only provide them with "such information about Cyprus as [he has] gained during a fortnight's residence in it." What follows is a pejorative description of every facet of Cypriot life and the British administration in Cyprus. He informs those who hope to gain government employment that all posts "have already been filled." He writes that "those who see El Dorado" in Cyprus are gravely mistaken. Perhaps some business opportunities may present themselves in the future, he admits, but he advises all those who hope to find their fortunes in Cyprus, to wait for at least one year before venturing forth; and even then, "they must harden their hearts, and prepare for many disappointments, and to be content with modest success."[74] He reaffirms that the island is definitely unhealthy, that "typhoid fever is always present, more or less" and so is phthisis, pneumonia, dropsy, ophthalmia, diphtheria and malaria. Echoing the great majority of scholars, travelers and journalists, he writes that "Cyprus may confidently be backed against the world for ugly women." "I begin to think," he continues in disgust, "that if I stay here long I shall come to regard the pig-faced lady as passable." He complains that the Greeks overcharge the British enormous amounts of money for rent, and this has forced Wolseley and his staff to build their own headquarters in a camp. Forbes closes his letter by indicating that he intends to travel "through the western regions of the island" next, and as "there are no postal communications of any kind there," his next letter might be submitted belatedly. Two weeks later, however, several British newspapers announced that "Mr. Archibald Forbes, whose telegrams in the *Daily News* from Cyprus have been read with so much interest, has unfortunately caught the fever prevailing there, and will have to leave the island."[75]

Forbes's correspondences for *The Daily News* significantly altered the public's initial enthusiastic reception of the acquisition of Cyprus. His more unequivocal denunciation, however, was published shortly after his return from the island in the October issue of *The Nineteenth Century*. Under the allusive title "The 'Fiasco' of Cyprus," the article provided, by far, the most scathing critique of the occupation up to that point, and Forbes's claims were widely discussed both in the daily press and the parliament. He argues that the attempt to "improve Cypriotes out of their existing state of semi-barbarism into a condition of pseudo-civilisation" was simply incidental; it was certainly not what the Anglo-Turkish convention aimed for. "I discovered, to my disgust," Forbes writes, "that so far from being the proud owners of a new acquisition, we are mere tenants at will."[76] The British, he continues, have become "the vassals, the tributaries of a battered and broken barbarian power," of the Ottoman Empire, which still controls the land and which could reclaim the island at any point. The natives, whom the British desired to usher out of barbarity, are still Ottoman subjects. Poking fun at the assertion that the object of the occupation was the defense against a potential Russian aggression, he writes that "it is from the fever-stricken camp of Chiflick, and the miasmatic 'sanatorium' of Dali, the Lord Beaconsfield, like a modern Canute—*absit omen!*—says to Russia, 'Thus far and no further.'"[77] Dismissing the frequently repeated argument that Cyprus was acquired because of its strategic position, he writes that the island

> possesses no harbour; it has but one anchorage, Larnaca, that is practically unavailable; Limassol is away in a corner, and the heavy swell renders Kyrenea [*sic*] too uncertain to be relied on. It produces nothing to speak of; ten thousand men would consume its spare provisions in less than a month. It is so unhealthy that before the unhealthy season proper had fairly set in, 25 per cent. or one-fourth, of the total strength of the troops on it were officially reported on the sick list.[78]

The island, Forbes continues, was so unhealthy that the sanatorium the British built at Dali to deal with the sickness had proven unhealthier than the camp itself. Even the Goorkas, "children of the sun," could not withstand the climate of Cyprus.[79] Referring to Rostovitz and M'Lean's report, which he had read in *The Times*, he writes that, in Cyprus, from June to October, "there is not a family which has not one or more members down with fever."[80] The position and the condition of the island render the British occupation completely useless: it has "no more influence . . . than if Cyprus were in the moon."[81] Britain, Forbes concludes, must "evacuate Cyprus."[82] And if the administration is truly concerned with Russian aggression, they must look to occupying Afghanistan, not "a miserable island in a dead angle of the Mediterranean."[83]

Unsurprisingly, the daily press had a field day with Forbes's condemnation of Cyprus. His article was reprinted, summarized and commented upon widely by several newspapers and magazines. "Mr. Forbes," the *Cambridge Independent Press* wrote, "has drawn up an indictment against the policy of the Government which it will be impossible to answer. He proves conclusively that in an economical and strategical view our occupation of Cyprus is a most serious blunder."[84] In another, rather characteristic, editorial commentary, the *South Wales Daily News* noted:

> Mr. Archibald Forbes has tried Cyprus, and it does not agree with him. He has, therefore come forward to suggest that the Government should give him a taste of Afghanistan. That is the moral of his article on the "Fiasco of Cyprus" which appeared in the new number of the *Nineteen Century.* His hatred of Cyprus and all its surroundings, his anger at the Government for what they have done, and the way they have done it, his contempt at their apologies, and his scorn at the their lack of adequate information, is of the blackest and most unrelieved sort. According to him there is nothing that Cyprus is good for.[85]

Though most newspapers simply reported Forbes's arguments, the more conservative ones urged for caution. *Lloyd's Weekly Newspaper*, for example, rejected Forbes's sensationalism: "it seems," the editors emphatically noted, "Mr. Hepworth Dixon is on his way thither [i.e., to Cyprus], to set the world right on the subject, so that Mr. Forbes can expect only a brief season for his fireworks."[86] *The Western Daily Press* also urged for caution, commenting that "the issues are too vast to be settled by the free and easy stroke of the pen of the special correspondent."[87] *The Yorkshire Post and Leeds Intelligencer* was more blunt, accusing Forbes of "feverish irritability and hasty deductions"; his health, the editors noted, in an apparent reference to the reports that he caught the fever in Cyprus, "has been too much tried by long hardship to permit of his exercising the calm discrimination which such an inquiry demands."[88] But the most creative of all the responses was, undoubtedly, a poem, "The Fiasco of Cyprus" (see Archibald Forbes's article in the *Nineteenth Century*), that appeared in the satirical magazine *Punch*, which "was suspicious of Beaconsfield's foreign policies and steadfastly supported William Gladstone":[89]

> WHEN FORBES, stout Special, his recital
> Of blunder thus baptises,
> As to the meaning of the title
> Perhaps, some doubt arises.
>
> *Fiasco*'s Italian for "bottle."

But "mull" means metaphorically;
Why?—it would puzzle ARISTOTLE
To answer categorically.

But Cyprus wine, or Cyprus mull,
Cost, fever, and the rest of it,
There's only one course for JOHN BULL,—
To gulp, and make the best of it.[90]

As Andrekos Varnava writes, "*Punch* was mature about the 'fiasco'—the English nation, as represented by John Bull, had to make the best of a bad situation."[91] By the time Gladstone would rise to power, however, the initial enthusiasm that surrounded the island's acquisition was indeed replaced by extreme doubt.

Despite Forbes's condemnation of the government's handling of Cyprus, his relationship with the military remained relatively respectful and amiable. Forbes died on March 30, 1900, and, soon afterwards, a preliminary committee was formed whose task was to secure funds for the design and placement of a memorial in honor of Archibald Forbes in St. Paul's Cathedral. Apart from prominent journalists, the committee included some of the top-ranking military officers of the time: Rear-Admiral Charles Beresford, General Evelyn Wood, General Redvers Buller, General Henry Brackenbury, and, of course, Viscount Wolseley himself.[92] The great accomplishments of all these men were, at some point or another, described by Forbes in his correspondences and in his books. He had sung the praise of Charles Beresford and his brother, William, in his essay "Bill Beresford and the Victoria Cross";[93] he did the same for Evelyn Wood and Redvers Buller in *Memories and Studies of War and Peace*, and elsewhere;[94] and, most importantly, Wolseley and Brackenbury were part of that "gang" that he so memorably mythologized in his character sketch of the General. On Saturday, May 31, 1902, the memorial was unveiled in the crypt of St. Paul's Cathedral. Wolseley, who was also one of the donors, led the unveiling and spoke to the crowd of journalists, politicians and military men in attendance. He described Forbes as an "old friend . . . whom he knew very well," praised his "military knowledge," and underlined the fact that he enlisted in the Royal Dragoons, an experience which taught him "the A B C in military matters and in the working of an army."[95] As in the case of the Sudan Correspondents' memorial, the concluding words of Wolseley's eulogy bear testimony to the interdependent and intimate relationship between the press and the military in Victorian England:

> [Forbes] always spoke of the British soldier in the highest terms, and he could compare him with the men found in the armies of foreign countries in a manner which others could not do. He was a man of great force of character, of great determination, but a man who, at the same time, had great power of

> recording on paper, in the most vigorous English, the deeds passing around him. He was one of those very few men who, in extreme danger, exposed to a heavy fire, could sit down and write clearly and forcibly all that was passing around him, so that anyone could see as in a picture the events which were recorded. . . . I would be ridiculous . . . to recount the many campaigns and the risks he ran—deliberately ran—for a good purpose; and, indeed, when one thought of these, he could not help feeling he expressed the feelings of the large majority of the people of England who read his letters . . . [and] followed every incident he described. When he was taken from them they lost a man who wrote not only a vigorous English but who brought to bear on his profession an enormous amount of daring, courage, and determination.[96]

NOTES

1. *Western Gazette*, April 6, 1900, p. 5.
2. Arthur, *Letters of Lord and Lady Wolseley*, 31.
3. Thomas Seccombe, "Archibald Forbes," in *Dictionary of National Biography: Supplement Vol. 2.* Eds. Leslie Stephen and Sidney Lee (London: Smith, Elder and Co., 1901), 222.
4. J.S.R. Phillips, "The Growth of Journalism," in *The Cambridge History of English Literature. Vol. 14: The Nineteenth Century, Part 3,* eds. Adolphus William Ward and Alfred Rayney Waller (Cambridge: Cambridge University Press, 1964), 190.
5. Ibid.
6. For more information on Forbes's reports from war-zones see W. Hamish Fraser, *The Wars of Archibald Forbes* (Aberdeen: Aberdeen University Press, 2015).
7. William Henry Rideing, *Many Celebrities and a Few Others: A Bundle of Reminiscences* (New York: Doubleday, Page and Co., 1912), 268.
8. *Fifeshire Advertiser*, April 6, 1878, p. 1.
9. For Twain's introduction of Forbes see the *Hartford Weekly Times*, November 23, 1881, p. 2.
10. For Forbes's rivalry with Wilde and their quarrels during their lecture tours in America see: Richard Ellmann, *Oscar Wilde* (New York: Vintage, 1988). In his *Souvenirs of Some Continents* Forbes writes: "An interesting phase of American society is its keen sympathy with things artistic. Mr. Oscar Wilde went to America with a sham and self-constituted mission, to infuse into its benighted people the principles of what he and the paltry filigree-work school of which he is an accident, prate about as 'true art.' He found to his discomfiture that cultured Americans knew a great deal more about the principles of art than he could tell them; and that they had learned in a school the canons of which inculcated a higher ideal than could be attained by what lavishness soever in sunflower and lily decorations, spite of what he called the 'gaudy leonine beauty' of the former vegetable, and the 'tender grace' of the latter." Archibald Forbes, *Souvenirs of Some Continents* (London: Macmillan and Co., 1885), 249.
11. Lee M. Edwards, "Hubert Herkomer in America," *American Art Journal* 21, no. 3 (1989): 50.
12. *Western Gazette*, April 6, 1900, p. 5.
13. "Archibald Forbes and his Reminiscences." *The Review of Reviews* 4 (1891): 295.
14. HC Deb, 15 August 1879, vol. 249, cc1036–7.
15. HC Deb, 08 February 1915, vol. 69, cc337–38.
16. Archibald Forbes, "The Fiasco of Cyprus," *The Nineteenth Century: A Monthly Review* 4 (1878): 609.
17. Ibid.
18. *A Handbook for Travellers in Turkey in Asia*, 4th ed. (London: John Murray, 1878), 177.
19. Forbes, "Fiasco," 609. Apart from geographical and historical information, the pre-1878 versions of the handbook include the following ominous commentary: "All the prosperity for which it was of old renowned has vanished under the destructive influence of Ottoman rule; yet

not even this can wholly obliterate the traces of what has been, or the indications of what might be, were good government ever to become the lot of the people" *A Handbook for Travellers in Turkey*, 3rd ed. (London: John Murray, 1854), 259.

20. *Daily News*, July 18, 1878, p. 5.
21. *Daily News*, July 19, 1878, p. 5.
22. *Daily News,* August 8, 1878, p. 5.
23. *Daily News*, August 8, 1878, p. 5.
24. *Daily News*, August 8, 1878, p. 5.
25. *Daily News*, August 9, 1878, p. 5.
26. *Daily News*, August 9, 1878, p. 5.
27. *Daily News*, August 9, 1878, p. 5.
28. *Daily News*, August 7, 1878, p. 5.
29. *Daily News*, August 1, 1878, p. 5.
30. *Daily News*, August 12, 1878, p. 5.
31. *Daily News*, August 15, 1878, p. 5.
32. *Daily News*, August 15, 1878, p. 5.
33. *Daily News*, August 15, 1878, p. 5.
34. *Daily News*, August 15, 1878, p. 5.
35. Neville Lloyd Walford, *Mr. Archibald Forbes and the Zulu War* (London: Samuel Tinsley and Co., 1880), 3.
36. *Daily News*, August 10, 1878, p. 5.
37. *Evening Telegraph*, August 19, 1878, p. 2.
38. *Daily News*, July 23, 1878, p. 5.
39. *Daily News*, July 26, 1878, p. 5.
40. *Daily News*, July 27, 1878, p. 5.
41. *Daily News*, August 5, 1878, p. 5.
42. *Daily News*, August 8, 1878, p. 5.
43. *Daily News*, August 12, 1878, p. 5.
44. *Daily News*, August 15, 1878, p. 5. The report was composed on August 3.
45. *Daily News*, August 16, 1878, p. 5. In the same report, Forbes informs his readers that, apart from the long list of white soldiers who were sick, "Mr Baring [was also] ill with fever."
46. *Daily News*, August 13, 1878, p.6.
47. HC Deb, 16 August 1878, vol. 242, cc2089.
48. HC Deb, 16 August 1878, vol. 242, cc2089–90.
49. HC Deb, 16 August 1878, vol. 242, cc2089–90.
50. Archibald Forbes, "My Campaign in Pall Mall," *The Universal Review* 3 (1889): 375–76. Also included in Archibald Forbes, *Barracks, Bivouacs, and Battles* (London: Macmillan and Co., 1891).
51. *Daily News*, August 27, 1878, p. 5.
52. Forbes, "My Campaign," 376.
53. Forbes's article "My Campaign in Pall Mall" outlines in detail this strained relationship between war correspondents and the British officials. See Forbes, *Baracks*, 307–28.
54. Januarius Aloysius MacGahan and Eugene Schuyler, *The Turkish Atrocities in Bulgaria: Letters of the Special Commissioner of the "Daily News," J.A. MacGahan* (London: Bradbury, Agnew and Co., 1876), 60.
55. Forbes does describe Baring as "a man of exceptional experience in knowledge of Turkish laws" (*Daily News*, August 13, 1878, p. 6).
56. Wolseley, *Cyprus 1878*, 37.
57. Ibid.
58. *Standard*, September 5, 1878, p. 5.
59. *Illustrated London News*, Vol. 73, October 19, 1878, p. 378.
60. Archibald Forbes, "A War Correspondents Reminiscences," *The Nineteenth Century* 30 (1891): 414.
61. Forbes, *Souvenirs*, 123–24.
62. Forbes *Baracks*, 310. There is some truth in Forbes's understanding that Baring came to verify MacGahan's findings in Bulgaria. MacGahan's report, which constantly juxtaposes Bar-

ing's findings with his own, probably left no room for Baring to manoeuvre out of the very difficult position of supporting the Turkish government's assertions.

63. *Daily News*, August 12, 1878, p. 5.
64. *Daily News*, August 12, 1878, p. 5.
65. Archibald Forbes, *Memories and Studies of War and Peace* (London: Cassell and Co., 1895), 354–56; Forbes, *Souvenirs*, 158–19; Forbes, *Baracks*, 307–8.
66. Reprinted in Forbes, *Souvenirs*.
67. Forbes, *Souvenirs*, 170.
68. Ibid.
69. Ibid., 171.
70. Ibid., 176.
71. Ibid., 177. Segments of Forbes's complimentary depiction of Wolseley were widely reprinted or summarized by the press. One negative outcome of his depiction, however, related to his claim that Wolseley had planted the flag on the Mess-house in the Siege of Lucknow. Several authorities, including Wolseley himself, publicly refuted the claim and Forbes was forced to retract it. For more information see Morgan Fenwolf, "Who planted the Flag on the Mess-house at Lucknow?" *The Army and Nave Magazine* 10 (1885): 338–47.
72. *Daily News*, August 27, 1878, p. 5.
73. *Daily News*, August 27, 1878, p. 5.
74. *Daily News*, August 27, 1878, p. 5.
75. *Sheffield and Rotherham Independent*, August 24, 1878, p. 10.
76. Forbes, "Fiasco," 610.
77. Ibid., 615.
78. Ibid., 617.
79. Ibid., 618.
80. Ibid., 625.
81. Ibid., 623.
82. Ibid., 625.
83. Ibid., 626.
84. *Cambridge Independent Press*, October 5, 1878, p. 5.
85. *South Wales Daily News*, September 30, 1878, p. 2.
86. *Lloyd's Weekly Newspaper* – October 6, 1878, p. 6.
87. *Western Daily Press*, September 30, 1878, p. 3.
88. *Yorkshire Post and Leeds Intelligencer*, October 3, 1878, p. 4.
89. Varnava, "*Punch*," 168.
90. "The Fiasco of Cyprus," *Punch* 75 (October 19, 1878): 173.
91. Varnava, "*Punch*," 178.
92. *Western Times*, May 9, 1901, p. 4.
93. Forbes, *Baracks*, 129–50.
94. See Forbes, *Memories and Studies*.
95. *Aberdeen Weekly Journal*, June 2, 1902, p. 6.
96. *Aberdeen Weekly Journal*, June 2, 1902, p. 6.

Chapter Five

John Augustus O'Shea and *The London Evening Standard*

The Irish journalist John Augustus O'Shea was thirty-nine years old, about the same age as Archibald Forbes, when he traveled to Cyprus to cover the occupation on behalf of *The Standard.* Though he was not as famous as his esteemed colleague of *The Daily News*, he was still one of the most prominent special correspondents in Britain and the "raciest of all the Irish journalists in London."[1] Whatever his fame was among the English public and his fellow London correspondents, his own countrymen regarded him as "one of the leading, but also one of the most adventurous, pressmen of modern times."[2] Forbes and O'Shea knew each other well and had covered, as special correspondents, many of the same historical events. They both reported the events of the Franco-German War, the Paris Commune, the Carlist Wars in Spain, and the famine in Bengal. Frederick Villiers—arguably one of the most legendary sketch artists of his times—described O'Shea as "a dear, delightful character, full of innocent fun."[3] He further narrates a chance meeting between Forbes and O'Shea, on a steamship sailing from India, where the two correspondents traveled to cover the Bengal famine. Forbes had run to the rescue of O'Shea when the latter's clothes and money were stolen by a thief.[4] He was also a family friend of the Vizetelly family,[5] particularly Frank Vizetelly, whose nephew, Edward, covered the Cyprus occupation as a special correspondent on behalf of *The Glasgow Herald.*[6] O'Shea signed many of his early articles with the pseudonym "Irish Bohemian," and among his friends he was known as funny and witty; they jokingly called him "The Gineral," "in virtue as much of a long and fierce looking moustache as of his military experiences."[7] His literary background is well-documented in his correspondences, his short stories and his books. Much of his understanding of distant colonies or Britain's wars around the globe are filtered through countless references to the British literary tradition or the Western literary canon. At one point, O'Shea crossed swords with Ireland's most esteemed poet, W. B. Yeats, when the latter misattributed a French popular story adapted and translated by O'Shea to an Irish legend.[8]

Like Forbes, O'Shea had some military experience, having joined the Papal Catholic Army in 1860; he "fought at the Siege of Ancona and elsewhere, was wounded, and finally surrendered with the rest of the army."[9] His deep devotion to the army and his restless exploits as a special war correspondent were noted by the satirical magazine *Punch*, which published the following poem, on January 17, 1885, as a commentary on O'Shea's book *Leaves from the Life of a Special Correspondent*:

> Oh bright and lively is O'Shea—that is this John Augustus is—
> His book as bright and lively as the author, you may trust us, is
> He discourseth of NAPOLEON, tobacco and philology;
> Of Paris and of pugilists, Lord WOLSELEY and zoology;
> Of GAMBETTA and of CALCRAFT, of cookery and quackery;
> Of SINNETT and balloonacy, of SALA and of THACKERAY
> With "special" journeys to and fro, direct, delayed, and round-about,
> For here and there and everywhere this Special loves to bound about!
> With most things he is conversant, from monkey unto mineral—
> And talks on warlike matters like a modern Meejor Gineral!

Indeed, O'Shea's writing, as well as his personality, are emblematic of the soldier-journalist type that was common among Victorian England's war correspondents. Like many of his colleagues, he was deeply offended by Wolseley's well-known despise of war correspondents. In *Leaves from the life of a special correspondent*, O'Shea refers to the special correspondents who lost their lives while performing their duties and raises them to the same level of gallantry as the combatants themselves. He then proceeds to discuss Wolseley's famous condemnation of correspondents in the *Soldier's Pocket Book*:

> And yet it is this order which one Colonel Sir Garnet Wolseley, C.B. K.C.M.G., writing at Montreal in 1869, stigmatizes as "newly invented curses to armies"—under the rose, I perhaps may agree with him to some extent—and counsels general officers to use as a medium for spreading false news to deceive the enemy—not a nice but a thoroughly legitimate expedient; and finally, most absurdly and unjustly dismisses as "a race of drones who are an incumbrance, who eat the rations of fighting men and *do no work at all*. I am confident the riper judgment of Lord Wolseley of Cairo would not endorse the immature opinion about a most industrious set of gentlemen, expressed by his namesake, the staff colonel.[10]

Apparently, O'Shea blamed Wolseley's derogative opinion of correspondents on his youthful immaturity, though the general was hardly a novice when he wrote the *Soldier's Pocket Book* (he was thirty-six years old and had already led many battles). But even in his disagreement with Wolseley, O'Shea recognizes, in some respects, both the legitimacy and spirit of Wolseley's statement. Furthermore, his references to Wolseley in his reports from Cyprus, as well as in his articles, are generally congenial and respectful.

O'Shea's journey to Cyprus is a kind of amusing quixotic endeavor that reflects the profound excitement of journalists and other intellectuals following the acquisition of the island. His first report on Cyprus, on behalf of *The Standard*, was written from Bari, in Italy, on July 13, a mere four days after the official announcement of the acquisition, and it begins with the following enthusiastic statement:

> Everybody who has any pretention to be anybody would now be ashamed not to be able to talk glibly of Cyprus, our new possession. Since that Monday morning, when the news was spread in London that the island had been transferred to us, how we have all furbished up our knowledge respecting it. It is no longer a *terra incognita*. Limassol, Famagosta [*sic*], Nicosia, and Larnaca by this time must have grown familiar in men's mouths as Putney and Mile-end, Camberwell and Hammersmith.[11]

Estimating that in a year's time, "there will be personally conducted excursions *en masse*" to the island, he informs his readers that he rejected to follow the standard route to Cyprus (via Brindisi and Smyrna) and opted instead "to go on to Malta, by way of Syracuse."[12] Using his good relationship with the army—"a few old friendships and new letters of introduction"—he hoped that he would be able to join the troops bound for Cyprus and sail with them in their historic journey. His plan, of course, was to arrive there before General Wolseley in order to report on his much-anticipated entry into Cyprus. "Surely," he wrote in anticipation of this momentous event, "there will be more of the ceremony that should attend an historic act when the hero of the Red river and Coomassie arrives. If such there be, I shall see it, and shall be, in a humble way, one of its historiographers."[13] Dismissing all the "nonsense" reported in England about Cyprus, he emphatically stresses that "there is no question that its situation for us is all that could be desired," that "it is the very place we wanted, the most valuable acquisition we have made since Aden," and that "Sir Garnet Wolseley is the right man in the right place."[14] His excitement is such that he feels obliged to inform his readers that "the coloquintida, figured as the essence of bitterness by Shakespeare, is a product of the island" and that the Crusaders bestowed upon the island "the name of Makaria, or the Happy Land, because of its abundance, healthfulness, and smiling homesteads."[15] Yet all this excitement is clearly fueled, first, by O'Shea's admiration of imperial might and, second, by his conviction that the Empire has added to its long list of possessions an island whose history has been long connected to the British history and literary tradition. The population of the island is completely irrelevant to his discussion of any future prospects. In this first correspondence, he describes the inhabitants of Cyprus as an "effete population of fawning and pilfering, bland and lying, affable and treacherous semi-Greeks."[16]

The following day, July 14, O'Shea found his way to Syracuse and caught a steamer to Valetta. Having reached Malta, he tried to secure a passage to Cyprus on one of the navy's ships. For the next few days he reported on the army's preparations for the Cyprus journey and he continued to fantasize about the condition of the island. He contemplated, for example, that "there will be some roughing it for the first few weeks" but living in a tent could not be so bad, especially if that tent is fixed in the famous groves of Cyprus: "They say that there are thickets of oak and fir, and clumps of cherry, carob, and walnut there. But if it be but a legend! The truth is nobody knows anything of Cyprus—the garrison library has been ransacked to no purpose."[17] On July 17, Wolseley arrives in Valetta on board the *Madura*. Showing his intimate knowledge of the general's character, O'Shea explained to his readers that Wolseley, as he could personally attest, "dislikes unnecessary parade."[18] Owing to his army connections and some letters of introduction, he did, eventually, secure a passage to Cyprus, albeit not with the general's armada, as he had hoped, which was scheduled to depart on the 18th, but with the steamer *St. Osyth* that was scheduled to sail on the 19th. However, the steamer's departure was further delayed and on the 22nd O'Shea was still sailing towards Cyprus, somewhere off the coast of Crete, lamenting the fact that he would miss Wolseley's historic arrival. Ironically, a few days later, when he would arrive in Cyprus at last, he would also miss Wolseley's historic entry into the island's capital because he was unable "to charter a conveyance."[19]

Still on his way to Cyprus, and having nothing better to describe, O'Shea veers off subject and discusses several trivial matters. In one of his most telling off-subject descriptions—one that points to the indisputable colonial mind-set that characterizes much of the Victorian era's journalistic descriptions—he begins to compare the Indian regiment on board the steamer with "European" (i.e., white) troops:

> The Indian troops are fine . . . but to say that they are equal to any European troops is to make of them a laughable stock, to insult them by fulsome flattery, to lessen their sterling merits, by raising an exaggerated conception of unreal ones. The Indians are good soldiers, but it is an utter illusion to put them on a level with good European soldiers. If they were all this, how is it we have conquered them; how is it we keep them in check? Their cavalry are excellent, and they and a couple of the infantry regiments of the contingent might probably be employed in a European campaign; but as for the remainder, they would be an embarrassment in winter; the cold would kill them off like so many flies.[20]

Figure 5.1. "The occupation of Cyprus: Indian troops at work." ***Source: The Graphic*****, July 27, 1878.**

This comparison between Indian and European troops was a common topic of debate among politicians, journalists, and army personnel during the second half of the nineteenth century in Britain. The deeper concern here—as it emerges from O'Shea's position as well—goes far beyond the question of the Indian army's efficiency or potential; these statements represent a categorical justification of the imperial conquering of the "inferior races" and of the right of the Empire to rule over them. It is not surprising, for example, that the interest of the British press in the participation of the Indian troops, in the first weeks of the Cyprus occupation, was commonly discussed in the context of a hierarchical comparison between them and the British "white" troops. The topic certainly deserves a separate examination in itself; a few examples of this representation, however, can be revealing. A couple of weeks into the occupation of the island, the British press was already discussing the usefulness of keeping a large contingence of Indian troops in Cyprus, and the British Parliament debated whether the Indians should be sent home. By August 7, Archibald Forbes was writing that the presence of the Indian troops in Cyprus is utterly useless: Sir Garnet Wolseley, he wrote, "could part with them with perfect serenity."[21] Other newspapers, responding to this debate, noted sarcastically that, like Cyprus, "India . . . is also hot, and not wholly free from reptiles, and it seemed reasonable to hope that the Indian troops would soon be quite at home in their new quarters."[22] This dismissive attitude towards the Indian troops in Cyprus, and the deeper reason behind the interest of the British press, was rooted in the debate, which intensified just a few weeks prior to the island's occupation, on the propriety of deploying native troops in territories outside the colonies. The issue arose when the British government deployed Indian troops to Malta, in 1878, without the prior consent of the Parliament. These were, of course, the same troops that would be deployed to Cyprus; the move of the government, however, was without precedent. The Liberals accused the ruling government of violating the constitution and brought the issue to both Houses of Parliament. Responding to this crisis, some newspapers complained of the severe moral consequences of the move. "It is a bad sign," wrote the *Dundee Courier* on May 13, "when we are summoning inferior races to assist us in fighting our battles . . . and we are treated to the story of the Roman decadence in similar circumstances."[23] Another correspondent asserted that the Indian troops are in fact as war-like and able as the English and European troops. What they need "as it is expected," is a "great deal of 'leading'"; as long as these troops were led by English officers, they would be "ready and able if need be to defend the integrity of our Empire at home and abroad."[24] In the House of Lords, the debate on the deployment of native troops abroad ranged from complaints that native officers seem to exercise more authority on native soldiers than the European officers (Robert Adair, 1st Baron Waveney), to statements that "the Army of Southern India could not fairly and properly be presented on the field of battle unless there were European officers in connection with every company" (Lord Napier and Ettrick) or that "it would be an evil day for the Indian Army and for ourselves if, under any pretext, we were to revert to a system which had weakened and deteriorated European influence on the Native mind" (Lord John Lawrence).[25] O'Shea's ruminations then, on board the *St. Osyth*, are part of a wider debate on how to manage Britain's vast empire in the context of the evident superiority—military, racial, or technological—of the colonizers over the colonized.

On the evening of July 25, O'Shea arrived in Cyprus—the land he likens to California or Australia during the "gold fever"[26]—as the steamer "dropped anchor in the midst of the proud and powerful fleet that bears the Union Jack bravely."[27] His first view of Cyprus, much like that of his fellow correspondents, is rather disheartening:

> At dawn the fog cleared away, and we had our first view of Cyprus—a range of stony eminences, greyish-blue, irregular, bare of herbage. As the sun burst forth in terrible strength and blinding glare we could distinguish palm trees

> standing sentinel-like alone on the beach; but no meadows, no groves, no rivulets; no flocks or herds. A dry uninviting land.[28]

In fact, for O'Shea, the most magnificent sight in Cyprus in this first encounter with the island, was the fleet anchored in the sea: "a panorama of formidable beauty, of diversity, and active life!"[29] Once he disembarks the *St. Osyth* and enters the city of Larnaca, his discontent is perhaps unrivaled among the correspondents who covered the occupation. His initial excitement, equally unrivaled among the Cyprus correspondents, turned into disgust:

> What a wretched decayed congeries of ruinous white-washed cabins! A whited sepulchre! Suez is half century before it in civilization. Narrow, uneven streets; a few rugged side paths; tenements hastily run up of lath and plaster; here and there a pretentious house of worship with semi-globular dome; a bazaar of the usual Asiatic type, with a patched awning of mats, a ragged fretwork overhead; wide arched and groined barn-like stores, as yet guiltless of merchandise; cobblers' benches, smiths' forges, stalls with stuffs, pipes, curiosities; unpleasant odours, offal, flies, dogs. Such is Larnaca![30]

This utterly depressing space was populated, according to O'Shea, by an equally dismal-looking people who came from all the corners of the earth:

> Jewish gabardines, baggy trousers, Egyptians in multi-buttoned short jackets, shrouded Mahometan [*sic*] women in yashmaks, bare-headed Christian girls who decidedly are not of the progeny of Venus, Turks in fez and back broadcloth, and Franks in topee and thin white tunics, Greek priests in brimless cylindrical headgear and Oxford-like gowns, and soldiers—Indian, European, and Turkish.[31]

Interestingly, this multicultural representation of the subalterns, which O'Shea finds so abhorrent, was, to a large extent, a result of colonialism itself, much like the sudden and ephemeral commercial activity in the small town of Larnaca. But the standard by which O'Shea measures the island's degree of civilization is clearly filtered through his position as a white privileged and educated man. For one thing, his parallelisms, throughout his writing from Cyprus, are devoid of any cultural, social, or historical considerations: hence, the traditional tunics of the Greek priests are described as Oxford-like gowns and the Greek girls as not the progeny of Venus. One of his most telling descriptions is his complaint that there are no amusements on the island—the understanding, of course, being that amusements are either linked to Western perceptions of entertainment or that designating enough time for entertainment is a sign of civilization: "The amusements here are *nil*; there is no music; I am advised there is but one piano on the island; there is no society; there is no resort for an afternoon stroll; true, there is one English billiard-table, but there is no chalk! But civilisation is sure to bring its adjuncts."[32] The absence of billiard tables and chalk, pianos, and afternoon strolls were, for O'Shea, signs of a backward and uncivilized society. But throughout his experiences in Cyprus, and despite his persistent depiction of the island as uncivilized, he is always certain of the progress that the British occupation will bring to the island. The island "can and will be made handsome and I trust prosperous, in a few years," he writes in the same correspondence.[33]

Like many of his fellow correspondents and most of the British travelers to the island, O'Shea reserves his most vitriolic description for the island's inhabitants. "The inhabitants," he writes after a two-week stay on the island, "generally are peacefully disposed, lazy, tolerant to strangers, fond of pleasure, and somewhat addicted to intemperance, but robbery and murder are unknown among them."[34] In a rather common paternalistic tone, he suggests that, despite the Greek inhabitants' desire to unite the island with Greece, "the bulk of the inhabitants who have brains to understand the transfer are satisfied."[35] By mid-August, after a three-week stay on the island, his derogatory view of the inhabitants becomes even more categorical. There is absolutely nothing remarkable in their character, he observes. They are ignorant, and they kill time on benches. The Greeks—the "Orientalised Greeks" as he describes them—are dirty and the Christian women dress slatternly and age early. The Muslim women are always covered but under their veil, he detects a desirous look towards the new strangers (i.e., the British).[36]

Like his *Daily News* colleague, Forbes, O'Shea was appalled by both the island's desolation and the inhabitants' way of life. But unlike his famous friend, he does not deduce that this dismal state of affairs points to either a political blunder in the acquisition of the island or to a less prosperous future for the newest British colony. On the contrary, many of his correspondences include optimistic expressions of a bright future that is certain to arrive now that the British administer the island. "That the good time will come is a certainty," he wrote on August 11; in time, "Cyprus, of course, will become a stronghold."[37] Responding to the liberal M.P., Bernhard Samuelson, and his concerns regarding the occupation of Cyprus—the absence of prober ports, the severe draught and the necessary expenses for the building of barracks for the soldiers[38]—he suggests that "the very drawbacks that exercise the mind of Mr. Samuelson, M.P. will render its armament more easy. The fewer the good anchorages, the fewer fortifications will have to be erected to protect its coastline."[39] He blames all the negativity regarding the occupation on opportunist politicians and disappointed travelers. In one of his common usages of the Western literary tradition in the context of describing the occupation of the island, he writes:

> Certes, this is not the land that Demodocus sang to Ulysses, the land of soft shores, blooming groves, and balmy skies. Nor are the men of Cyprus the

> "noble swelling spirits" whom Iago "flusrer'd with flowing cups." But, on the other hand, it would be wrong to run away with the idea which seems to have taken possession of members of both our Legislative Houses, who undervalue our new acquisition undeservedly in the debates, the reports of which are to hand.[40]

For O'Shea, there were two main problems that exasperated the situation in Cyprus and led to the unfair critique of journalists and politicians alike regarding the occupation. The first was the utter disappointment of merchants and emigrants who had hoped to find prosperity on the island. Having seen enough of the island's desolation, by mid-August, he tells his readers, as Forbes did, that he "would not advise Englishmen to come" and those who insist on moving to Cyprus, should be "used to tropical climates" and should not be "afraid to rough it."[41] When his military friends told him of the inquiries they receive about potential "nice openings" in Cyprus for young British men, he responds that "emphatically there are no 'nice' openings for anybody. . . . There is much work to be done, but beardless and aspiring younger sons are not those to do it at the moment."[42] Those who came to the island in a rush, he continues, "are going away again" and return to England "inveighing bitterly against the island" and giving "the gloomiest accounts of it." He advises his readers not to give them credit: "They were the wrong men for the place, and hung out the flag for distress at the first challenge—a touch of low fever, an ill-cooked meal, a few degrees of heat extra, or a trifle of that kind."[43] By the end of August, he was reporting that "adventurers are still arriving in large numbers, but not in such numbers as they are going away"[44] and that "Englishmen come by every steamer—and by every steamer other Englishmen depart, chicken-hearted adventurers, dismayed under the very lintel of the gate."[45] Apparently, his attitude towards the work that needed to be done in Cyprus was in line with his soldierly view of correspondents. What the British administration of Cyprus needed, in this transitional time, were strong and able soldiers, men who are accustomed to "roughing it" under extremely difficult circumstances. Though, in his first correspondences, he had bemoaned the lack of entertainment in Cyprus, he now writes that those who were disappointed were weak-hearted, spoiled and too accustomed to the luxuries of England. Expressing his confidence that Cyprus will eventually become civilized under British rule, he claims that "when the simple-minded peasantry realise the value of the reforms which are to be introduced, there will be universal jubilee here, and the croakers in England who wish for political motives that our adoption of the island should be disastrous will hang their heads in shame."[46] Finally, putting his faith in the valiant British army and the leadership qualities of Wolseley, he writes that the high commissioner "is not letting the grass grow under his feet";[47] he "has been multiplying himself since his arrival . . . he has been accumulating information from every source, and infusing some of his own restless energy into the officials that surround him."[48]

The second problem that O'Shea confronts in his response to the critics of the occupation is the perennial subject of the island's unhealthiness. As expected, his correspondences in *The Standard* persistently understate the prevalence of disease on the island. Cyprus, he insists, is "hot, but not unhealthy so much as uncomfortable" and malaria is nowhere to be found.[49] Three weeks into his stay, he reports that the island is not "so unhealthy as represented; there is comparatively little dangerous fever, though there is much a weakening and depressing form. Malaria exists only during certain months and in certain districts."[50] Though he does report on the number of sick soldiers, he dismisses any claims that the Cyprus fever amounted to an epidemic. "A very large number of British soldiers—forty-four in one regiment alone—put in an appearance before the doctor yesterday," he wrote on August 16. But he blamed their sickness on "the diurnal heat and nocturnal dew under the wretched single cloth bell tents."[51] At some point, he admits that he himself had fallen sick from fever, and that he wrote some of his correspondences while feverish; nevertheless, he insists, the Cyprus fever is not dangerous at all.[52] By the end of August he informed *The Standard*'s readers that "the fever which was prevalent is on the decline"[53] and, perhaps responding to Forbes's estimates, he put the total number of sick soldiers at "under nine per cent."[54]

The sharp contradiction between Forbes's and O'Shea's accounts of Cyprus's unhealthiness did not go unnoticed by the British press. On August 20, *The Nottingham Evening Post* published an extensive commentary on the conflicting information regarding sickness as described by the two correspondents:

> One of the most engrossing topics of discussion in the metropolis just now is the nature of the climate of Cyprus, and the health of our troops there stationed. . . . This controversy has arisen chiefly from the startling statements made by the special correspondent of one of the London daily papers, and their contradiction by the special correspondent of another. Mr. Forbes, who represents the *Daily News*, has been writing home such accounts of the island as would lead one to regard the place as a pit of pestilence; whilst on the other hand Mr. O'Shea who is out there for the *Standard*, states the climate of the island is genial, its soil prolific, its scenery superb, its inhabitants healthy, and the condition of the troops satisfactory. When doctors differ who shall decide? Both Mr. Forbes and Mr. O'Shea are men of acknowledged ability, and both, no doubt, are doing the best they can, each in the interest of the journal which he represents. They are both, although tolerably young men, veterans of the pen, having passed through many campaigns and chronicled those events which have decided the fates of nations.[55]

The anonymous writer ends his report by wishing that O'Shea's version is the more correct, "for the sake of mere humanity." That two of Britain's leading correspondents disagreed on the healthiness of Cyprus should not be surprising at all; after all, this sharp division was also reflected in the parliamentary debates and became part of the political divisions that separated Liberals and Conservatives in 1878. But O'Shea's firm belief in the prospects of Cyprus's colonization is more rooted, much like Leger Herbert's, in his intimate relationship with the British Army; a congenial relationship he repeatedly stresses in his letters and telegrams from the island. Even his response to the critics of the occupation bears the marks of a military response: in short, those who were disappointed with the occupation were just too weak, consequently, unable to "rough it." When he returned to England from Cyprus, sometime in late September, O'Shea met a fellow correspondent from the *Aberdeen Weekly Journal* who recounted this meeting in the October 1 edition of the newspaper. The "universally popular press man," recounted the journalist, looked as if he had just returned from a vacation in the south coast of England. Apparently, O'Shea told him that "he had never a day's illness during his stay," a statement contradicted by his own correspondences from the island. "The complaints against the climate of our latest possession," O'Shea informed him, repeating his much-stated conclusion, "have principally been by 'finicking' gentlemen not used to roughing it"; But for a man like himself, "who has lived through the cold of a Norwegian winter, the hunger of a Parisian siege, and the fever of India in the sultry season, to say nothing of such trifles as sleeping in a barge on the Danube during the Vienna Exhibition, camping on the hills of Navarre with the Carlist Guerillas, does not much heed scant accommodation in Cyprian villages, or the inconveniences of 92 degrees in the shade at six in the morning."[56] Owing to his experiences in Cyprus, the article concludes, O'Shea was asked to deliver some lectures in London but he was "obliged to decline temporarily pending the prospect of a run to Cabul."

Paradoxically, eight years after his Cyprus adventure, a curious incident took place during one of O'Shea's public lectures, that completely undermined his insistence that the Cyprus fever was a rather trivial affair exaggerated by weaker men. In December 1886, he was invited to deliver a lecture in Scotland, on his experience of the Paris Siege, under the title "The Humours of Paris Besieged."[57] During the lecture, the audience complained that his voice was too soft and "the utterance was very indistinct, making it difficult for the audience to follow him." When the situation did not improve, the audience became impatient and noisy. Some decided to leave as O'Shea was speaking, and others found "great amusement in stamping their feet by way of applauding those who retired." Trying to explain his low voice, O'Shea told the audience, according to one newspaper's account, that he had lost it "through a trouble he had caught in Cyprus." Eventually, the lecture ended abruptly when the lights went out, presumably after the interference of a disgruntled attendee.

It seems that years after his brief sojourn, O'Shea's Cyprus experience was still very much with him—be it as an excuse or as an actual chronic illness. He would revisit the subject of Cyprus on several occasions after his return from the island. As I will discuss shortly, in December 1886, when the incident described above took place in Scotland, he had just published an autobiographical short story about Cyprus. In the spring of 1879, O'Shea returned to the subject of Cyprus, in the context of reviewing one of the most popular travel books on Cyprus, Hepworth Dixon's *British Cyprus.* Seen alongside his correspondences, this review, published in the May 1879 issue of *Tinsley's* magazine, verifies, in the most definite way, his appreciation of the colonial work of the British Army, as well as his admitted friendship with many of the officers. One of the most offensive aspects of Dixon's book, O'Shea wrote, was his habit of calling officers—"many of them my personal friends"[58]—without their first names or honorifics. He finds Dixon a mediocre writer who got all the military and historical events that took place during the first months of the Cyprus occupation completely wrong, and who does not have the proper respect for the army and its officers. Though his excitement over the prospects of the island is more measured in this review, it also constitutes a reaffirmation of his belief that what is needed in Cyprus is a kind of paternal despotism. "White men, not natives, can never till its fields," he writes, "but white men with capital can *supervise their culture* and make profit out of the harvests."[59] Both unequivocally and unapologetically, what he underlines here are the two pillars of imperial policy: the making of profit and the empire's civilizing mission.

The irony in O'Shea's critique of *British Cyprus* lies in the fact that his own recollections of the island are as much filtered through an exaggerated colonial discourse as Dixon's are. O'Shea wrote two extensive articles that reflect on his Cyprus experience and describe particular incidents that took place during his stay there. In the February 1883 issue of *Tinsley's* magazine, O'Shea published a story under the title "A Little Dinner at Kiko." It depicts an incident that happened to a certain Irish character named McGillicuddy—presumably an autobiographical persona—who worked for "*The Banner*, a London daily paper."[60] In this story, Sir Garnet Wolseley invites this McGillicuddy to an official dinner, but the journalist has no proper attire to wear for this formal event. He hastily visits the local bazaar, in Nicosia, and buys a rather strange coat he finds on sale. When he attends dinner, Wolseley asks him how he finds Cyprus. He responds reluctantly, careful not to make any statement that would offend the "Chief," that he finds the island excessively hot. The high commissioner agrees with him and suggests that he takes off his coat. The punch line of the story is that McGillicuddy may have bought a coat but he wears nothing underneath. The dinner party bursts out laughing and Wolseley expresses his indebtedness: "'McGillicuddy,' he said, 'I am indebted to you for the most cheerful moment I have had since I came to the island.'"[61] The joke is apparently a fine example of Victorian humor: it is a rather naïve joke based on the violation of a formality. O'Shea's story provides us with many of the finer details regarding the British occupation of the island: the influx of journalists who were sent to cover the historic acquisition of Cyprus, the presence of the Indian forces—one of the main characters belongs to the Goorkas—the legend-like status of Wolseley among military men and journalists, etc. Most importantly, it reveals, in several passages, O'Shea's view of an almost natural coexistence between journalists and military men. The story opens with a group of men—military officers and journalists—sitting together at the Army and Navy Hotel in Nicosia; one of them, in fact, occupies both positions: he is "a retired captain of artillery who was acting as correspondent of a London illustrated paper."[62] The journalist he is most likely referring to is Samuel Pasfield Oliver, who was indeed working for *The Illustrated London News* and he had just retired from the army. The story concludes with yet another group of men—again, officers and journalists—sitting around Wolseley and discussing politics. This happy relationship, epitomized in the figure of the journalist-soldier, appears in a rather brief but highly symbolic moment: when McGillicuddy unbuttons his coat, he explains his nakedness to Wolseley by saying that he, a journalist, has adopted the advice from the *Soldier's Pocket Book*, Wolseley's famous manual of instructions, and "never carried more impedimenta" that he could possibly do without.

O'Shea's second Cyprus story, "The Phantom Piper," was published, rather emblematically, in the December 1886 issue of *The Army and Navy Magazine*, eight years after his stay on the island.[63] The story begins with a reference to Wolseley; O'Shea praises the general's suggestion that a memorial should be raised in honor of the Black Watch, the famous infantry battalion of the Royal Regiment of Scotland, and describes Wolseley's enthusiastic support for the regiment's conduct in the field of action.[64] Like his first Cyprus story, this is also a humorous reminiscence of an incident that took place in the north of the island, the town of Kyrenia. Indeed, O'Shea's correspondences from Cyprus verify the fact that, in mid-August 1878, he was staying with the Royal Highlanders in a camp outside Kyrenia.[65] The central plot of the story is fairly simple and it belongs to the genre of the fantastic, as Tzvetan Todorov would have it, where a story continuously wavers between a supernatural and a pragmatic explanation of a certain event. The "event" here is the following: every time the bagpiper of the regiment plays a tune, the music is strangely echoed in the surrounding landscape. The soldiers deduce that this is not an actual echo but an extensive repetition of the music the bagpiper performs. When the same incident is repeated for three consecutive nights, some of them reach the conclusion that it must be a spirit, or a fairy, that repeats the tune (hence, the "Phantom Piper" of the story's title). Years later, in 1886, O'Shea relates how he met a certain man who was with him in Cyprus and who confesses that during his stay there he was learning to play the bagpipes. In fact, he tried to imitate the regiment's official bagpiper, he confesses, but he couldn't. In confessing this, O'Shea concludes, the man "had unconsciously stuck a pin into the wind-bag of the supernatural."[66] The joke, apparently, is the perception of the real as supernatural: an event that overstepped the boundaries of reality is eventually explained in the most banal terms.

Here, again, we are presented with a journalist who mingles happily with the soldiers and the officers. Unlike the first story, however, which is devoid of any references to the people of Cyprus, or to the conditions on the ground in this transition from Ottoman to British rule, the "Phantom Piper" is much more detailed in its presentation of both. O'Shea informs his reader, for example, of the dreadful conditions soldiers had to endure during the early days of the occupation: the unbearable heat, the rodents, snakes, spiders and cockroaches in the camps, the malarious fever, etc. During his camping with the Scottish Regiment, he takes several excursions in the area surrounding the town of Kyrenia, and he describes both the landscape and the people he encounters. Here is his take on the Cypriots in a passage that appeared, verbatim, both in the September 4, 1878, edition of *The Standard* and, eight years later, in "The Phantom Piper":

> I strolled out to take notes of the aborigines. They were poor, but not paupers; civil, ignorant, and much given to killing time on wooden benches, pipe in mouth. The males are muscular, and have brown, regular countenances, with the straight Greek nose; but they are Orientalised Greeks, with a forbearance, if not a love, for dirt. The females have large limpid eyes; dress in a Frankish style, more slatternly than elegant; age early, and have sickly yellowish complexions. As for the Moslem women, they are as careful not to show themselves as the prophet Mokanna himself. They raised their breast-curtains to their nostrils when they met me, but the moment my back was turned I felt that the natural Eve got the better of Fatima, and that she took a long look at the receding Giaour. Jock and Duncan, Davie and Sandie, were not likely to lose their hearts to these jealousy-shaded lights of the harem.[67]

Colonial discourse in this passage is not simply filtered through O'Shea's Western notions of beauty or civility that persistently place the Orientals at the antipodes of civilization (they are portrayed as filthy, apathetic, ugly, sickly, etc.). The literary references implied here are part of the orientalizing discourse that O'Shea, like most scholars of his generation, was intimately familiar with. "Prophet Mokanna" is a reference to the eighth-century heretic al-Muquanna, whom Thomas Moore made immensely famous in his celebrated oriental romance *Lalla-Rookh* (1817). In Moore's poem, he is known as the "Veiled Prophet," as he covers his face with a "Silver Veil" to hide his monstrous appearance (which bears "features horribler than Hell e'er trac'd").[68] The "Giaour" is a reference to Lord Byron's famous poem of the same title, which was published four years before Moore's *Lalla-Rookh*. In the poem, Leila, a woman in the harem of Pasha Hassan, falls in love with a Christian infidel, the Giaour. Both poems, written by two close friends who often discussed their interest in oriental tales, are exemplary pieces of romantic orientalism and have been extensively discussed in the context of British Romanticism's fascination with the Orient.

O'Shea's inclusion of these cultural references serves the purpose of filtering the differences between *us* and *them* through what is apparently familiar and intimate to his readers: the veiled Muslim woman covers her face, like Mokanna, not because of religious custom but because her appearance is appalling; and O'Shea presents himself as the Giaour, the infidel towards whom the desire of the Muslim woman is directed. Such strange metaphors, which function as ways of making the exotic, or the unknown, familiar to both the writer and his readers, are scattered throughout O'Shea's "Phantom Piper." In order to praise the Scottish bagpiper as both a soldier and an artist, he turns to Byron's *Childe Harold's Pilgrimage*. The corporal of the 42nd regiment that O'Shea accompanies to Kyrenia is reading Walter Scott's novels; another young soldier is reciting a poem by Robert Burns. When O'Shea sees the "northern sierras" of Cyprus (i.e., the mountain range Pentadaktylos), he recalls Lord Tennyson's *Idylls of the Kings* and Merlin, who made Camelot "spire to heaven."[69] Apart from the legacy of Romantic orientalism, O'Shea's correspondences, like these stories, are full of references drawn from the British literary tradition—from Shakespeare's *Othello* to Elizabeth Barrett Browning's "Wine of Cyprus." In this filtering through the literary tradition of the colonizer, both the colonial subjects and the landscape they inhabit are forcefully placed in the colonizers' familiar narrative, which expresses itself through an intimately familiar literature.

Ultimately, as was the case in the majority of war correspondents of the Victorian era, O'Shea's opinion of the Cyprus occupation rests on the congenial and intimate relationship between the army and the press. He firmly believed that the colonization of the island would be crowned a success only if the army—the Empire's civilizing machine—would be allowed to proceed undisturbed in applying the kind of paternal despotism necessary for ushering Cyprus out of the misery and the darkness that consumed it. Everyone else—the weak-hearted merchants, the travelers, the tourists and even the politicians—should step aside until the army completes its mission. Accordingly, every opinion he expresses during his stay in Cyprus or, later on, in his writings about the island, remain faithful to this principle. His work constitutes, at the same time, a tribute to the British soldier and an apotheosis of the journalist who behaves *like* a soldier. It is not surprising that, for example, throughout his writings, he casually offers his opinion on military matters: from the thickness of the garments officers wear in the unbearable heat of Cyprus to the tents they brought with them; or that, in one of his last reports from the island, he asks his readers to send English magazines or newspapers to Colonel White, the civil commissioner of Larnaca, who would distribute them to the sick soldiers, our "poor lads" as he calls them, in Cyprus.[70] Perhaps one of the finest examples of his affection for the Empire's soldiers—an affection which is in sharp contrast to his description of colonial subjects—is his description of the death of Sergeant M'Gaw. I have already discussed the symbolism of the first British casualty in Cyprus, in the context of Archibald Forbes's dramatic and sensational description of the event. M'Gaw died on July 22, 1878. On that day, O'Shea was somewhere off the coast of Crete, still sailing on the *St. Osyth* to Cyprus. Yet, he reports the sergeant's death, five days *after* the event, in the same sensational tone as Forbes did. M'Gaw, in O'Shea's description, is a gallant, courageous, devoted veteran who died because "a foolish guide led the men astray."[71] In Forbes's letter it was in fact "a Turk" who misdirected the soldiers and was responsible for their getting lost. But despite the differences between the two versions of the event—which include a rather bad misspelling of the sergeant's name by *The Standard* as Macan, instead of M'Gaw—the conclusion of both narratives is indicative of the admiration, the respect and the empathy both journalists felt towards the soldiers. "M'Gaw's body," Forbes wrote, "was buried on the Tuesday afternoon; and it may be said that a good and staunch soldier had hanselled the little burial plot under the locust tree."[72] O'Shea's description of the sergeant's death is strikingly similar and perhaps inspired by Forbes: "The following evening, soon after sunset, he was laid to rest in a lonely grave, under a gnarled tree near the camp—the first tenant of a British cemetery in our new possession."[73] This memorialization of the British soldier, who rests alone under a crooked locust tree, a casualty of the perils imperial soldiers had to endure in the service of colonialism, depended entirely on the mutual appreciation between soldiers and correspondents. And it was precisely based on such sympathetic descriptions, independently of whether they were first- or secondhand accounts, that dozens of newspapers in England copied, reprinted and disseminated these sensational accounts for the education of the British public.

NOTES

1. Eugene Davis, "Irish writers in London," *Donahoe's Magazine* 29 (1893): 687.
2. *Weekly Nation*, February 2, 1889, p. 4.
3. Frederic Villiers, *Peaceful Personalities and Warriors Bold* (London: Harper and Brothers, 1907), 121.
4. Ibid.

5. Henry Vizetelly, *Glances Back Through Seventy Years: Autobiographical and Other Reminiscences* (London: Kegan Paul, Trench, Trubner and Co., 1893), 98–99.

6. During his coverage of the Carlist Wars, O'Shea's "chief companion" was Frank, whose nephew, Edward, also traveled to Cyprus to cover the occupation. For the relationship between O'Shea and the Vizetelly family see: Ernest Alfred Vizetelly, *In Seven Lands: Germany, Austria, Hungary, Bohemia, Spain, Portugal, Italy* (New York: Duffield and Co.,1916), 306; John W. McDonald, *A Soldier of Fortune: The Life and Adventures of General Henry Ronald Maciver* (New York: The New York News Company, 1888), 249; John Augustus O'Shea, *Roundabout Recollections* (London: Ward and Downey, 1892).

7. *North and South Shields Daily Gazette and Shipping Telegraph*, September 24, 1887, p. 2.

8. William Butler Yeats, *The Collected Works of W.B. Yeats, Vol. 2: The Plays* (New York: Scribner, 2001), 728.

9. "Romance of War Corresponding." *To-day: A Weekly Magazine-Journal* 16 (1897): 102.

10. John Augustus O'Shea, *Leaves from the Life of a Special Correspondent* (London: Ward and Downey, 1885), 242–43.

11. *Standard*, July 18, 1878, p. 5.
12. *Standard*, July 18, 1878, p. 5.
13. *Standard*, July 18, 1878, p. 5.
14. *Standard*, July 18, 1878, p. 5.
15. *Standard*, July 18, 1878, p. 5.
16. *Standard*, July 18, 1878, p. 5.
17. *Standard*, July 23, 1878, p. 5.
18. *Standard*, July 24, 1878, p. 5.
19. *Standard*, August 15, 1878, p. 5.
20. *Standard*, August 7, 1878, p. 5.
21. *Daily News*, August 7, 1878, p. 5.
22. *Sussex Advertiser, Surrey Gazette and West Kent Courier*, August 13, 1878, p. 4.
23. *Dundee Courier and Argus*, May 13, 1878, p. 2.
24. *Fife Herald*, May 16, 1878, p. 2.
25. See HL Deb, 15 July 1878, vol. 241, cc1449–62.
26. *Standard*, August 7, 1878, p. 5.
27. *Standard*, August 7, 1878, p. 5.
28. *Standard*, August 7, 1878, p. 5.
29. *Standard*, August 7, 1878, p. 6.
30. *Standard*, August 8, 1878, p. 5.
31. *Standard*, August 8, 1878, p. 5.
32. *Standard*, August 8, 1878, p. 5.
33. *Standard*, August 8, 1878, p. 5.
34. *Standard*, August 14, 1878, p. 5.
35. *Standard*, August 14, 1878, p. 5.
36. *Standard*, September 4, 1878, p. 2.
37. *Standard*, August 1 4, 1878, p. 5.
38. HC Deb, 11 July 1878, vol. 241, cc1242.
39. *Standard*, August 14, 1878, p. 5.
40. *Standard*, August 27, 1878, p. 3.
41. *Standard*, August 14, 1878, p. 5.
42. *Standard*, August 27, 1878, p. 3.
43. *Standard*, August 27, 1878, p. 3.
44. *Standard*, September 5, 1878, p. 5.
45. *Standard*, September 14, 1878, p. 3.
46. *Standard*, September 6, 1878, p. 2.
47. *Standard*, August 7, 1878, p. 5.
48. *Standard*, August 15, 1878, p. 5.
49. *Standard*, August 14, 1878, p. 5.

50. *Standard*, August 16, 1878, p. 5.
51. *Standard*, August 20, 1878, p. 5.
52. *Standard*, August 28, 1878, p. 5 and September 6, 1878, p. 2.
53. *Standard*, August 29, 1878, p. 5.
54. *Standard*, September 10, 1878, p. 2.
55. *Nottingham Evening Post*, August 20, 1878, p. 2.
56. *Aberdeen Weekly Journal*, October 1, 1878, p. 3.
57. For a full account of the incident see *Falkirk Herald*, December 11, 1886, p. 5.
58. John Augustus O'Shea, "About Cyprus," *Tinsley's* 24 (1879): 440.
59. Ibid., 442. My emphasis.
60. John Augustus O'Shea, "A Little Dinner in Kiko," *Tinsley's* 32 (1883): 193.
61. Ibid., 198. In 1899, *The Sketch* summarized this incident suggesting that it had happened to O'Shea himself. See "Small Talk of the Week," *The Sketch* 28, no. 360 (December 20, 1899): 321.
62. O'Shea, "A Little Dinner in Kiko," 193.
63. John Augustus O'Shea, "The Phantom Piper: a Legend of the Black Watch." *The Army and Navy Magazine* 13 (1887): 168–78.
64. O'Shea's quotations of Wolseley are from a letter the general sent to a member of the Parliament, Sir Donald Currie, which was circulating in the Press a few months before "The Phantom Piper" was published. See "Lord Wolseley and the Black Watch," *New Zealand Herald*, July 24, 1886, p. 2.
65. *Standard*, September 4, 1878, p. 2.
66. O'Shea, "Phantom Piper," 178.
67. Ibid., 173. Also see *Standard*, September 4, 1878, p. 2.
68. Thomas Moore, *The Poetical Works of Thomas Moore* (London: Longman, Brown, Green, and Longmans, 1853), 320, 345.
69. O'Shea, "Phantom Piper," 171.
70. *Standard*, September 17, 1878, p. 2.
71. *Standard*, August 8, 1878, p. 5.
72. *Daily News*, August 10, 1878, p. 5.
73. *Standard*, August 8, 1878, p. 5.

Chapter Six

Edward Henry Vizetelly and *The Glasgow Herald*

Edward Henry Vizetelly (1847–1903), like Leger Herbert, was twenty-nine years old when he traveled to Cyprus to cover the occupation on behalf of *The Glasgow Herald.* Despite his youth, however, he had already covered, as a war correspondent, some of the important events of his time: like Archibald Forbes and John Augustus O'Shea, he had reported on "the Franco-Prussian War for the *Daily News* and the *New York Times*." He also covered "the 1876 Turko-Serbian War and then the Russo-Turkish War for the *London Standard*."[1] His post-Cyprus career included the coverage of the British bombardment of Alexandria, in 1881, on behalf of *The Daily News*, and the coverage of the celebrated return of the explorer Henry Morton Stanley from the African interior for *The New York Herald.*[2] Vizetelly considered Sir John Robinson, the "veteran and popular manager of *The Daily News*," his "journalistic father."[3] In the case of the Cyprus occupation, however, *The Daily News* opted to use the more experienced, and immensely more famous, Archibald Forbes as special correspondent; hence, Vizetelly accepted a commission from the Scottish *Glasgow Herald* and restricted his collaboration with *The Daily News* to the submission of "occasional telegrams" from the island.[4]

Vizetelly belonged to a well-known family of publishers and correspondents. His father, Henry Richard Vizetelly, a well-established publisher, among other endeavors in his illustrious career, edited two newspapers (*The Pictorial Times* and *The Illustrated Times*), and served as a correspondent for *The Illustrated London News*, in France. His brother, Ernest Alfred (1853–97), was also a correspondent for *The Illustrated London News*, as well as for *The Pall Mall Gazette*, and *The Daily News*. His half brother, Frank Horace (1864–1938), from Henry Richard's second marriage, was a lexicographer who also served as a correspondent for *The Illustrated London News*. His uncle, Frank Vizetelly (1830–83), worked for *The Illustrated Times, The Illustrated London News* and *The Times*, and was one of the seven journalists commemorated in the War Correspondents' Memorial in St. Paul's Cathedral, along with St. Leger Herbert. A rather good example of the family's deep immersion in the production and distribution of news in England is the fact that at least three members of the Vizetelly family covered the Franco-Prussian War of 1870–71 for major newspapers in London: Edward and his brother, Ernest, for *The Daily News* and their father, Henry Richard, for *The Illustrated London News*.

In many ways, Vizetelly's correspondences from Cyprus are rather exceptional in comparison with his fellow correspondents who covered the occupation. To begin with, he was the only journalist who was not commissioned by a major London newspaper. Though *The Glasgow Herald*'s political position often shifted from liberal to conservative and back, most of its readers were Scots, and Glasgow was certainly far from the divisive political atmosphere of London. One of the most pronounced characteristics that sets his descriptions apart is the fact that he does not venerate the British Army, and it seems that he lacks access to proper sources of information (i.e., to the army hierarchy who provided much of the information on the colonial government's actions or plans). As we will see, his descriptions are often critical of the military and even dismissive of entrusting it with civil affairs. Compared to other correspondents, Vizetelly is also the only journalist who stayed in Cyprus even after his commission as a correspondent expired. He arrived on the island in August 1878 and departed in February 1882. In other words, he was the only journalist who emigrated to Cyprus and was able to witness the process of development longer than most of the early travelers, and certainly far longer than any of his colleagues. Though his reports for *The Glasgow Herald* lasted for about seven months—from August 1878 to February 1879—he later published a book where he offers some of the most detailed descriptions we have of the early days of the British occupation. Published in 1901, *From Cyprus to Zanzibar by the Egyptian Delta* is a remarkably detailed account of both Vizetelly's life on the island and his subsequent adventures in Egypt and Zanzibar.

Vizetelly was in Athens when he learned of the Anglo-Turkish treaty and the celebrated occupation of Cyprus by Britain.[5] He immediately secured a commission to cover the occupation on behalf of *The Glasgow Herald* and by the afternoon of July 31 he was on his way to the island, on board the Austrian Lloyd's steamer *Ceres*. The steamer, carrying 111 passengers, passed through Gallipoli and the Dardanelles, and, passing the islands of Tenedos and Mytilene, it reached Smyrna on August 2. On the next day, it departed from Smyrna, stopped at the island of Rhodes, and reached the port of Larnaca, in Cyprus, at daybreak on August 6. In the afternoon of the same day, Vizetelly composed his first correspondence for *The Glasgow Herald*, in which he described this weeklong journey, as well as the excitement of his fellow passengers who were flocking to the "Eldorado of the Levant" and "expecting to find the streets of Larnaca and Lefcossia [*sic*] paved with gold."[6] Even in this first report, one can sense the marked difference between Vizetelly's experience and that of his fellow correspondents. Unlike Forbes and Herbert, who traveled on the same ship as Wolseley to the island, and unlike O'Shea, who used his military connections to secure a place on one of the steamers accompanying the high commissioner, Vizetelly traveled alone and along a very different route. Even more importantly, he does not seem to be nearly as excited as his colleagues regarding the occupation. Though he concedes that the acquisition of the island was indeed a victory for British diplomacy, he simultaneously takes a distance from all the excitement generated by the acquisition. Instead of expressing his own sentiments, he describes the expectations and enthusiasm of his fellow travelers.

In his book, he explains that the day after his disembarkment from the *Ceres* he looked to make a profit by joining a French baker from Alexandria who was trying to secure a contract with the authorities to supply the army with bread.[7] Vizetelly, who knew French quite well, acted as his translator and they both visited the camp at Chiflik Pasha to make the arrangements. However, the proposed venture failed, since the army had already signed a contract with an English Smyrniot baker. This incident is, again, indicative of Vizetelly's vastly different perception of his move to Cyprus compared to other journalists: he was participating in the occupation both as a correspondent and as an emigrant; the bread business was, in fact, one of the many ventures he would attempt during his three-and-a-half-year stay on the island.

His second report from Cyprus was composed eight days after his arrival and was published on August 28. There, he gives readers his first impressions of the town of Larnaca, describing it as dirty with "the burned up appearance of almost all Asiatic and African towns."[8] He complains about the inflated prices on the island and explains that there are hundreds of new immigrants looking for jobs in Larnaca, but there is no employment anywhere. Echoing most journalists and travelers to the island, he also expresses his disdain for "the horrible Greek dialect that is spoken in this island, and which an Athenian would only understand with difficulty."[9] Despite his often-condescending tone in describing both the island and its inhabitants, Vizetelly's subsequent reports concentrate more on deeply personal impressions rather than descriptions of colonial policies or even of events. He rarely participates or describes any of the symbolic ceremonies that the administration arranged, and he rarely mentions Wolseley or other administrators in his reports. Once again, he seems to be excluded from the deeply intimate alliance between the military and the press.

This lack of veneration for the army expresses itself rather explicitly in his reports to *The Glasgow Herald*. Three weeks after his arrival, he was writing that the "administrative department of our army was destined ever to be defective" and that the civil department was "infinitely worst."[10] Part of the problem, as Vizetelly saw it, was the fact that the army was entrusted with the civic administration of the island when their knowledge and expertise had nothing to do with governance. But his accusations go far beyond the disagreement with the political arrangements in Cyprus. In sharp contrast to O'Shea, whose reports amount to an apotheosis of the British military, his critique is entirely dismissive of the army and, on some occasions, full of conceit. When he hears soldiers complain that they are suffering, that they eat bad bread, dirty meat and diseased potatoes, threatening to expose their treatment by the authorities to the press, he responds in the following way:

> Judging from the appearance of the English troops who are here, it is my opinion that they are too well fed. In fact, they all look fat and flabby. No army in the world costs its country so much feed as the English army does, whether in time of peace or war, and I am afraid we shall find that our men will die like flies the first time the chances of war subject them to serious privations. [11]

His critique does not stop here. He finds that General Watsen "resides in one of the best houses on the Marina" of Larnaca, but "does not seem to trouble himself about anything at all."[12] He often talks of the total disorganization and mentions particular examples of what he perceives as the military government's mismanagement: he accuses the administration, for example, of wasting money and time by initially trying to build the road from Larnaca to Nicosia and then abruptly abandoning the project. When he visits a camp outside the town of Kyrenia, he finds it utterly banal and disinteresting: "At the camp there was, of course, nothing to see. I hardly know what one can say about a camp beyond the fact that you see a number of bell-shaped tents and a number of men in flannel shirts, helmets, and trousers, engaged in cleaning their accoutrements or lothing about. The present instance was no exception."[13] Interestingly, this was the same camp that O'Shea had described in deep admiration—since it was occupied by the Black Watch regiment—and which formed the background for his story "The Phantom Piper." On another occasion, Vizetelly describes the appearance and attitude of the officers supervising the loading and unloading of boats at the small port of Kyrenia, as that of masters towards slaves: these officers looked to him "more like-slave drivers than anything else."[14]

Vizetelly finds the privileged position of the army in the occupation and the administration of Cyprus irritating. He writes of the civilians' total lack of health facilities and the absence of medicine in the early days of the occupation, comparing it with the privileged access of soldiers to four military hospitals. "The military," he writes poignantly, "have everything that could be desired in the shape of hospitals, doctors, medicines, and attendance."[15] One of his most critical reports was composed on January 22, towards the end his of commission with *The Glasgow Herald*. There, he blames much of the sickness in Cyprus on the military government's failure to protect soldiers from the intense heat of the summer. But part of the problem, he claims, is the very nature of the British soldier himself who is "not up to the standard he used to attain." British soldiers, he writes, are "fat and podgy" and "they looked as if they ate too much pudding and drank too much beer, and I believe they do. There can be no doubt that the British soldier is better cared for than any other in the world."[16] He even goes so far as to blame the death of British soldiers in Cyprus to their spoiled and totally feeble nature:

> In Cyprus I have heard soldiers complaining because the beef was tough and the bread brown, while many were most indignant because they were only allowed to take a pint of strong beer in the morning and another at night in the canteen. This kind of flabby, overfed men were not at all likely to bear the heat of a Cyprus summer with impunity, and it is by no means a matter of surprise that many of them should have fallen ill, and that some should have died.[17]

British soldiers are not the only ones who receive this kind of contemptuous treatment by Vizetelly. Despite the staunch support for a transition from a military to a civil administration, his description of the Greek population is equally dismissive. His December 11 report is entirely devoted to what he describes as "the discontent among the Greeks of Cyprus," and it begins with an essentialist description of both the "peculiar" Greeks and the "half-bred" Greek-Cypriots:

> The Greeks were ever a discontented people. The Greeks of Greece have been discontented for centuries. They were discontented under the Romans, discontented under the Turks; they have been discontented with their Ministers, with their king, with their old rulers the Turks, with England, and even with France; and I think that anyone who has resided for any length of time among these peculiar people will frankly admit that it would not merely be extremely difficult, but almost impossible, to content them. The Cyprian Greeks, although they speak a jargon which bears some slight resemblance to the Greek language, are but miserable shadows when compared with their Grecian cousins. They are like them, however, in one respect: they are inveterate grumblers and malcontents.[18]

Vizetelly's portrayal of the Turk is as essentialist as that of the Greeks, but it is far from being a negative one. Though he writes that "most people are agreed that the Turks are bad rulers" and that they are responsible for the present condition of the island, he still believes that "they are not naturally the oppressive brutes they have so often been painted in British literature."[19] The emphasis here is on what he understands to be the "natural" traits of the Turkish people: "*Naturally* they are neither cruel not corrupt."[20] This juxtaposition of the Turks and the Greeks is common among the writings of both journalists and travelers in Cyprus in the early years of the occupation and it can also be traced, even more lucidly, in Hepworth Dixon's *British Cyprus* and Garnet Wolseley's positive opinion of the Turkish legal system. As an orientalist trope, it points to the complicated conditions in Cyprus where the Turks represent a declining, yet respected, Empire and the Greeks a kind of fallen people, whose claim to ancient glory is essentially misguided. Even worse, the Greeks of Cyprus—who are "miserable shadows when compared with their Grecian cousins"[21]—are twice removed from any claims of greatness. They speak a Greek jargon, they are half-bred and they have inherited the worst characteristics of their modern fellow brethren.

Yet, Vizetelly's most adverse depiction, and one that eventually got him into trouble, was not centered on British soldiers, Greeks, or Turks. Early in his reporting from the island, he expresses his bewilderment with the mass emigration of British merchants and civilians to the island. "It seems strange," he wrote on September 5, "that so many people out of England should have allowed themselves to be persuaded that Cyprus, figuratively speaking was a mine of gold."[22] Everyone with a small capital, or with no money at all, "seemed to have thought that he had only to come to Cyprus to make money." Vizetelly sees this as a grave mistake. He describes unemployed people "half starving" in the streets and "scores of others" who "have accepted menial positions" in order to survive.[23] Though he concedes that the island "will be a very nice place in a few years," he maintains that "it is simple folly for people to come out here now unless they have money."[24] His disdain for the thoughtless rush of merchants is underlined in the description of certain business ventures. He finds it ridiculous, for example, that a certain Mr. Sky decided to open a "zinc house" company in Cyprus. Considering the extremely hot weather conditions on the island, he deduces, "why he should have brought a zinc house out to a country like this is beyond my comprehension."[25] In other instances, he complains that stores "were almost wholly devoted to the sale of cheap Manchester goods,"[26] or that many of the businesses in Cyprus are managed by people with no experience; as an example, he offers the case of a young Cornish man, whose experience at running a bar "consisted of a passing flirtation with a bar maid."[27]

By mid-November, his disdain for the "English element" in Cyprus became such that he describes it as "neither the best educated not the most intelligent of its class." "One hears of fearful riots in public houses," he continues, "of people getting punches-in-the-eyes, of savage biting and kicking—riots, in fact, that more resemble wild beast fights than anything else."[28] This behavior, according to Vizetelly, was a result of the English immigrants' overconsumption of alcohol: "I am sorry to say," he reports, "that there is more drink consumed by our countrymen than anything else."[29] His correspondence was published in *The Glasgow Herald* on November 25. About a month later, he returned to the subject of the "drunken habits and riotous behaviour" of the Englishmen in Cyprus, complaining that his report infuriated some of his countrymen on the island.[30] According to Vizetelly, a certain anonymous correspondent found a copy of *The Glasgow Herald* containing his article in Paris and mailed it anonymously from Amsterdam to an Englishman in Cyprus (the inexperienced bar owner from Cornish, mentioned above). Consequently, several of his countrymen threatened Vizetelly who responded with the following commentary:

> These are the rowdies, although not the only ones, who think themselves aggrieved because I considered it my duty to picture to your readers some of the Englishmen who had come out here to colonise the island. I have been threatened with violence by several of them, but Providence having blessed me with tolerably large bones and the courage of this scum of Great Britain, I can think of no more suitable term for them—being unequal to their language, they leave me alone.[31]

The issue of drunken Englishmen in Cyprus deserves a closer consideration since it became a rather contested issue in Britain, even prior to Vizetelly's report. In September 1878, several major newspapers in England printed, or summarized, a letter submitted by Alfred Sargant, secretary of the Church of England Temperance Society. The letter was signed by the head of the Church of England, the Archbishop of Canterbury, who served as president of the Temperance Society, and the Bishop of Gibraltar, vice-president of the Society, and it was addressed to the "Governor of the Island of Cyprus," Sir Garnet Wolseley. This "memorial," as the authors call it, was essentially written in response to several correspondences from the island, which described the sale of strong drinks as one of the changes the occupation brought about. Though England, they write, has been able to carry "the blessings of Christianity and civilization" to her dependencies, "she has introduced among the native populations her own prominent vices, and chiefly and at the root of it all, her intemperance."[32] Suggesting that the lives of soldiers are often "in striking contrast to the precepts of the Gospel of Christ," they expressed their concern that Muslim countries, where alcohol was traditionally forbidden, were now in danger, under English influence, of developing the traffic of strong drinks. As Cyprus was now a model of good English governance for other Asiatic countries still under Ottoman rule, they continued, the sale of alcohol should be discouraged, the increase of public houses should be prevented, and temperance should be encouraged among natives and foreigners.

It was, in fact, Leger Herbert, under his authority as the high commissioner's private secretary, who was tasked with the duty of responding to the Society's "memorial." The response also found its way to several English newspapers. "His Excellency," Herbert wrote, in reference to Wolseley, "desires me to beg that you will tender to the executive committee of the society his sincere thanks for this expression of their concern for the well being of the population of Cyprus, and to assure them of his Excellency's clear recognition of the evils that intemperance engenders, and of the warm interest that he takes in all measures calculated to encourage sobriety."[33] In another response, reprinted by several British newspapers, the local newspaper *Cyprus* wrote, rather sarcastically, that wine shops selling local "poison" were present in the marina of Larnaca long before the arrival of the British. Now foreigners owned most of the shops and sell "good English Beer." The only consequence of the English arrival is that getting drunk was now more expensive in Cyprus.[34]

Regulations concerning the sale of alcohol were, indeed, some of the first to be imposed by the British colonial administration in Cyprus. The first proclamation of the Municipal Council of Larnaca (August 1), signed by General Watsen, the civil commissioner, and Dr. Heidenstam, the temporary mayor, was meant to regulate trade by announcing three classes of annual licenses merchants could obtain. It was submitted by John Augustus O'Shea to *The Standard*, and published on August 20, 1878:

> The first class pay 10l, for these licences,
> The second class pay 5l, for these licences,
> The third class pay 2l, for these licences.
> To the first class belong all such shops in which spirits, wine, and beer are sold, also all casinos, theatres, hotels or other places of entertainment or amusement.
> (Cafes in which coffee only is sold excepted)
> Second Class,—Shops for the sale of beer or Cyprus wine (Cyprus spirits not included), European wares of all sorts.
> Third Class,—Shops for the sale of country produce, and for the manufacturing or repair of goods, furniture, clothing, such as tailor, bootmakers, & c.[35]

The proclamation was undoubtedly aimed at capitalizing on the presence of a large number of English immigrants in Cyprus, the establishment of hotels and other places of entertainment, and the eventual arrival of tourists. Hence, the most expensive licenses were those regulating accommodation and the consumption of alcohol. In addition to these regulations, the municipality had already decreed, as O'Shea also reported, that "no alcoholic liquors, or beer, should be sold to soldiers under pain of the immediate closing of the premises."[36] The consumption of alcohol by the British was so rampant in the early days of the Cyprus occupation that one of the foremost authorities on the history of the island, Hamilton Lang, connected the reports of fever in Cyprus with drinking. In a passage that was widely quoted by English newspapers, Lang wrote: "But to what country, with the thermometer generally about 90° in the shade, can Englishmen, with their national love of heavy eating and alcoholic liquors, be sent without incurring a considerable risk of sickness of some kind?"[37]

Evidently, Vizetelly's description of drunken and raucous English immigrants in Cyprus was a continuation of an already intense discussion in England concerning the consumption of alcohol. By the late 1870s, the temperance movement, which advocated for the restriction of, or even the total ban on, alcohol, had gained significant ground. Yet, the consumption of alcohol remained widespread in Britain, with the medical establishment suggesting that "moderate beer-drinking was healthy," with beer commonly served to children from a young age and with several workers drinking beer both before and after work.[38] In his book, *From Cyprus to Zanzibar by the Egyptian Delta*, Vizetelly offers further explanation for the rampant consumption of alcohol—particularly whiskey and beer—by English immigrants. They came to Cyprus, he explains, expecting to find employment, but they found nothing to do instead. Therefore, they "strolled from bar to bar and talked and drank" during the day, and they continued to drink in the music hall, the club, and the few hotels, through the night.[39]

Whatever the reason behind his distaste for the behavior of his fellow countrymen in Cyprus, his derogatory description of them sets him apart from the rest of the journalists who were covering the occupation. At the same time, one should note that Vizetelly criticizes practically everyone—from the military administration to the Greeks and the English immigrants—with the notable exception of the Turks, with whom he was intimately familiar since he joined, as a soldier, the Ottoman irregular troops (the Bashi Bazouk) in the Russo-Turkish War of 1877–78. This critique, however, never rises to the level of a rejection of the British colonial project. As in the case of the Temperance Society's "memorial," the problem, as he perceives it, is the behavior of Englishmen as *savages*; it is, in other words, their degeneration and fall to the level of the colonized. His belief in the civilizing mission and the might of the British Empire is reflected in the concluding lines of his book, *From Cyprus to Zanzibar by the Egyptian Delta*:

> Our glorious flag streams gaily breeze at Alexandria, Cairo, Khartoum, Fashoda, Sobat, Uganda. The Nile is ours from source to estuary. It has cost us countless valued lives, enormous treasure, to gain control of that noble waterway; but ours it is, and ours it shall remain. Advance Britannia![40]

Interestingly, the expression "Advance Britannia" was made popular during the Crimean War in an inspirational military song which ended with the following verse:

> The mem'ry of the deeds we've done
> In aiding the oppress'd,
> Will bind, in ages yet to come,
> The nations of the West!

Seen through the prism of colonialism's destructive aftermath, in Cyprus and elsewhere, these lines constitute a haunting statement in which the original intention is entirely reversed.

Perhaps Vizetelly's most noteworthy correspondence, and one that exemplifies his nuanced view of the occupation, was one of the last he published in *The Glasgow Herald*. It appeared in the February 3, 1879, edition of the newspaper under the title "The Prospects of Cyprus."[41] He begins by addressing the "contradictory reports" concerning the occupation of Cyprus with some writers "lauding it immoderately" and others "abusing it beyond all reason." He suggests that most writers who resided in Cyprus, such as Cesnola, von Löher, and Lang, speak positively about the island. Those who resided for a short time, like Archibald Forbes and Lewis Farley, denounce it. His critique of Forbes and Farley centers on the opinions expressed in two works: the former's article "The Fiasco of Cyprus," which had been recently published in the *Nineteenth Century*, and the latter's travel book, *Egypt, Cyprus and Asiatic-Turkey*, which was also published in 1878.[42] He complains that a person cannot really form an objective opinion about the condition of the island, or its future prospects, by visiting it for two months in July and August. Referring directly to Forbes's article, he concludes that the celebrated correspondent visited the island during the worst possible time of the year—the unbearably hot months of July and August—and was thus misled into forming a generalized opinion of it. To support his argument, he cites extensively from von Löher's book, *Cyprus, Historical and Descriptive*, "the work of an unprejudiced and impartial author, who quite recently visited the island, and who may, therefore, be accepted as an authority, to show that Cyprus is not so black as has been painted." A big part of the Cyprus health problem, he insists, is the fact that military authorities had not taken steps to protect the soldiers from the heat. Finally, he expresses his certainty that Cyprus will become prosperous in the future and that time will prove both Forbes and Farley wrong.

The discussion on the island's healthiness, which, as we have seen, became an important point of contention between Forbes and O'Shea, becomes, in Vizetelly's correspondences, a peripheral issue: neither politicized nor sensationalized, it is simply described as one of the many obstacles one has to anticipate once they arrive in Cyprus. Taking a direct hit, perhaps at

O'Shea, he suggests that catching the Cyprus fever is not a matter of being able to "rough it"; fever on the island, he claims, comes unprovoked and independently of any precautions.[43] Since he caught fever himself, he provides his readers with a detailed account of the symptoms he experienced as well as the long-lasting effects it had on his energy and his ability to write. Vizetelly writes about fever but refrains from placing the event within the context of the ongoing debates on the healthiness of the island or the value of Britain's new acquisition. In fact, much of his reporting from the island is historically detached: his reports are almost entirely devoid of proper historical observations. They are empirical and personal: we learn of the places his visited, the different landscapes of the island, how he experienced fever, what he ate and how much it cost, where he stayed, and how much rent he paid. This detachment is, of course, partly due to his distance from any significant sources of information. At the same time, his lack of access to the colonial military authorities gives his reports a more accurate account of the British experience in Cyprus.

As Mary Roussou-Sinclair has written, in describing Vizetelly's *From Cyprus to Zanzibar*, his "caricature of the Briton," particularly the British soldier we might add, "reveals the weaknesses inherent in the attempt at colonizing certain territories."[44] Indeed, the reality on the ground, as experienced by Vizetelly, was very different from the British fantasy of the island prior to the occupation; it was also very different from the government's attempt to convince the British Public of the eventual transformation of the island and even from the opposition's entirely negative depiction of the island and its future prospects. As I have been arguing, however, it is precisely within the boundaries of intimacy and personal description, that colonialism makes itself more manifest. One such moment in Vizetelly's book comes towards the end of his stay in Cyprus and is related to his decision to stop criticizing the military government of Cyprus. But before we get to that point, it is important to follow his life on the island immediately after his commission with *The Glasgow Herald.*

Vizetelly's final report to *The Glasgow Herald* is submitted in February 1879, presumably because the public's interest in the occupation of Cyprus had subsided considerably. He had also secured some income by transcribing petitions, with the help of a translator, to be submitted by Cypriots to the British colonial authorities. As he wrote, "the business paid very well for a time" due to the "mania" of Larnaca Cypriots "for petitioning the authorities."[45] After his collaboration with *The Glasgow Herald* ended, and when Henry S. King and Co. confiscated the premises of the first Cypriot newspaper, *Kypros-Cyprus*, Mr. Killerby, the company's director, offered him the editorship of the newspaper, which was by then published solely in English, under the title *Cyprus*. Living off the small amount of money he made from these ventures and from his savings, he moved to a cottage in the village of

Livadia, outside Larnaca, where he also bred poultry. Once again, he contracted fever and, once he recovered, moved back to Larnaca.

Vizetelly quit his position as the editor of *Cyprus* when the mayor and police magistrate of Larnaca, Dr. Heidenstam, employed him as his private secretary. He continued to work for Heidenstam for the next three years, "writing all his medical and medico-legal reports from his dictation, as well as those on the cattle plague in the island, which were issued to Parliament in the form of Blue Books."[46] At the advice of his patron, he also took on a position in the office of the district commissioner, under Claude Delaval Cobham at first, and then under Colonel White. He was then transferred to the office of the assistant district commissioner, Robert Fisher, and worked as a clerk in the Larnaca High Court of Justice. In 1880, dissatisfied with both his salary and the conditions in the civil service, Vizetelly quit his job with the district commissioner and collaborated with a local Cypriot barrister, Nicolas Rossos, to print the English-language weekly newspaper, *Cyprus Times*. Meanwhile, he continued to work for the Larnaca municipality, under Heidenstam. The collaboration with Rossos didn't last long, and soon Vizetelly found himself the sole editor of the *Cyprus Times*. His newspaper, as he claimed, ran on the liberal policy of "government by civilians, and military men back to their regiments."[47] In other words, it ran contrary to the status quo in Cyprus where most administrators, from the high commissioner to the civil commissioners in each district, were, in fact, military men. As expected, the government was irritated with some of the positions his newspaper took and asked Heidenstam to fire him from the municipality. Hence, having lost yet another governmental job, Vizetelly became a teacher of English and kept the editorship of the *Cyprus Times*, as well as his position as Heidenstam's private secretary (outside the municipality).

The *Cyprus Times* project was short-lived, lasting from May 1, 1880, to December 17, 1881. But, judging by the reports that appeared in the English press at the time, Vizetelly's newspaper was indeed critical of the British government and his caustic and constant attacks found their way in the columns of the British press. When the newspaper first appeared in 1880, *The Daily News*, a newspaper that occasionally employed Vizetelly, welcomed its publication and described it as a "well written" paper that "expresses the feeling of the population, and demands justice reform and civil Government."[48] Similarly, *The Illustrated London News*—perhaps due to the Vizetelly family's long-standing collaboration with it—also welcomed the news of its publication and described it as "a very well printed and vivacious little sheet, and decidedly strong in its comments on current local politics."[49] In comparing three Cypriote newspapers—*Cyprus*, *Cyprus Times* and *Neon Kition*—*The Pall Mall Gazette* found the latter to be too ethnocentric in the expression of the desire to unite the island with Greece and that, *Cyprus* seems to "have the most confidence of the three in the good intentions of the

English Government towards the island."[50] It also noted that Vizetelly's newspaper, the *Cyprus Times*, "fiercely abuses the *Cyprus*" which aligned its politics around the official line of the colonial government.

Other British newspapers simply reprinted or referred to the *Cyprus Times*' indictment of the colonial government. In November 1880, *The Daily News* referred, for example, to *The Cyprus Times*' criticism of the government's failed plan to organize the "Cyprus Pioneer Corps."[51] Similarly, in December 1880, *The Nottingham Evening Post* reprinted one of the most scathing attacks, by *The Cyprus Times*, on the colonial government of Cyprus, which included accusations against the "military administrators of the island" for failing to produce a realistic plan in regards to the occupation. Consequently, "justice is being parodied; the introduction of capital and labour is impeded; the arrival of foreigners is jealously watched; cold water is thrown on the expression of public opinion; and all the future of the island is being deliberately and hopelessly blighted."[52] *The Liverpool Mercury* informed its readers, in July 1881, that *The Cyprus Times* thoroughly investigated the complaint of "the unfortunate Cypriots" that "they are now treated as badly as they ever were—for the old Turkish system has been necessarily continued so far as the local authorities are concerned—and they have no legal right of appeal."[53]

Apart from the more serious investigations that Vizetelly's newspaper conducted, it also printed several comical and sarcastic commentaries and poems aimed at ridiculing the colonial government and its administrators. It printed, for example, an absurd "imaginary burlesque," which featured Sir Robert Biddulph, who had by then replaced Wolseley as high commissioner, holding a baby in his arms; when the chief secretary, Colonel Falkland Warren, who was wearing a monocle, pats the baby's cheeks, the infant is frightened and starts crying. Biddulph sways the baby and starts to sing (with an evident reference to Warren's monocle):

> He won't bite,
> Though a fright,
> With his perspicacious stare.[54]

Apparently, the government reacted to Vizetelly's persistent attacks by firing him from his job at the municipality of Larnaca. Then, the chief secretary of the colonial administration, Colonel Falkland Warren himself, met with him in the mountains of Troodos and intervened on the government's behalf. As Vizetelly recollects, the colonel attempted to bribe him by offering him another governmental position. And it worked:

> I passed the night at his house, and in a long chat we had together, he urged me to moderate the tone of the *Cyprus Times*; promising me, if I would do so, that on the return from England of the High Commissioner then imminent, he would talk the matter over with him, and endeavour to obtain some support for

> me, from the Government of the island. I confess I was becoming tired of fighting, and I undertook to do as the Colonel wished.[55]

The following morning, when the colonel left for his office, his wife warned Vizetelly that her husband is "sincere" but he should not be too hopeful: "I know as a positive fact," she told him, "that if Sir Robert Biddulph, or Mr. Cobham, could work you some terrible harm, ruin you irretrievably, neither of them would hesitate to do so."[56] Despite this warning, Vizetelly decided to soften his tone, as he had promised, and printed a "conciliatory article" in the next edition of the newspaper. When Constantinides's newspaper, the *Neon Kition*, reacted critically to this dramatically changed tone, Vizetelly responded by printing a sarcastic poem in which he presented Cyprus as the land where "cholera morbus" is abundant, the price of soap is enormous (presumably because everyone is filthy), "fever is sublime," people are indolent, women are ugly, and where slanderers and brute European Levantines reside. "The Cypriots went mad," Vizetelly recollects, and some local young men vowed to give him a beating. The print-house where he published *The Cyprus Times* demanded that he settles his account immediately before he would allow the printing of the next issue. Feeling that he "had quite enough of Cyprus one way or another," Vizetelly decided to leave for Alexandria.

There are several important points to be made in what is, apparently, Vizetelly's final act before his departure from the island. His admission of what basically constitutes a blatant case of nepotism—the government supporting him in exchange for his silence—was not uncommon in Victorian England. As Philip Harling observes, Victorian society was slow "to accept the principles of competitive recruitment" and "nepotism remained a noticeable feature of the system" until the end of the century.[57] In fact, as we have seen in the cases of other journalists who covered the Cyprus occupation, the production and distribution of news in Victorian England was caught up in a network of intimate relationships that significantly affected the opinions of journalists. If the case of Vizetelly is interesting, it is because he seems to be excluded from this network, at least to the extent that he does not enjoy the same intimate relationship with the army as his fellow correspondents. Yet, the very promise of such intimacy—the promise that the high commissioner would "obtain some support" for him—was enough for him to abandon his presumably more ethical stance of demanding civil reforms in Cyprus. In essence, his changed position, which is encapsulated in the repetition of the standard stereotypes concerning Cyprus (i.e., it's a filthy place, the women are ugly, the natives are indolent, etc.), aligns his positions with those of his fellow correspondents.

If there was ever a public relations officer in the early years of the British occupation of Cyprus, this was certainly Colonel Falkland Warren, whose intervention convinced Vizetelly to abandon his harsh critique of the military government.[58] The owner of the *Cyprus Times* was not, of course, the only British visitor to fall under the spell of the colonel's charm. Warren had first gained his reputation on the island as the great reformer of the town of Limassol. In August 1879, he was appointed chief secretary of the government, a promotion that increased his authority and influence over excavations on the island since he also acted as "Superintendent of Excavations for the Government" and, later, as an honorary keeper for the newly established Cyprus Museum.[59] In what appears to be an astounding apotheosis of Warren, the overwhelming majority of travelers and journalists who visited Cyprus praised both his character and his ingenuity. Much of the information they obtained came, in fact, from Warren himself.

Hepworth Dixon, who had acted as Cyprus correspondent for several provincial newspapers in Britain, became intimately familiar with the colonel while he was in Cyprus, in 1878, and devoted an entire chapter on his achievements in his volume, *British Cyprus* (1879), under the unmistakable title "A Reformer" (this, of course, was in reference to Warren's "cleaning-up" of Limassol). He further expressed his deep admiration for Warren and found in him "the genius and the instinct of a true reformer."[60] In his correspondences for *The Standard*, John Augustus O'Shea praised Warren as an "active and keen" guardian of British interests in Cyprus.[61] Warren was also well familiar with the Brasseys—the powerful member of the British Parliament, Thomas Brassey, and his wife, Annie—and had previously traveled with them to Russia. In 1878, when they arrived in Cyprus on their yacht, the *Sunbeam*, which Annie Brassey had made famous in her best-seller *A Voyage in the Sunbeam* (1878),[62] Colonel Warren acted as their guide. Annie Brassey writes that the colonel "takes great interest in his work, which is of the most arduous and varied description, as his jurisdiction extends over several hundred square miles of country."[63] Underlining Warren's interest in both archaeology and current news, she also writes that they exchanged "*new* newspapers for *old* pots and earthenware vases, some of beautiful shape."[64] The colonel was subsequently commissioned by Annie Brassey to conduct excavations on her behalf in Cyprus and in 1884 she exhibited her "Cypriot curiosities" at her husband's institute in London.[65] And when Warren was criticized for the draconian measures he enforced in Cyprus, particularly for his actions as civil commissioner of Limassol, Thomas Brassey defended him fiercely in the House of Commons.[66] Samuel Baker, who stayed with Warren and his family for sixteen days in 1879, when the colonel was district commissioner of Limassol, credits Warren with cleaning up the town: he "was an officer of great energy and ability and he had grappled vigorously with every difficulty and cleansed the Augean stables thoroughly."[67] When he was promoted to chief of staff, Baker writes, and consequently left Limassol, the district "lost its leading spirit."[68] Warren, according to Baker, was ahead of his time and if he got into trouble with the locals it was precisely because "he was determined to administer the laws without fear or favour to all classes."[69] The English novelist, William Hurrell Mallock (1849–1923), who stayed in Cyprus for three months, in 1888, also as a guest of Colonel Warren in his house in Nicosia,[70] describes him as "an ardent antiquarian" who was "eager to tell me whatever he knew of the architectural curiosities of the island ancient and medieval."[71] In fact, as it becomes evident in Mallock's *In an Enchanted Island* (1889), the Warrens, and particularly Mrs. Warren, did not merely open their house to Mallock; they practically acted as tour guides who gave him "a glimpse of the unknown world [he] was living in."[72]

This overwhelming show of support for Colonel Falkland Warren by English travelers, as well as the intimacy with which they describe their interactions with him, signifies his relentless effort to present an image of both himself and the government of Cyprus as reformers who would usher the island into Western civilization. This carefully constructed image of Warren, however, was drastically challenged in at least two occasions. The first time the colonel found himself in trouble was when the bishop of Citium accused him, in an 1879 letter submitted to Wolseley, of several violations in administering his duties as district commissioner of Limassol.[73] The most important accusations included the harsh and disproportionate punishment of Christian subjects by Warren, who quadrupled, or even sextupled, their original punishments of Christians by the Court of Justice; the fact that Warren refused to accept petitions or correspondence in Greek, even when he was provided with a translator, stating that "the official language of the Government in Cyprus is Turkish"; the unwarranted punishment of poor natives; and the unlawful infliction of harsh fines on the population. "On the whole," the bishop of Citium concluded in the memorandum submitted to Wolseley, "the Governor of Limassol has conducted, and still conducts, himself in a manner spreading desperation, without any exception, to all the inhabitants of that portion of the island, having exalted on a high throne the terror amidst a mild people, exemplary submissive to the authority."[74] These accusations were widely reported by the British press and were much-discussed in the British Parliament. The entire administration of Cyprus—from Wolseley to the district commissioners—rallied behind Warren and, as Samuel Baker wrote, "the case was investigated by a special court of inquiry, and terminated, . . . completely in favour of Colonel Warren."[75] Warren came out of this crisis victorious and, within a few months, he was promoted to chief secretary of the colonial government.

It was in this capacity, that the second crisis unfolded for Warren, in 1885–86, and it was, once again, related to his abuse of power. As chief commissioner, the colonel was now responsible for approving archaeological excavations in Cyprus. As an archaeology enthusiast and an avid collector himself, Warren found himself in a perfect position to take advantage of his new role and to amass a considerable number of ancient Cypriot artifacts. As Michael Given writes, through a circuitous bureaucratic procedure, Warren would apply for permission to excavate a site and end up approving the application himself; the countersignature of the high commissioner was simply a formality.[76] Consequently, Warren managed to acquire permission to excavate an area, in which Charles Watkins, the director of the Imperial Ottoman Bank, was already authorized to excavate. When Warren proceeded with the excavation, Watkins took the chief secretary to court and demanded part of the artifacts he discovered. As in the case of the bishop's accusations, the court found nothing illegal in the actions of Warren; naturally, the judge who acquitted the colonel, Charles Walpole, was Warren's subordinate in the government.[77] As Given writes, "archaeology in the early days of colonial rule in Cyprus was clearly driven by greed, power and self-display as much as by scholarly interest or academic enthusiasm."[78] Apart from the excavations that were indeed driven by "greed, power and self-display," we should add the apparent use of Cypriot artifacts as mediums through which power and self-promotion were consolidated: Warren often displayed his collection to visitors, lent parts of it to museums and, most importantly, gave several objects as gifts to the travelers who visited the island.

Vizetelly was certainly not aware of Watkins's accusations against Warren since the events took place about three years after his departure from the island. Even though he was probably aware of the bishop's accusation against Warren, his low opinion of the Greeks, whom he saw as a discontented people, did not permit him to take these accusations seriously. He was well-acquainted, however, with the colonel's powerful position in the government hierarchy and the intricate network of associations he had built during his tenure in Cyprus. The acceptance of the colonel's proposal to tone down his accusations of the government seems to be a result of the function of this intimate network, where personal ambition and public duty become indistinguishable. Vizetelly's reports from Cyprus testify to his isolation from the center of activity, his marginalization by the military government of Cyprus, as well as his attempt—unique among correspondents—to make a living in Cyprus through other means. When he saw a glimmer of hope that would, at long last, alleviate his financial troubles and give him access to the inner workings of the establishment, he accepted it. He ended up departing from Cyprus as marginalized as he arrived. Ironically, as the British press widely reported, he died alone, at the age of fifty-six, under "sad circumstances."[79] For unknown reasons, he had ended up at "Rowton House," in Whitechapel, a philanthropic hostel where one could acquire cheap accommodation. There, he caught pneumonia and passed away in April 1903. As several newspapers reported, "the deceased had been in straitened circumstances."[80] Dr. King-Houchin, the coroner who inquired into Vizetelly's death, stated that it seemed "very sad that such a renowned man should have drifted down to live in a lodging house" and that this was probably due to the fact that "his circumstances must have been restricted."[81]

NOTES

1. Michael P. Roth, *Historical Dictionary of War Journalism* (London: Greenwood Press, 1997), 328.
2. Ibid.
3. Edward Henry Vizetelly, *The Reminiscenses of a Bashi-Bazouk* (Bristol: J. W. Arrowsmith, 1897), 202–3.
4. Vizetelly, *From Cyprus to Zanzibar*, 17.
5. Ibid., 3.
6. *Glasgow Herald*, August 15, 1878, p. 3.
7. Vizetelly, *From Cyprus to Zanzibar*, 6.
8. *Glasgow Herald*, August 28, 1878, p. 5.
9. *Glasgow Herald*, August 28, 1878, p. 5.
10. *Glasgow Herald*, September 2, 1878, p. 4.
11. *Glasgow Herald*, September 2, 1878, p. 4.
12. *Glasgow Herald*, September 2, 1878, p. 4.
13. *Glasgow Herald*, November 19, 1878, p. 7.
14. *Glasgow Herald*, November 19, 1878, p. 7.
15. *Glasgow Herald*, January 30, 1879, p. 5.
16. *Glasgow Herald*, February 3, 1879, p. 9.
17. *Glasgow Herald*, February 3, 1879, p. 9.
18. *Glasgow Herald*, February 3, 1879, p. 9.
19. *Glasgow Herald*, February 3, 1879, p. 9.
20. *Glasgow Herald*, February 3, 1879, p. 9. My emphasis.
21. *Glasgow Herald*, December 26, 1878, p. 5.
22. *Glasgow Herald*, September 16, 1878, p. 5.
23. *Glasgow Herald*, September 16, 1878, p. 5.
24. *Glasgow Herald*, October 7, 1878, p. 4.
25. *Glasgow Herald*, November 25, 1878, p. 5.
26. *Glasgow Herald*, November 19, 1878, p. 7.
27. *Glasgow Herald*, November 25, 1878, p. 5.
28. *Glasgow Herald*, November 25, 1878, p. 5.
29. *Glasgow Herald*, November 25, 1878, p. 5.
30. *Glasgow Herald*, January 2, 1879, p. 2.
31. *Glasgow Herald*, January 2, 1879, p. 2.
32. *Daily News*, September 11, 1878, p. 6.
33. *Nottingham Evening Post*, October 30, 1878, p. 1
34. *Cardiff Times and South Wales Weekly News*, October 26, 1878, p. 3.
35. *Standard*, August 20, 1878, p. 5.
36. *Standard*, August 15, 1878, p. 5.
37. Lang, *Cyprus*, 321–22.
38. Susie L. Steinbach, *Understanding the Victorians: Politics, Culture and Society in Nineteenth-Century Britain*, 2nd ed. (London: Routledge, 2016), 149.
39. Vizetelly, *From Cyprus to Zanzibar*, 11.
40. Ibid., 473–74.
41. *Glasgow Herald*, February 3, 1879, p. 9.
42. James Lewis Farley, *Egypt, Cyprus and Asiatic Turkey* (London: Trubner and Company, 1878).
43. *Glasgow Herald*, October 7, 1878, p. 4
44. Roussou-Sinclair, *Victorian Travellers*, 86.
45. Vizetelly, *From Cyprus to Zanzibar*, 8.

46. Ibid., 24.
47. Ibid., 38.
48. *Daily News*, May 11, 1880, p. 5.
49. *Illustrated London News*, December 11, 1880, p. 563.
50. *Pall Mall Gazette*, September 20, 1880, p. 4.
51. *Daily News*, November 23, 1880, p. 5.
52. *Nottingham Evening Post*, December 28, 1880, p. 4.
53. *Liverpool Mercury*, July 1, 1881, p. 5
54. Vizetelly, *From Cyprus to Zanzibar*, 45.
55. Ibid., 47.
56. Ibid.
57. Philip Harling, "The Powers of the Victorian State," in *Liberty and Authority in Victorian Britain*, ed. Peter Mandler (Oxford: Oxford University Press, 2006), 30.
58. For more on Colonel Warren's tenure in Cyprus see H.-G. Buchholz, "Falkland Warren," in *Cyprus in the 19th Century AD: Fact, Fancy and Fiction*, ed. Veronica Tatton-Brown (Oxford: Oxbow Books, 2001).
59. Max Hermann Ohnefalsch-Richter, "Dr. Ohnefalsch-Richter's Record," *The Art Collector* 4, no.15 (June 1893): 234.
60. Dixon, *British Cyprus*, 335.
61. *Standard*, October 3, 1878, p. 3.
62. Annie Brassey, *A Voyage in the 'Sunbeam'*, 4th ed. (London: Longmans, Green, and Co., 1878).
63. Brassey, *Sunshine and Storm*, 259.
64. Ibid.
65. *Hastings and St Leonard's Observer*, November 22, 1884, p. 7.
66. HC Deb, 24 March 1879, vol. 244, cc1553–1557.
67. Baker, *Cyprus as I Saw it*, 256–57.
68. Ibid., 412.
69. Ibid.
70. William Hurrell Mallock, *Memoirs of Life and Literature* (New York: Harper and Brothers, 1920), 229.
71. Ibid., 230–31.
72. William Hurrell Mallock, *In an Enchanted Island: Or, A Winter's Retreat in Cyprus* (London: Richard Bentley and Son, 1889), 81.
73. See U.K. Parliament, *Correspondence Respecting Complaints*.
74. Ibid.
75. Baker, *Cyprus as I Saw it*, 412.
76. Michael Given, "The fight for the past: Watkins vs. Warren (1885–86) and the control of excavation," in *Cyprus in the 19th Century AD: Fact, Fancy and Fiction*, ed. Veronica Tatton-Brown (Oxford: Oxbow Books, 2001), 255.
77. Ibid., 258.
78. Ibid., 259.
79. *St. James's Gazette*, April 15, 1903, p. 9.
80. *St. James's Gazette*, April 15, 1903, p. 9.
81. *St. James's Gazette*, April 15, 1903, p. 9.

Chapter Seven

Samuel Pasfield Oliver and *The Illustrated London News*

As Kate Flint has argued, "the dissemination of images, whether photographic or engraved, was made possible by the development of the press and the diminishing costs of newsprint and printing technologies."[1] But most importantly, perhaps, it was a result of the Victorians' fascination with the image, which the invention of photography had essentially turned into a fetish. In the context of colonialism, the proliferation of the image satisfied the British public's desire for the visualization of exotic lands, the glorious battles of the Empire, the depiction of the "barbaric" as opposed to the "civilized," and, more generally, it allowed for the differentiation between the familiar and the foreign. This process of differentiation, which Edward Said persistently defines as *ontological*, was made available to a vastly larger number of people by utilizing the more basic medium of the image in combination with the art of description. Though the two most important illustrated newspapers that covered the occupation of Cyprus were *The Illustrate London News* and *The Graphic*, the description of a particular image, published in the August 24, 1878, edition of *The Illustrated Police News*, would serve as a good starting point in exploring the central role of illustrated newspapers in Victorian Britain; it would also serve as a good example of the fantasies the acquisition of the island elicited in the British public's imagination.

Founded in 1864 by the publisher George Purkess, *The Illustrated Police News* was a prototype of today's tabloid news—known as "penny newspapers" at the time—and its sketches of violence were visually provocative, even by today's standards. It was devoted to descriptions "of the leading murders, suicides, offences, and casualties of the week," and it had reached such wide circulation and notoriety that, in 1886, the readers of *The Pall Mall Gazette* voted it as "the worst newspaper in England."[2] The cover of its

August 24, 1878, edition features drawings of several sensational events: two illustrations of a murder-suicide that took place in Stepney; two illustrations of another murder-suicide that took place in Hampstead; an illustration of the vivisection of a dog (see figure 7.1); an illustration of a fatal bicycle accident; a group of individuals entertaining themselves in a cemetery (playing games, smoking, lying on tombstones, etc.), under the heading "shocking scene at burial ground" (see figure 7.2); and an illustration of a fatal gas explosion that took place in Stockton. Most of these are depictions of the moment of death: under the caption "The fatal shot," in the case of the Hampstead murder-suicide, we see a man shooting a pistol pointed at a woman's head; under the caption "Finding the bodies" we witness a man bending over two bloodied bodies lying on the ground; in the case of the two accidents, bodies are depicted bending, thrown unnaturally off-balance by the force exercised on them; and the vivisected dog is depicted lying on a table, with a knife sticking out of his body and four men (apparently scientists) watching as a fifth man dissects the animal.

All of these violent images are accompanied by more elaborate descriptions of the events they depict, in the second page of the newspaper. Astoundingly, most of the space on this page, alongside the descriptions of these sensational events, is devoted to the occupation of Cyprus. In order to give its readers as accurate an understanding of Britain's new possession as

Figure 7.1. "A dog vivisected—dissected alive and tortured with no anaesthetic." ***Source: The Illustrated Police News*, August 24, 1878.**

Figure 7.2. "Shocking scene at a burial ground." ***Source: The Illustrated Police News*****, August 24, 1878.**

possible, the fourth page of *The Illustrated Police News* includes a full-page sketch titled "Cyprus Illustrated" (see figure 7.3). On the top of the page, immediately under the heading, the sketch depicts three landscape views of the island. The center sketch takes most of the space and it shows a distinguished-looking General Wolseley taking over the administration of the island. He stands visibly to the foreground holding his helmet in one hand and a book in the other, as a second man, presumably Admiral Hay, reads from a declaration. Immediately behind Wolseley are his men, standing attentively, and behind them, a number of turbaned natives in disarray, scrambling to get a good view of Wolseley and his men. The most grotesque orientalist depictions included here are of the island's supposedly most representative types: a bride wearing a burqa, a turbaned porter, an odalisque, a peasant girl, a married woman, a eunuch, and an officer. At a first glance, the attire of these characters points to an exaggerated combination, in the British fantasies of the Cypriots, between Ottoman and ancient Greek culture.

The depictions on this sketch, the editors note, were taken from "a rare and valuable work in the Royal Library." "All the pictures in the book," they continue, "are reproductions from water colour drawings, made from the life. There cannot, therefore, be any doubt about their accuracy."[3] Though they do

Figure 7.3. "Cyprus Illustrated." ***Source: The Illustrated Police News*, August 24, 1878.**

not mention the title of this "rare and valuable work" that inspired these depictions of the natives, it appears that their source is a book of engravings published in 1802 under the title *The Costume of Turkey.* The book includes a total of sixty engravings, "made on the spot" in 1798, by the French artist Octavian Dalvimart.[4] They all depict costumes, as well as brief descriptions, in both English and French, of the Ottoman characters who wear them. All but one of the character sketches included in *The Illustrated Police News*'s rendition are copied from specific drawings in this book: The drawing of "the bride" is copied from an image describing "a Turkish lady in her wedding dress" (see figure 7.4). The drawing of "the porter" is copied from the engraving of "a hamal, or common porter." The image of the "odalisk" is copied from the plate depicting "a sultana, or odalisk" (see figure 7.5). The Cypriot "married woman" of the *Illustrated Police News*' illustration is, in fact, a copy of an engraving depicting "a Greek woman from the island of Marmora," without any reference to her marital status (see figure 7.6). The depiction of the "eunuch" is a rather faithful copy of "the Kislar Aga, or the first black unuch of the seraglio," and, finally, the image of the "officer" is copied from the engraving of the "officers of the grand signior."

"The Orient," Said writes, "was Orientalized not only because it was discovered to be 'Oriental' in all those ways considered common-place by an average nineteenth-century European, but also because it *could be*—that is, submitted to being—made Oriental."[5] What the recycling of old images in *The Illustrated Police News*' sketch tells us is that, likewise, the Cypriots were orientalized simply because they "*could be*—that is, submitted to being—made Oriental." Much like other newspapers turned to existing entries on Cyprus in British encyclopedias, the editors of *The Illustrated Police News* turned to depictions that were already in circulation and that they imagined to be relevant to the newly acquired colony. It didn't quite matter whether the depiction of a Cypriot woman was originally drawn to represent a "Greek woman from the island of Marmora," whether the Cypriot eunuch was the Kislar Aga, or if there was even a harem in Cyprus. As subjects of an Ottoman territory, the natives were expected to wear the same clothes, perform the same roles and represent the same types as the natives of Constantinople or Asia Minor. But it is the fact that these supposedly representative types, these "prototypes," were presented alongside violent shootings, suicides, an animal dissection, fatal accidents or immoral behaviors, that points to the remarkable impact that the acquisition of Cyprus had on the British public. The public's "blind, brutal, . . . bestial thirst for blood,"[6] to recall Kipling's phrase, was thus satisfied through the peculiar mixture of the exotic and the violent, the oriental and the deviant. This is precisely the ontological function that colonialism performed. What connects the masses' crime obsession with their mania over Cyprus is the fact that they both functioned as voyeuristic loci where difference could be enacted, where otherness could

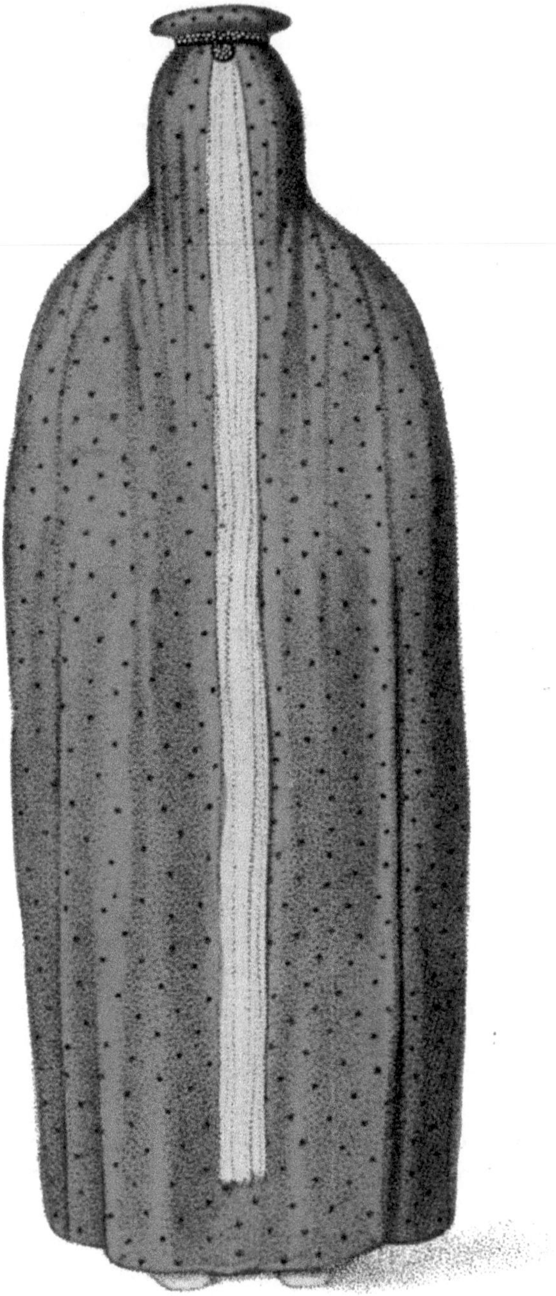

Figure 7.4. "A Turkish lady in her wedding dress." ***Source: The Costume of Turkey*** **(London: William Miller, 1802), Plate 57.**

Figure 7.5. "A sultana, or odalisk." ***Source: The Costume of Turkey*** **(London: William Miller, 1802), Plate 2.**

Figure 7.6. "A Greek woman from the island of Marmora." ***Source: The Costume of Turkey*** **(London: William Miller, 1802), Plate 13.**

Figure 7.7. "Officers of the Grand Signior." ***Source: The Costume of Turkey*** **(London: William Miller, 1802), Plate 3.**

be constituted, where the lines separating the human from the animal, the moral from the immoral, or the Empire from its colonies, could be clearly drawn. The emphatic declaration that these depictions of the Cypriot natives are "made from the life" and that "there cannot . . . be any doubt about their accuracy" can also be applied to the illustrations of crime. Both are grotesque representations of the human body and they both belong to the same ontological space that differentiates normalcy from deviance.

Though not as hyperbolic or sensational in their depictions of Cyprus and its people as *The Illustrated Police News*, *The Graphic* and the *Illustrated*

London News' representations are equally replete with orientalist connotations. And though all three newspapers were tremendously popular, *The Illustrated London News* was, by far, the most successful newspaper in Victorian England. Founded in 1841, by the 1860s it had reached an astounding circulation of about 300,000 copies per week; by comparison, the more prestigious *Times*' circulation was about 70,000 copies and the *Daily News*' 4,500 copies.[7] Its enormous success was largely due to the energy and entrepreneurship of its founder, Herbert Ingram, and his colleague Henry Vizetelly, who was Edward Vizetelly's father.[8] Naturally, the frenzy that followed the acquisition of Cyprus became a central topic, which was both depicted and described in detail, in both *The Illustrated London News* and *The Graphic*. As Rita Severis noted, "the July-December 1878 editions of both newspapers/magazines contain extensive reports [on Cyprus] and altogether 90 illustrations."[9] Underlining what I have been describing as an intimate relationship between the army and the press, many of these illustrations were submitted by "military personnel with artistic interest, already based in Cyprus . . . : Lieutenant G. H. Lane of the 101st Regiment, Captain R. Coveny of the 42nd Regiment, Lieutenant Alan Gilmore of the 61st Regiment who was later local commander of the military police of Nicosia, Captain McCalmont, and W. J. Eastman of the Royal Marine Artillery were but a few."[10]

Before discussing the reports and the sketches that appeared in *The Illustrated London News*, it would be useful, I believe, to consider briefly an illustration in *The Graphic*, as it pertains to both the process of the news' dissemination and the central role of special correspondents in this process. While the newspaper chose not to dispatch a special correspondent to Cyprus, its coverage of the occupation was as detailed as most of the major London newspapers. Beginning on July 13, 1878, it published Cyprus-related articles, illustrations, summaries of parliamentary discussions and general commentaries in successive issues. The newspaper's fascination with the island was rather short-lived; it lasted for about four months, as illustrations appeared continuously until mid-November and, from then on, they became much more sporadic. The central pieces of *The Graphic*'s presentation were the illustrations, which were accompanied by brief descriptions. Most of these were published anonymously, though a select few were described as sketches submitted by specific soldiers or officers who were serving in Cyprus. The cover of the August 17 issue of the newspaper includes a sketch of the famous correspondent, Archibald Forbes, and is accompanied by the following description:

> [Illustration] No 4. shows Mr. Forbes, the *Daily News* 'special,' riding into camp upon a Cyprian donkey, which, he says, took four hours to get over the five miles from Larnaca to the camp, and on the return journey lay down to

Figure 7.8. "Arrival in Camp of Mr. Forbes." ***Source: The Graphic*****, August 17, 1878.**

> rest, and was left enjoying a peaceful slumber, Mr. Forbes making his way back on foot.[11]

The sketch shows Forbes sitting sideways on the donkey as he enters the camp (see figure 7.8). The donkey's back feet seem to buckle under the weight it carries. Military officers and soldiers, dressed in kilts, appear to welcome Forbes wholeheartedly, and several of them give him a military salute. This warm welcome of the most famous of the correspondents who traveled to Cyprus exemplifies, of course, the congenial relationship between the army and the press. Forbes is essentially welcomed, by both officers and soldiers, as one of their own. In fact, this depiction is unmistakably one of reverence and respect: it would perhaps be uncanny, yet not extravagant, to compare this illustration of Forbes entering the British military headquarters in Cyprus on his donkey, with that of Christ as he triumphantly enters Jerusalem, also riding a donkey as the crowd around him cheers. Whatever association this image evokes, the celebratory atmosphere it captures, as well as the soldiers' salutations, are clear markers of both respect and veneration towards Forbes.

This sketch, as well as its accompanying description, were clearly inspired by Forbes's correspondence, which was published on August 10 in

The Daily News—that is, a week prior to *The Graphic*'s sketch. It is unclear whether it was produced after reading the correspondence or if it was drawn by a soldier or officer who was present at the Chiflik Camp during Forbes's visit. Be that as it may, Forbes's report does describe several of the details depicted in the sketch: the soldiers, for example, are in kilts because, as Forbes informs us, they belonged to the famous 42nd Regiment (i.e., the Royal Highlanders). Forbes, who was Scottish himself, discusses the symbols of their Scottishness in detail: from their kilts to their bagpipes. The description of the Cypriot donkey, which *The Graphic* summarizes briefly, is one of the most prominent and comical aspects in Forbes's correspondence. Other details that find their way from Forbes's correspondence to *The Graphic*'s sketch include his description of the shaded sentries, the camp's bell-tents, and Forbes's stick, a necessary tool since "the Cyprus donkey," as he writes, "requires steady and emphatic beating to make him move at all."[12] The significance of this movement from narrative to image—that is, from Forbes's correspondence to *The Graphic*'s illustration of it—is in many ways exemplary of the way stories, opinions, and perceptions of the colonized proliferated, and of how they were repeated and disseminated widely, in Victorian England. The sketches of Cyprus in the illustrated newspapers are posited, in this manner, as accompanying popular visualizations of the narratives which were already in wide circulation. Most importantly, these complimentary depictions clearly serve as ways through which public perception—even the uneducated masses—could understand and appropriate the colonized land and its inhabitants as parts of the mighty British Empire. To state the obvious, there is nothing Cypriot in this depiction of Forbes riding a donkey into a British camp to meet the 42nd Regiment, except perhaps for the wretched donkey. As in the case of the British flag, which is often depicted in these illustrations, the celebrated war correspondent and the renowned Royal Highlanders serve as familiar symbols of Britishness. If such a seemingly peripheral scene is worthy enough to be described and illustrated, if it is important enough to be printed and disseminated in both word and image, it is precisely because it is symbolically familiar. In this context, the sketches which appeared in *The Illustrated London News* are even more interesting since they present us, simultaneously, with both the image and the text of the scenes they aim to represent.

Unlike Forbes's critical position on Cyprus, *The Illustrated London News* maintained a rather positive stance in relation to the occupation of the island. In fact, when Forbes's "The Fiasco of Cyprus" appeared in the *Nineteenth Century*, the newspaper published a brief but equally scathing commentary on it:

> The sensational article of the *Nineteenth Century* of this month is Mr. Forbes's paper on the "Fiasco of Cyprus," which must itself be pronounced a fiasco. It

> is surprisingly deficient in the item of personal experience, and is, in fact, hardly anything else than a restatement of those obvious exceptions against the moral and strategical significance of our occupation, which could be and have been perfectly well discovered at home.[13]

For its own coverage of the occupation, *The Illustrated London News* chose a rather unfamiliar name in journalistic circles, Samuel Pasfield Oliver, who would perform the dual function of being both a special artist *and* a correspondent. As in the case of *The Graphic*, the coverage of Cyprus began on July 13 with lengthy commentaries, in different columns, on the Anglo-Turkish treaty and the "Cyprus frenzy" in England, a summary of the Parliamentary discussion on the subject, a brief history of the island copied from "Murray's Handbook for Travellers," and the actual text of the Anglo-Turkish treaty. The cover of the following issue, published on July 20, featured an illustration of "Famagosta [*sic*], the ancient Venetian port of Cyprus."[14] It also included several other illustrations of Cypriot landscapes and towns, scattered information about the occupation (such as Wolseley's arrival in Malta, en route to the island), its first Cyprus-related advertisement (for the perfume Eau de Chypre), a detailed map of the island, and a rather extensive overview of the island's history. The July 27 issue, the third successive issue on Cyprus, featured two illustrations of the island's coast on its cover, and several more inside, a synopsis of the Parliamentary debate about the occupation, commentaries on the significance of the acquisition and another lengthy account describing the situation in Cyprus since Wolseley's arrival. In this issue, it was also announced that the editors of *The Illustrated London News* "have already dispatched a Special Artist to furnish [the] journal with illustrations of the commencement of British rule in Cyprus."[15] This statement was repeated in the following issue, published on August 3, and a week later, the newspaper started publishing Samuel Pasfield Oliver's correspondences, along with his illustrations of the island.

The choice of Oliver as a correspondent was in some ways peculiar. Like some of the correspondents who covered the occupation, he was a military man who had served in the army for almost twenty years.[16] He had graduated from the Royal Military Academy and joined the Royal Artillery in 1859, serving, among other places, in China, Mauritius, Madagascar and Central America. His explorations in archaeology, botany, geography and ethnography were largely acknowledged by the scholarly societies in London, before his Cyprus journey: he became a Fellow of the Royal Geographical Society in 1866, a fellow of the Ethnological Society in 1869, and a Fellow of the Society of Antiquaries (FSA) in 1874. By the time he traveled to Cyprus, he was already an established scholar and known as a specialist on Madagascar, a country that he explored throughout his scholarly career. In 1878, just before he set out for Cyprus, he resigned from his position in the army.

Although he was a prolific scholar and had extensive experience in military expeditions, his commission with *The Illustrated London News* was essentially his first venture into journalism.

Oliver arrived in Cyprus on July 25, 1878, and departed sometime in October of the same year. He submitted a total of six correspondences to *The Illustrated London News*; the first one was composed on the day of his arrival and the last on September 7. His journey, as detailed in his first correspondence from Cyprus, begins with a remarkably thorough account of the route he followed: from the offices of *The Illustrated London News*, to Waterloo, to Southampton and across the channel to Le Havre, France. From there he continued to Paris and then, changing railway lines, he traveled southwards, to the port of Marseilles. Boarding the *Saint Marc*, a boat owned by Compagnie Fraissinet, he proceeded to Malta where he arranged, with the help of his friends in the army, for a transport to Cyprus. On July 25, after two weeks of traveling, he arrived in Larnaca, a day after the arrival of High Commissioner Wolseley. What emerges from this first report submitted by Oliver is his extraordinary attention to detail and his profound affection for the army. "With British officers as *compagnons de voyage*," he writes on board the steamer heading to Malta, "there is always some pleasant society."[17] He praises a group of military officers on board: a colonel who was "a great linguist," a captain who was an exceptional musical performer and "a smart Adjunct" as "good specimens of our Army men." He also takes the opportunity, while in Valetta, to visit "old acquaintances and fellow officers."[18]

In his next letter, composed three days after his arrival and published on August 17, he expresses his indebtedness to Admiral William Luard for arranging his passage from Malta to Cyprus. His deep knowledge of the army becomes apparent as he provides his readers with the long list of all the names of ships harbored in Cyprus (a total of about thirty vessels), along with the regiments on board each one of them as well as the names of the vessels' commanding officers. As this description is rather characteristic of both Oliver's style and his attention to detail—particularly in military matters—it is worth quoting in full, tedious as it might appear:

> The fleet is arranged as follows:—In the outer line (that is, furthest from the shore of the long shallow bay forming the Larnaca roadstead) is the Channel Squadron, consisting of H.M.S. Black Prince, commanded by H.R.H. the Duke of Edinburgh; H.M.S. Minotaur (flagship of Admiral Lord John Hay); H.M.S. Raleigh, H.M.S. Invincible, and H.M.S. Monarch. In the second line are the Government troop-ships—namely, H.M.S. Tamar, which brought the 71st Highlanders; H.M.S. Orontes, which brought the 1st Bombay Lancers and the 9th Bombay Native Infantry; and H.M.S. Himalaya, onboard of which are Sir Garnet Wolseley and his staff, with the 101st Fusiliers and the 42nd Highlanders. Next to these lies the despatch-boat H.M.S. Salamis; and H.M.S. Simoom, with the Royal Engineers, from Southampton, has a place here reserved for

> her. In the third line are ten hired transport steamers, which I mention by their numbers and names, with the regiments carried by each, and with their present destinations:—no. 5, the St. Osyth, with part of the 2nd Ghoorkas, for Larnaca; No 6, Malda, with another battalion of the same regiment, for Larnaca; no. 7, Madura, with the 31st Punjaub [*sic*] Infantry, for Limasol; no. 8, Goa, with the 13th Bengal Native Infantry; no. 9, Macedonia, with the 1st Bombay Lancers; no. 12, Nankin, with the 25th Madras Native Infantry, and no. 15, Marina, with part of that regiment, both for Kyrenia; no. 16, Suez, is now gone to Beyrout for horses; no. 23, Bengal, is here with the 13th Bengal Native Infantry, for Baffo; and no. 27, Trinacria, with the commissariat stores for Larnaca. The Canara has return to Malta for troops, and H.M.S. Simoom is daily expected. In the fourth line, nearest the shore, are the seven hired sailing transports, viz.:—No 2, the Hospodar; no. 3, Clydesdale; no. 11, Seaforth; no. 19, Citadel; no. 20, Aros Bay; no. 22, Kilkerran; and no. 24, Brambletye. Inside of these is a small steamer belonging to the Eastern Telegraph Company, which, with one or two small trading vessels, Turkish and Greek, makes up the shipping in the bay.[19]

This enumeration of the ships harbored in the small bay of Larnaca, was accompanied by a sketch, which the newspaper chose to publish in their next edition, a week later (August 24).[20] This remarkably extensive catalog—the modern equivalent of the Homeric catalog of ships—is indeed illustrative of Oliver's intimate knowledge of the army; more importantly, perhaps, it is exemplary of his tendency towards lengthy and, oftentimes, trivial descriptions. Though the information he receives from the army, as well as his already extensive knowledge of its nature, seems to be unrivaled among correspondents, it is impossible for him, perhaps due to his inexperience in journalism, to hierarchize this information. Similar catalogs or tedious descriptions are also published in his other correspondences from Cyprus. In almost every report he submits, he informs his readers which ships have left Larnaca and for which destination. In one report he provides his readers with a description of the "Chevlik Camp," the headquarters of the British forces, with the precise location of each regiment. He also reports on the activities and the health of several secondary officers: Colonel Prendergast of the Indian Engineers sailed to Bombay on board the *Trinacria* and, the last Oliver saw him, he tells his readers, he was suffering with the Cyprus fever; Lieutenant-Colonel J. Popham Magnay, of the Royal Engineers, is active in Nicosia and responsible for constructing wooden frames for the soldiers' tents; Young Bethel and Lieutenant A. H. Bagnold discovered sites in Cyprus which could serve as sanatoria or cantonments; Major Maitland "is over in the hills near Beyrout, suffering from dysentery, an old complaint, which should have prevented his coming out here."[21]

Oliver's itinerary in Cyprus was contingent upon his army connections and the military expeditions organized by the colonial government of Cyprus. His first three reports are written from Larnaca. From there he proceeds to Nicosia, where, with the help of a letter from the Larnaca Consul, he procures accommodation at the house of the governor's dragoman, where Wolseley's close associate, Colonel Biddulph, Cyprus's second high commissioner, was also residing. On August 8, he briefly meets with Wolseley in Nicosia, and describes the general as "genial and kind as he always is."[22] He then returns to Larnaca and charters a boat to explore "the eastern shores of the island."[23] On the same day he arrives in Famagusta where he meets the district commissioner of the town, Captain L. V. Swaine, and Captain Inglis, the assistant commissioner. As the editors of *The Illustrated London News* reported, Swaine kindly permitted Oliver to accompany him "in this round of administrative inspection."[24] In this tour of the district, which was undoubtedly Oliver's most intimate experience of the island, they were also accompanied by the commissioner's secretary and interpreter, a certain Mr. Cambettino, as well as baggage mules and muleteers, and two Turkish zaptiehs. Together they visit several villages and monuments and hear the complaints of villagers. One of the most dramatic episodes that he narrates during this trip is Captain Swaine's "triumphal entry" into the village of Levconico [*sic*], a description which was accompanied, in the same issue, with a sketch (see figure 7.9). As Swaine approached the village, Oliver hurried to the front, to gain a good vantage point, and described the following scene. This is probably his most convoluted and dramatic episode in his experience of Cyprus, and I include it here in its entirety:

> Many hundreds [of people] soon collected together in the street, and also on the roofs of all the houses which commanded a view of the scene. A good many priests and other leading men of the town went out some distance to meet the Kaimakam on his arrival, and a regular triumphal procession was formed; but there was no cheering, no noise of any description, except that of the bells ringing. In front rode the brigand-like zaptiehs, looking as important as possible, and then came Captain Swaine and his interpreter on their ponies, surrounded by a motley crowd of townsfolk, which increased in numbers as they moved along. Under the window from which I surveyed the scene were collected a large number of women, who on the like occasions always keep together, and hold aloof from the men, awaiting the approach of the procession, which came on at a rapid pace. Priests and all were on the trot, kicking up no end of dust, but, as I said before, without noise. This noiseless crowd had a curious effect; it must have numbered at least six or seven hundred, and such a tumultuous running and jostling crowd would in England and most parts of Europe have been accompanied by shouts, hurrahs, and other cries. But all these people were so serious and quiet that the contrast was peculiar. Captain Swaine was quite taken aback by his reception, but preserved his imperturbable demeanour; in fact, he looked every inch the Kaimakam. The scene would have been almost ludicrous if it had not suggested the painful thought of what these silent, reserved people had suffered under former Kaimakams and of what they looked forward to under British rulers.[25]

The description is rather uncanny. This "running and jolting crowd" of villagers is essentially rendered as mute. It is, to repeat Oliver's words, noiseless, serious, quiet, and reserved. What makes the scene uncanny is the fact that this muteness is in sharp contrast with the general urgency of the scene: that is, the ringing of churchbells, the rapid pace of the procession, the great number of people rushing to witness the arrival of their new rulers. Both Swaine and Oliver seem to be taken aback by the peculiar antithesis captured in this mute spectacle. Oliver's explanation is that that the crowd's reservation is due to their suffering under the previous rulers, the Turks. Yet, what seems to be even more uncanny in this scene is his evident slip of the pen, in the description of Swaine as looking "every inch the Kaimakam." In persistently using the Ottoman term for the governor of a province, or the local archon, Oliver inadvertently parallels the past with the present rulers: to put it bluntly, if the villagers suffered under the Kaimakams, and if Swaine "looked every inch the Kaimakam," then this reception seems to indicate the crowd's reserved attitude towards their new rulers. Far from pointing to a "looking forward" under the new administration, as Oliver concludes, the silence of this "ludicrous" spectacle points to the unconscious yet profoundly tragic position of the colonized vis-à-vis the colonizer. In the civilized West, he suggests, this scene would certainly be accompanied by a vociferous

Figure 7.9. "British occupation of Cyprus: Triumphal entry of Captain Swaine into Levconico." ***Source: The Illustrated London News*****, October 12, 1878.**

welcome; after all, in the standard narrative of the occupation of Cyprus, the British saw themselves as emancipators who had put an end to the people's suffering under the seemingly brutal Ottomans. Instead, what we are presented with in this scene are all the signs of a rightfully anxious crowd which is utterly uncertain about the intentions of their new rulers. Oliver's sketch, in fact, captures this anxiety very well. Without the accompanying description, the scene is less the depiction of a triumphal entry into a Cypriot village and more expressive of the anxiety, perhaps even the panic, of the conquered in encountering their conquerors for the first time: what we see is a procession of armed men speedily entering the village on their horses, and literally looking down on the people who are "running and jolting" in utter disarray.

Compared with the other correspondents covering the occupation of Cyprus, Oliver's reports seem to be less flamboyant or dramatic and far more composed, albeit exceedingly detailed and even tedious at times. Most of the subjects he covers are relatively neutral: he describes the landscape of the island, its cities and its ruins, the movements of the army, the comings and goings of ships, or the actions of the high commissioner, usually without judgment. His position, for example, on one of the most contested topics in the occupation of Cyprus—that of the rampant fever, which was gradually turning into an epidemic—is indicative of his overtly scholarly approach to journalism. In one report, dated August 7, he writes that "we hear of no sickness among the inhabitants" and that "it is not possible to see a more healthy lot of country folk than these cheery Cyprians [*sic*]."[26] The very next day, he reports on the existence of the "expected malarious fever" in Cyprus and admits that in his experience of the Chinese, Indian and Central American summers, he had never suffered "more from heat and vermin."[27] His judgment, however, does not lead him to a reassessment of the occupation's value. Instead, after admitting the existence of fever in Cyprus, he veers off into a meteorological discussion on atmospheric temperature in the Levant in comparison with the rest of the Mediterranean, in order to assess the cause of it. There are, of course, several moments where he interferes to comment on a certain observation or to pass judgment on a subject; but, once again, compared with his fellow correspondents, these moments are less frequent and rather peripheral. Echoing a widely held orientalist perception, for example, he writes that "the present hurry and bustle [at the marina of Larnaca] is all European. The phlegmatic Turks are as impassive and unconcerned as if it was no business of theirs."[28] When he travels with Swaine to inspect the District of Famagusta, after merely seeing a handful of Cypriot villages, he emphatically concludes that "as all these villages are alike, there is little to describe—they are merely a collection of mud huts."[29] Instead of politicizing the occupation, as many of the other correspondents did, he simply observes that the future of Cyprus is linked to the question of what the British can practically do with the island. He suggests, for example, that the island might be used to school Turkish officers in modern warfare. If the Anglo-Turkish treaty was based on the desire to protect Turkey from the advances of Russia, then "if we are to protect Turkey, Turkey must be taught how to protect itself."[30] Cyprus's position, he concludes, as well as its geographical features, render it ideal for such a "camp of instruction."

One of Oliver's most ardent criticisms in Cyprus is, interestingly, against the military administration of the island. Even though he is not as absolute as Vizetelly in his preference towards a transition to civil (rather than military) government, he still perceives the current state of affairs in Cyprus as utterly confusing. In a report composed on August 28 he writes:

> All officialdom is in the hands of interpreters, and most unsatisfactory interpreters too. Justice and the administration of the government must suffer. A proper staff of Turkish-speaking Foreign Office officials, from Constantinople and Cairo, should be sent here. It is an up-hill job for Sir Garnet Wolseley, with a raw staff, utterly ignorant of the requirements of a strange people, to administer the government. The whole administration will fall into disrepute if we are not alive to our interests which suffer now. Our Treasury is robbed with impunity, as no one knows accurately what should be paid in and what the revenues are; and that can never be arrived at as things are carried on at present.[31]

"It may seem presumptuous for me to say so," Oliver continues in his usual reserved manner, "but I cannot help thinking that the Executive has too much of the military element in it at present." Military officers, he suggests, have plenty of energy and goodwill, and they certainly work hard, but they are not fit to do the job of civil servants. In fact, as he sees it, "a staff of experienced Indian civil servants would have been far superior." Elsewhere, he observes that in this "semi-military, semi-civilian administration of this unfortunate island," no appointments are permanent and this leads to a "general feeling of mistrust" and prevents a "settling into a state of security."[32]

One of the most noteworthy events Oliver covers during his stay in Cyprus is the ceremony of hoisting the British flag at the monastery of Kikko, in Nicosia, near the army's headquarters. Its significance lies in the fact that it was covered by three special correspondents in Cyprus—Herbert, O'Shea and Oliver—and it was also described by Wolseley in his personal diary. The ceremony took place on Sunday, August 18, 1878, at the monastery of Kikko, in Nicosia. None of these descriptions is as acrimonious and scornful as the one provided by Wolseley. Part of the reason, of course, is linked to the fact that this account was recorded in the general's private journal; in other words, it was meant for a private reading and not for public consumption. Nevertheless, it is an account worth reading in our attempt to piece together the grand narrative of Cyprus's colonization, since, in all the other descriptions, the presence of Wolseley at this ceremony is, as we shall see, of paramount importance:

> Went to the monastery church to attend a great function in honour of hoisting the English flag upon it: first we had Mass—Such a mockery of everything sacred, dirty greasy priests attempting to intone some dreary dirges that were utterly devoid of music or melody. . . . After the mass which was very long some of the congregation advanced to the screen which hides the altar and kissed the pictures of the Virgin and some ugly looking saints. . . . The whole ceremony was like a penny peep show very badly done by very inferior showmen. . . . We all proceeded to the door of the church where on the steps there was more intoning and then at last the Abbot stepped forward and took the British Jack from the table where it had been lying while these incantations were being gone through and incense being burnt over it. As if our flag required any purification—and opened and fastened it to the halliards and it was hauled up amidst loud "Zitas" [*sic*] from the ugly crowds. Cheers were given for the Queen and, the ceremony over, went back to breakfast.[33]

Wolseley, whose *Soldier's Pocket Book* gives testimony to the great attention he paid to ceremonial procedures in the military, was scandalized by what he perceived as a "mockery of everything sacred" in this ceremony. Beyond his apparent disdain for the priests, the orthodox liturgy, the crowds and their saints, his description points to the admittedly ludicrous spectacle underlining the ceremony: in what appears to be an ironic reversal, the leaders of the colonized, that is the priests led by the abbot, consecrated the flag of the colonizers.

Five days after this ceremony, John Augustus O'Shea wrote his own description of it which appeared in the September 5 edition of *The Standard.* Like Wolseley, he describes the mass as a combination of "much genuflection and much nasal vocalism, half recitative, half humming, [and] doleful" but adds that it was "not unmelodious."[34] He also makes note of the "gilt throne" arranged for Wolseley and observes that the general "did not occupy this throne, but stood beside it, looking a little uneasy." After describing the blessing of the flag and its clumsy hoisting by a young Cypriot, he proceeds to criticize the ceremony as completely inappropriate:

> To my thinking this whole military movement was wrong, impolitic, and a stretch of courtesy to the tearing-point. The Governor [*sic*] attended out of pure kindness to the monks who have good-naturedly given up a part of their premises to him as offices. But was it absolutely necessary to bless the flag before hoisting, and will not the attendance of the Governor at the ceremony tend to beget in the Greeks a delusion that we identify ourselves in sympathy with one race in this island to the contempt of the other, and that other the governing race from whom we got the island?[35]

Like Wolseley, O'Shea, whose reports are markedly sympathetic and respectful of the military, was appalled by the blessing and the hoisting of the flag by the non-British natives; he further perceived the great attention given by the colonial administration to such a minor event as sending the wrong signals to the two communities on the island.

The Times' correspondent, St. Leger Algernon Herbert, offered a much more composed description of the event on August 21, three days after the ceremony:

> Last Sunday the monastery of Zigo [*sic*], close to the Head-quarters Camp, was the scene of a ceremony which attracted numerous spectators from the villages in the neighbourhood and from Nicosia. The British flag was to be hoisted from a flagpole on the roof of the Greek church. The Abbot would not fly the flag till it had received consecration, and, accordingly, in the presence of Sir Garnet Wolseley and his Staff, a dense crowd filling the court-yard and lining its parapets, the ceremony was conducted at the church door. I cannot say that the intention of the monks was a triumph of musical modulation. Indeed, I heard it likened to a breeze from the bagpipes. When the service was concluded the flag was run up among enthusiastic cheers, led by the Abbot, and I believe a photograph was taken of the assemblage.[36]

Apart from his agreement with the high commissioner regarding the cacophony of the orthodox liturgy, Herbert attempts, at least implicitly, to absolve Wolseley of any responsibility regarding this apparently improper gesture of blessing the British flag. The flag was blessed, according to his account, because the abbot would not fly it "till it had received consecration."

Compared with these accounts—even with *The Times'* usual undramatic tone—Oliver's description is characteristic of his detached and reserved style:

> Our Special Artist in Cyprus, "S.P.O.," contributes a sketch of the scene at the door of the Greek Monastery Church at Kiko, two miles from Nicosia, adjacent to the headquarters' camp of General Sir Garnet Wolseley, on Sunday, the 18th ult., when the Most Reverend Archimandrite, with other Greek clergy, blessed the British flag. This ceremony was preceded by the performance of a high mass within the church. . . . A gilt chair of state was placed for the English Governor, a table, with a pair of tall candlesticks, for the clergy. Sir Garnet Wolseley declined to sit on the chair, which looked too much like a throne; but he stood behind it, while Colonel Brackenbury, Captain McCalmont, and Lord Gifford, members of his staff, were behind the chair. The monks and priests, with acolytes bearing the crucifix and censer and vessel of holy water, came out in procession, attired in gorgeous vestments, and chanting a solemn hymn. The flag was hallowed by the Archimandrite with a particular benediction, and was hoisted, rather clumsily, by one of the church attendants. Three cheers were given for Queen Victoria, for Sir Garnet Wolseley, and for the British nation. There was no parade of military force.[37]

In contrast to other British correspondents, Oliver chooses to emphasize the homage the natives paid to Queen Victoria, Sir Garnet Wolseley, and the British nation. He also underlines the humility of the colonizers: the gilt chair arranged for Wolseley looked too much like a throne and, therefore, the humble high commissioner declined to sit on it; additionally, after the conclusion of the ceremony, "there was no parade of military force." He does not find the priests' chant to be cacophonous, as Wolseley, O'Shea and Herbert did; he rather describes the archimandrite as "most reverend" and the clergy as "attired in gorgeous vestments." This is clearly a description that aims to highlight the Christian natives' reverence for their British rulers and their flag. The accompanying illustration is in fact indicative of this veneration: it depicts several priests crowding around the Union Jack, raising their censers and crosses towards the most venerable symbol of the British Nation (see figure 7.10). The priests and the large crowd of spectators, which spreads as far as the eye can see, are all turned towards the flag and a regiment of Indian natives—from England's most prized colony—executes the "present arms" drill. On the bell tower three priests attend to the ringing of the bell. In short, the Union Jack is at the center of attention in this depiction. Both Oliver's illustration and the accompanying description aim to emphasize the enthusiastic welcoming of the British by the Christian natives (as well as the Indians) and the unconditional submission of the colonial subjects to the British flag and its representatives. The illustration includes an additional fine but quite revealing detail: all the colonial subjects depicted in the illustration are wearing their hats or caps, whereas the colonial administrators (i.e., Wolseley and his staff) have taken them off and hold them in their hands. Independently of whether this depiction is historically accurate or not, this seemingly minor detail serves as a marker of the British civility, humility and veneration in the context of religious custom or vis-à-vis the flag. In fact, the handful of British officers watching the ceremony are distinctly set apart from the crowd. Their nonchalant posture seems to be in contrast with the general atmosphere of reverence. They are depicted as unwilling witnesses to a ceremony that, on the one hand, encapsulates the triumph of British colonialism and, on the other, the discomfort of allowing the native priests to consecrate and hoist the most venerable symbol of the Empire. Once again, this detail—the depiction of the hatless British officers and that of the covered natives—is not mentioned in Oliver's description. Yet, when the British public saw the sketch, it presumably emerged as a central marker of differentiating the colonizers from the colonized.

This ceremony, purely symbolic as it may have been, was widely reported by the British press through the republishing of the correspondences submitted by Herbert, O'Shea and Oliver. It was also mentioned by travelers and scholars who had not witnessed the event at all. In her famous travelogue *Sunshine and Storm in the East*, Lady Brassey, who arrived in Cyprus in

Figure 7.10. "The Occupation of Cyprus: Greek Priests Blessing the British Flag at Nicosia." ***Source: The Illustrated London News*****, September 21, 1878.**

November 1878, about three months after the ceremony took place, was evidently informed about it, most likely by Herbert, whom she met on several occasions in Cyprus, and noted that "the patriarch [*sic*] made a great ceremony of blessing [the flag] before allowing it to be hoisted, and had to send all the way to Kikko for his state robes, in which to officiate on the occasion."[38] As in the case of Herbert's description, Wolseley is absolved here of any direct involvement in the rather extraordinary decision of "blessing" the British flag. One of the most interesting commentaries on the ceremony of hoisting the flag was written by the military historian Charles Rathbone Low, whose popular biography of Wolseley was proofread by the general himself. Low writes that "the British flag, after consecration of the convent of Nicosia, was hoisted in the presence of Sir Garnet Wolseley and of the Christian classes of the community with imposing ceremonial and amid hearty acclamations."[39] In other words, he simply summarizes the ceremony as a magnanimous event in honor of the British and their leader in Cyprus, Garnet Wolseley. He then proceeds to write—with Wolseley's blessing, since the general read the manuscript proofs—that "with the greed of their race, the Greeks sought to make all the pecuniary gain possible out of their deliverers."[40] The explanation he gives to justify the Greeks' greed, is their demand for exuberantly high rents for the houses they provided to the colonial administration. The subject of the high prices for housing was indeed one of the main topics of discussion in British newspapers in the early months of the occupation. The conflation of the two issues, however—that of the ceremony and the demand for high rents—points to a narrative that we constantly encounter in the early years of British colonialism in Cyprus. The British, according to this narrative, delivered the Greek/Christian population from the oppression of the Ottomans, yet the "greedy Greeks" did not show any respect for this magnanimous act: instead, they demanded high rents. This passing reference captures well Wolseley's annoyance with what he perceived as the constant demands from the Greek community: complaints that they were mistreated by the British administration, that they were oppressed, that they were not allowed to use their language in official communications, etc. In his final report from Cyprus, Oliver does include an equally exuberant demand by the Greeks, when he describes one of Swaine's speeches during their tour of the Famagusta district. The "Kaimakam," he writes in reference to Swaine, told the people at the village of "Levkonico" [*sic*] that under their new rulers, all communities of the island (Turks and Greeks) would be treated equally. But the Greeks reacted demanding that "the two neighbouring Turkish villages should be destroyed, or rather that the Turks should be driven away from these two villages because they annoyed them, and stole their sheep, and they had never hitherto been able to get redress."[41] To Oliver, this is an example of "how little these people appreciate toleration."

About two weeks after the ceremony at Kikko, Oliver wrote his final two letters from Cyprus. In his conclusion he wrote that he was planning a visit to the village of Kouklia, near the town of Paphos, where two English settlers, Messrs. Sparrow and Bass, had bought a farm and they were planning to import "good breeds of English sheep."[42] This trip to the western part of the island was never realized. On October 26, two weeks after publishing Oliver's final two reports, *The Illustrated London News* reported that their "Special Artist in Cyprus, 'S.P.O.,' has been compelled by an attack of fever to seek refuge, for a week or two, in the salubrious high lands of the Lebanon, above Beyrout [*sic*], on the opposite shore of Syria."[43] In its next edition, on November 2, they repeated the announcement stating that Oliver "made an excursion to the western coast of the island, just before he was taken ill of fever, but was unable to go to Baffo, or to inspect the reputed site of the ancient Paphos, renowned in Greek mythology as the abode of Venus."[44] Captain Swaine, the Famagusta "Kaimakam" whom Oliver had accompanied during his stay in the island, was also stricken ill with fever. In late October, newspapers reported that Captain Swaine had "broken down, like most of his *confreres*, from exposure to the climate"[45] and that he returned to England, on board the *Tamar*,[46] "with a number of other invalids whose health has been affected."[47] Hence, Oliver's sojourn to Cyprus ended rather abruptly and ingloriously. His journey to Lebanon and Syria, where he traveled to convalesce from the Cyprus fever, was recorded in a series of articles submitted to *The Gardeners' Chronicle*, in 1879.[48] Upon his return to England, he continued to publish, mostly on the subject of Madagascar, until his death in 1907; however, apart from a brief response to the archaeological findings of David George Hogarth and Francis Henry Hill Guillemard, published in *The Athenaeum* in 1888, Oliver's description of Cyprus is restricted to his 1878 reports and does not feature prominently in his post-1878 work.

NOTES

1. Kate Flint, *The Victorians and the Visual Imagination* (Cambridge: Cambridge University Press, 2000), 3.
2. *Pall Mall Gazette*, November 23, 1886, pp. 1–2.
3. *Illustrated Police News*, August 24, 1878, p. 2.
4. *The Costume of Turkey* (London: William Miller, 1802).
5. Said, *Orientalism*, 5–6.
6. Kipling, *Selected Works*, 50.
7. Christopher Hibbert, *The Illustrated London News: A Social History of Victorian Britain* (London: Angus and Robertson, 1975), 13–14.
8. For more on Vizetelly's involvement see C. N. Williamson, "Illustrated Journalism in England," *The Magazine of Art*, 13 (1890): 297–301.
9. Rita. C. Severis, "Although to Sight Lost, to Memory Dear: Representations of Cyprus by Foreign Travellers/Artists (1700–1955)" (PhD. diss., University of Bristol, 1999), 154.
10. Ibid., 153.
11. *Graphic*, August 17, 1878, p. 155.
12. *Daily News*, August 10, 1878, p. 5.
13. *Illustrated London News*, vol. 73, October 12, 1878, p. 342.
14. *Illustrated London News*, July 20, 1878, p. 49.
15. *Illustrated London News*, July 27, 1878, p.85.
16. For a more extensive biography see G. S. Woods, "Oliver, Samuel Pasfield," in *Dictionary of National Biography (Second Supplement),* ed. Leslie Stephen and Sidney Lee (New York: The Macmillan Company, 1912): 44–45.
17. *Illustrated London News*, vol. 73, August 10, 1878, p. 123.
18. *Illustrated London News*, vol. 73, August 10, 1878, p. 123.
19. *Illustrated London News*, vol. 73, August 17, 1878, p. 162.
20. *Illustrated London News*, vol. 73, August 24, 1878, p. 185.
21. *Illustrated London News*, vol. 73, October 5, 1878, p. 314.
22. *Illustrated London News*, vol. 73, August 31, 1878, p. 210.
23. *Illustrated London News*, vol. 73, October 5, 1878, p. 312.
24. *Illustrated London News*, vol. 73, October 19, 1878, p. 378.
25. *Illustrated London News*, vol. 73, October 12, 1878, p. 350. My emphasis.
26. *Illustrated London News*, vol. 73, August 24, 1878, p. 186.
27. *Illustrated London News*, vol. 73, August 31, 1878, p. 210.
28. *Illustrated London News*, vol. 73, August 17, 1878, p. 162.
29. *Illustrated London News*, vol. 73, October 12, 1878, p. 350.
30. *Illustrated London News*, vol. 73, August 31, 1878, p. 310.
31. *Illustrated London News*, vol. 73, October 19, 1878, p. p. 378.
32. *Illustrated London News*, vol. 73, October 5, 1878, p. 313–14.
33. Wolseley, *Cyprus 1878*, 51–52.
34. *Standard*, September 5, 1878, p. 5.

35. *Standard*, September 5, 1878, p. 5.
36. *Times*, September 2, 1878, p. 8.
37. Oliver's description was not part of his correspondence. It was presumably submitted separately along with the illustration. *Illustrated London News*, vol. 73, September 21, 1878, p. 275.
38. Brassey, *Sunshine and Storm*, 295.
39. Low, *Lord Wolseley of Cairo*, 348.
40. Ibid.
41. *Illustrated London News*, vol. 73, October 12, 1878, p. 350.
42. *Illustrated London News*, vol. 73, October 12, 1878, p. 350.
43. *Illustrated London News*, vol. 73, October 26, 1878, p. 397.
44. *Illustrated London News*, vol. 73, November 2, 1878, p. 408.
45. *Naval & Military Gazette*, vol. 49, October 23, 1878, p. 331.
46. *Hampshire Telegraph and Sussex Chronicle*, November 6, 1878, p. 2.
47. *Morning Post*, October 21, 1878, p. 6.
48. See *The Gardeners' Chronicle: A Weekly Illustrated Journal* 12 (July to December, 1879).

Chapter Eight

Hepworth Dixon and the Provincial Press

When Hepworth Dixon visited Cyprus, in the autumn of 1878, he was already one of the most established and recognizable figures among literary circles in London. A prolific writer, Dixon was also an avid traveler, having journeyed to Portugal, Morocco, Palestine, the United States, the Baltic provinces, Russia, Switzerland, Spain, Germany and Canada. Apart from his travel books, which include *The Holy Land*, *New America*, *Free Russia*, *The Switzers*, *The White Conquest* and, of course, *British Cyprus*, Dixon wrote on a plethora of subjects. His first literary work, *The Azamoglan*, which he published at the young age of twenty-three, was a tragedy "founded on an incident in the Greek Revolution" of 1821 and very much influenced by Romantic philhellenism.[1] He proceeded to write several books and pamphlets on a wide range of topics: on the London prisons, the history of the representative system in England, the possibility of a French invasion, Mormon polygamy, Marx and Communism, four volumes on the history of the Tower of London, four volumes on Windsor Castle,[2] two works of fiction, as well as several biographies (e.g., on the Quaker philosopher William Penn, the seventeenth-century English admiral Robert Blake, the seventeenth-century philosopher Francis Bacon, the Irish novelist Lady Morgan, who had appointed him her literary executor, Queen Catherine of Aragon and Anne Boleyn).[3] Most importantly, Dixon was known for his editorship of one of the most popular and widely circulated British literary magazines of the nineteenth century, *The Athenaeum*, which he edited for sixteen years (1853–69).

While Dixon was one of the most popular writers of his time, he was also one of the most controversial. Even though his works went through many editions and the public apparently embraced them, the literary establishment often accused him of being inaccurate, hyperbolic or plainly wrong in relation to historical facts. In fact, he was so despised by certain critics that several obituaries that appeared in the press after his death, on December 27, 1879, commented on his offensive character, his frenetic publishing of mediocre books and the inaccuracies in his writing. "It is undeniable," one journalist wrote, "that, somehow or other, Mr. Hepworth Dixon managed to get himself thoroughly disliked among his literary contemporaries; indeed he was, perhaps, about the best abused man of his time in the world of letters."[4] Another journalist noted that his strange immunity from the vast majority of his readers was "the cause of the carelessness with which some of his works were compiled, and in which historical errors are found."[5] Yet another noted, more politely, that "Mr. Dixon's productions, both as a traveller and a historian, bore inevitable marks of haste."[6] One of the harshest judgments of Dixon's character was written by William Carew Hazlitt, the grandson of the celebrated essayist, literary critic, painter, and philosopher William Hazlitt:

> Dixon utilized his vacations by visiting some locality likely to yield marketable stuff for a book against the next winter season. One year he went to Cyprus, and after a six weeks' stay appeared in due course as the historian of that island and ancient seat of arts and government. . . .
>
> The author of *Spiritual Wives* was gifted with the art of quick study. He came, saw, and conquered. The history of an ancient empire or the picture of a latter-day heresy, it mattered little. He had the knack of disguising his lack of knowledge and information under a specious and flippant style emphatically Dixonian, and his object was achieved.[7]

Indeed, several nineteenth-century critics used the adjective "Dixonian" as equivalent to flippant writing and flamboyant rhetoric.[8] Once again, the majority of the late nineteenth-century readers, who apparently devoured everything Dixon published, did not share the harsh, albeit accurate, critique of the quality of his work.

Dixon's intention to travel to Cyprus was widely circulated in the British press. In August and September of 1878, several provincial newspapers announced that in early October they would begin publishing a series of letters from Cyprus by the distinguished litterateur and traveler, Mr. Hepworth Dixon. *The Western Mail* advertised Dixon's forthcoming letters under the title "Letters from Cyprus by Hepworth Dixon" and provided the following description:

> Mr. Hepworth Dixon has left England for Cyprus by way of Alexandria, and his present intention is to take Greece on his road home. In connection with this visit we are glad to announce that arrangements have been made with Mr. Dixon to supply the columns of this paper with interesting letters descriptive of the different places of interest on the island, as well as of the other peoples

> and countries which he proposes visiting. His contributions will, there can be no doubt, be eagerly looked for.[9]

Several provincial newspapers, including *The Aberdeen Weekly Journal*, *The Bristol Mercury*, *The Northern Echo*, and *The North British Daily Mail*, published similar advertisements. Dixon had followed the same tactic of serializing his travel impressions, in the form of letters, during his journey to the United States. In September and October of 1874, several newspapers had announced their intention of publishing a series of twenty letters by the "distinguished and popular writer" Mr. Hepworth Dixon, describing his impressions of America.[10]

Dixon published fifteen lengthy letters describing Cyprus to the British public. The fact that these letters did not appear in the more prestigious London newspapers but, rather, in several peripheral ones, is in some ways exemplary of the dissemination and popularization of colonial discourse. That is, the description of the colonies by the British press, along with the expression of the cultural supremacy that came along with it, was not restricted to the colonial metropoles but was dispersed throughout Britain through the pages of provincial newspapers. These newspapers either reprinted, summarized and commented upon the articles of the major London publications or, as in the case of Dixon's letters, secured their own correspondents by sharing the cost of commissioning a journalist. Most importantly, Dixon's letters are indicative of what I have described as a discourse founded on intimate relationships. If one compares Dixon's original letters from Cyprus with his book *British Cyprus*, which is, in some respects, an edited and expanded version of the letters, this intimacy comes to the foreground and reveals the ways colonial discourse is often entangled in an interpersonal and intersubjective exchange between men in power.

The relationship between Wolseley and Dixon, as it emerges in the former's journals and the latter's book on Cyprus, was, to say the least, a tense one. On October 4, 1878, Wolseley noted in his journal, in his usual mocking tone, that "a man calling himself Major Cesnola . . . who is brother to the man who called himself General Cesnola . . . had been excavating here although he was distinctly told he must not do so."[11] He further wrote that he gave orders to seize Cesnola's possessions and arrest him if "he was caught in the act."[12] As we will see, this incident was of pivotal importance in shaping Dixon's perception of both Wolseley and the administration's work in Cyprus. Wolseley ends the day's entry with the following comment, which points to the fact that Dixon's fame and reputation preceded him: "I hear that pompous ass Hepworth Dixon who arrived by the last mail steamer is with him [i.e., Cesnola] having come here to write a book about Cyprus."[13] Wolseley's description of his eventual meeting with Dixon, on October 20, is reflective of the deep resentment he felt towards him:

> The man himself is such an offensive snob, so thoroughly unlike everything in manner and bearing that one has been accustomed to regard as the characteristics of an English gentleman. So egotistical, so vain, so pompous, self satisfied, dirty and lying that one felt an itching about the toe to apply it to his stern.[14]

Wolseley proceeds to mock Dixon's declaration that he never reads books about a country he intended to visit, so as not to affect his judgment. He also claims, having heard this from one of his trusted men, that Dixon wrote a description of the Temple of Venus in Paphos without actually setting foot on the temple.[15] Wolseley's description of Admiral Lord John Hay was equally scornful: he describes him as a man full of "pompous ignorance," who laughs unpleasantly[16] and who is nothing than "a foolish idle child."[17] When he finds himself in the company of both men on the occasion of a dinner on board HMS *Minotaur*, his reaction is, again, one of outmost repulsion:

> Hay's hands and nails are always disgustingly filthy, which is, I presume, why he likes Mr. H. Dixon whose dirty appearance is very repulsive. That offensive liar was at dinner. He is one of those creatures—I cannot call him a man—whom soldiers feel a longing to kick at. I have difficulty in restraining my right boot from defiling itself against the seat of his filthy looking trousers. His voice as well as his unkempt and unmanly appearance are offensive. Sitting next to such a pompous fellow as Hay and having that filthy scribbler under my eye, it was a pleasure to see and talk to Hornby.[18]

In Wolseley's journals, every single reference to Dixon is much the same; he even suggests that scribblers like Dixon should be exiled from England to some republic where they cannot "proselytyze" [*sic*] "and where they can look around without being oppressed by the sight of men, better, stronger and socially of a different type and organization than themselves."[19]

Dixon's representation of Wolseley, on the other hand, is not nearly as negative; yet, there is a marked difference between the depiction of the general in the "Letters from Cyprus" and in his book *British Cyprus*. In the seventh chapter of his book, Dixon describes in detail the takeover of the island. He presents Admiral John Hay as an ingenious commander who, despite the advice to wait until the arrival of High Commissioner Wolseley, proceeded to form and execute an excellent plan that led to the peaceful transition from Ottoman to British rule. "Long before Sir Garnet Wolseley and his regiments arrived in Larnaca," Dixon concludes, "the work of taking over Cyprus from the Sultan to the Queen was done."[20] The new ruler of Cyprus is reduced to the margins of a story in which the protagonist is clearly Admiral Hay. Interestingly, in one of his first meetings with Lord Hay, Wolseley himself noted that "he has talked to me as if he had arranged all the affairs of the Island before I arrived, and that I had only to keep things going."[21] Undoubtedly, Dixon's informant in Cyprus was Admiral Hay.

The conversations between Dixon and Wolseley, as presented in *British Cyprus*, are similarly full of insinuations and unspoken contempt. Dixon presents himself as a learned advisor, or even an instructor, to Sir Garnet who is, again, reduced to merely agreeing with the author's didactic remarks on the history of the island. The letters, on the other hand, present us with a different story. In his first dispatch from the island, Dixon describes Lord Hay as "a mighty satrap" and Wolseley as "a peaceful and enlightened Pasha."[22] By the time the fifth letter is published, a little over a month after the first, Dixon expresses his concern that General Wolseley's "first experiment in civil government may be clogged and hampered by a wrangle with the United States."[23]

The story behind this shifting representation is, again, exemplary of the way intimate or personal relationships inform the propagation of colonial discourse. When Dixon arrived in Cyprus, as he informs his readers in both the letters and the book, he was hosted in the house of the famous Cesnola family. The Cesnola brothers, Luigi and Alessandro, were Italians who became naturalized as American citizens. Their names became intrinsically linked with Cypriot archaeology. Luigi Palma di Cesnola, the more famous of the two brothers, was appointed by President Lincoln as consul of the United States in Cyprus in the period immediately preceding the British occupation of the island (1865–77). It was during this time that he conducted many excavations around the island and amassed the largest collection of Cypriot antiquities of his time, which he subsequently sold to the newly founded Metropolitan Museum of Art in New York; in fact, Luigi Palma di Cesnola served as the Metropolitan Museum's first director from 1879 to 1904. The younger of the Cesnola brothers, Alessandro, went to Cyprus in 1873 and, upon the recommendation of his consul brother, was appointed "Vice-consul of the United States at Paphos."[24] For about two years, he assisted his brother in excavations as "chief digger and partner."[25] After Luigi's departure from Cyprus in 1876, Assesandro was hoping to be appointed as American consul in Cyprus, replacing his brother. That year, however, the American government abolished the consulate of Cyprus. Having been left without employment, he dedicated himself to excavating and selling Cypriot antiquities.

In Dixon's *British Cyprus*, references to Alessandro Palma di Cesnola are few: the Cesnola brothers appear in three passing moments in the book, and the only substantial reference concerns the most famous of the two, Luigi, who is described, rather hyperbolically, as "the most successful explorer of modern times."[26] Dixon's letters, however, tell a different story. The first four letters from Cyprus were written from Cesnola's retreat in the village of Ormidia, near Larnaca. In his first letter, Dixon discusses at length his friendship with Alessandro di Cesnola, whom he describes as his "good angel" and an "erudite and successful seeker after ancient treasures of art."[27] And much of the information he gives his readers in the next three letters directly relates to the Cesnola brothers: he laments the closure of the American Consulate in Cyprus, he praises the Metropolitan Museum for "snatching away" the Cypriot treasures from the great European museums, and he continues to sing the praise of his kind host, whom he considers a dear friend. Dixon's original plan was to travel around the island with his friend, Alessandro di Cesnola, but as soon as Admiral Hay learned of his arrival, he invited him to stay on board the *Minotaur*. Dixon decides to move his quarters to the *Minotaur*, but he soon proceeds to visit his friend's house in the village of Ormidia. On his way to the village, accompanied by Cesnola, he falls from his horse, breaks his collarbone, and is brought, once more, to Cesnola's house to recover.

The fifth letter is where we learn of the reason behind Dixon's change of attitude towards Wolseley. A "discarded servant" by the name of "Anastatios" [*sic*], Dixon writes, had stolen some pieces from Cesnola's collection and sold them to the English officers.[28] He was soon arrested on the charge of robbery, but after Cesnola's intervention, for humanitarian reasons (apparently, the servant had a wife and six children), the charges were dropped. The servant, however, testified against Cesnola, who was subsequently charged for violating Wolseley's order prohibiting excavations on the island. Although he was initially arrested and jailed, he was soon released, but the British authorities asked him to relinquish his entire collection of Cypriot antiquities. Cesnola refused to do so, claiming that his excavations were carried out before Wolseley issued his order. He also submitted a complaint to the American Consulate in Beirut. Dixon's concluding paragraph is indicative of his frustration with this turn of events:

> Here we are, a law abiding English people, acting in Cyprus for the benefit, as we hope, of all the world, slipping our feet and falling into trouble through the over zeal of a subordinate agent. I am sorry for Major di Cesnola: I am sorry for the cause of scholarship and learning here insulted in the person of her active and conscientious minister. But I am most of all concerned for Sir Garnet Wolseley: the young and brilliant soldier whose first experiment in civil government is likely to be clogged and hampered by a wrangle with the United States.[29]

After the Cesnola incident, Dixon's references to Wolseley are few but quite telling. He informs his readers, for example, that Wolseley named his residence "King Richard's camp" at his suggestion.[30] The most significant reference that points to Dixon's irritation with the inexperienced high commissioner is included in the ninth letter from Cyprus, where he castigates him for excluding the Greek orthodox bishop from administrative matters. He remarkably argues that the reason for Wolseley's scorn of the Greek Orthodox

Church is due to Sir Garnet's Catholicism; that is, the general is being revengeful towards the natives due to the mistreatment of Catholics by the Greeks in the fifteenth and sixteenth centuries. "Let the cause be what it may," he writes, "the step is taken on a downward path. The pasha was a wiser man."[31] In another remarkable moment of passive-aggressiveness towards Wolseley, in his book *British Cyprus* Dixon presents us with a Muslim character who imagines that if he were "to pluck Sir Garnet's beard" he might "become a hero" in a book written by an Englishman.[32]

Contrary to Dixon's dramatic description of the Cesnola incident, Wolseley's reference to it is much simpler and straightforward. In his journal, he notes that Major Cesnola "was distinctly told" he is not allowed to excavate, but he did so anyway. He was put on trial "strictly in accordance with Turkish law";[33] Brackenbury served as a prosecutor and the accused was found guilty. Though he objected and insisted to be tried as an American citizen, the court dismissed his plea. He was eventually fined "4 Liras and had all the curiosities in his possession confiscated."[34] Like Wolseley, *The Times* correspondent in Cyprus, Leger Herbert, also described the incident, in his October 9 and October 16 dispatches, in a far less dramatic tone, and put the blame on Cesnola's refusal to return the antiquities to the British authorities. In his first reference to the matter, Herbert informs his readers that:

> Mr. di Cesnola, a brother of the gentleman well known for his discovery of the antiquities of Cyprus, applied to Government of leave to conduct excavations in the island, and was informed that the leave could be granted him. It was subsequently reported that Mr. di Cesnola was digging for treasure in the Larnaca district. The law in force renders a person so transgressing liable to arrest and fine or imprisonment, and it was found necessary to apprehend Mr. di Cesnola, and bring him, with two mule-loads of antiquities he had amassed, into Larnaca, where he was cautioned against a repetition of his unlawful acts and was discharged.[35]

The publicity Dixon's version of the event had received, forced Herbert to return to the subject of Cesnola's arrest and imprisonment in his next correspondence, where he writes:

> I informed you in my last letter that Mr. di Cesnola had been arrested for contravention of the law regarding the excavation of antiquities. Mr. di Cesnola, having been arrested, was lodged in the konak of Larnaca on the 6th inst. where a room and every possible convenience were specially provided for him. Upon the following day he was released with a caution, and expressed the warmest thanks to the Commissioner of Larnaca for the kindness and consideration with which he had been treated. He subsequently asked for permission to be allowed to go to the village where some of the excavated antiquities remained in order to see that they were safely brought in. This indulgence was granted, and a permit was given Mr. di Cesnola authorizing him to remove the

> antiquities, his word of honour being given to deliver them up on their arrival in town. At a later date, Mr. di Cesnola returned the Civil Commissioners' permit, stating that he declined to use it, and that as an American citizen he had placed himself under the protection of his Government and had addressed a complaint to the American Consul at Beyrout. As Mr. di Cesnola seems to have some doubt as to the legality of the proceedings commenced against him, those proceedings will now be conducted to their close in accordance with the law against which he has offended, and he will be prosecuted before the Medjilias Davi of Larnaca.[36]

Dixon's exaggerated reporting of Cesnola's arrest and imprisonment caused an avalanche of reactions both in England and the United States. An incident that exemplified, at worst, an attempt to manage the transition from Ottoman to British law and to control the massive exportation of antiquities from the island, was turned—partly due to Dixon's reporting and partly due to political tensions in Britain—into an international scandal. In the United States, the incident, as described by Dixon, was widely reported in the mainstream press, which stressed the fact that the British authorities had allowed an American citizen to be tried under Ottoman Law. *The New York Times* published Dixon's entire report of the incident under the conspicuous title "Maj. Di Cesnola's Wrongs: Insolent treatment of an American in Cyprus."[37] *Frank Leslie's Illustrated Newspaper*'s report on the affair is indicative both of the American frustration with British behavior and of the orientalist perceptions of the differences that (should) separate the "civilized" West from the "heathen" East:

> The insolent treatment of Major A.P. di Cesnola by the British authorities at Cyprus calls for prompt action on the part of our Government. The major was engaged in excavating for antiquities. Upon complaint of a discarded servant he was arrested for alleged violation of a Turkish law, was thrown into the common prison, bail being refused, and when finally released, found that the whole of his antiquities had been sequestrated by the British officials. He protested loudly but all his remonstrances were treated with contempt. Mr. Hepworth Dixon, who was on the island at the time, says that the major violated no law, but simply an order issued by Sir Garnet Wolseley, of which he knew nothing. Mr. Dixon denounces the arrest and imprisonment as an unpardonable outrage, an insult to the cause of scholarship and learning which the United States cannot fail to resent, adding that Major di Cesnola has already referred the whole matter to the proper representatives of this Government for their consideration. It is well to remember, in connection with this case, that, under the consular capitulations signed by Turkey and the United States, American citizens were not subjected to Turkish law. No American was ever before, perhaps, imprisoned in Cyprus. It has been left for civilized England—the great Christian power of Europe—to open the doors of Turkish prisons to the citizens of free countries whose rights even heathen Turkey never once thought of invading.[38]

Apparently, part of the confusion and the frustration expressed in the report relates to the peculiar legal situation in Cyprus. The British were merely administrating an island, which still remained under Ottoman sovereignty. In addition, British officials, including Wolseley, considered it wiser not to abolish Ottoman Law from the onset.

Apart from the reaction of the American press, the Cesnola affair was also discussed in the House of Commons, in December 1878; in fact, it was one of Dixon's close friends, the Liberal M.P. Charles W. Dilke, who raised a series of questions concerning the treatment of Cesnola. Dixon had traveled with Dilke to the United States and had dedicated his book *New America* to him.[39] Addressing the Under Secretary of State for Foreign Affairs, Robert Bourke, Dilke inquired whether "Mr. di Cesnola, an American citizen was tried for an offense against Turkish law in digging up objects of antiquarian interest without a Firman"; he also inquired whether "the Court was presided over by a Turkish Cadi," whether "Mr. di Cesnola sentenced to a fine," whether the objects were confiscated and whether the accused made any protest.[40] Bourke confirmed the facts of the story and responded that "in regard to jurisdiction in Cyprus [i.e., Ottoman vs. English] . . . pending arrangements . . . are now in progress."[41]

The Cesnola affair, as described through Dixon's hyperbolic style, became a prime example of the Legal muddle that resulted from the process of transitioning from Ottoman to English Law. As early as November 1878, *The Law Magazine and Review* had published a lengthy and harsh critique of the administration's decision not to completely abolish Ottoman Law in Cyprus. The high commissioner of Cyprus, the magazine noted in protest, referring to Wolseley, is "consciously treating Cyprus as Ottoman soil."[42] In February 1879, after Dixon's letters, and after the Parliamentary debate between Dilke and Bourke appeared in several newspapers, the magazine published a second lengthy critique of the legal confusion in Cyprus under the title "Cyprus and the Capitulations." Making direct references to the parliamentary debate, the magazine lamented that in Cyprus there are no capitulations, no protections to foreigners (British or otherwise) and no process of appeal.[43]

Once again, this chain reaction was initiated by the slanted and rather exaggerated description of the incident by Dixon. By the time *British Cyprus* was published, the Cesnola affair was already well-known; most importantly, it was widely discussed in magazines and newspapers, as well as in the British parliament, raising questions regarding Ottoman and British Law, the relationship between Britain and the United States, the status of the agreement between England and the Ottoman Empire, the efficiency of Wolseley as a high commissioner, etc. In other words, what began as personal tension spiraled into proper colonial discourse. The treatment of Wolseley in Dixon's book—a kind of passive-aggressive disregard—is a result of this tension. In one of the most peculiar descriptions in *British Cyprus*, Dixon presents Wolseley as the most enthusiastic proponent of Ottoman Law. "I came out," the high commissioner supposedly tells Dixon, "under the impression that I might have to change the whole system of government."[44] But Wolseley discovered, Dixon continues, that "these laws [i.e., the Ottoman Laws] are very good. All that is wanted is to put them into force."[45] In fact, Dixon portrays the general as being pleasantly surprised at the "humanity" and "justice" of Turkish laws; he finds that "they are very clear and full" and that "they well adopted to an Oriental people." "In theory," he concludes, "I regard these laws and rules as perfect."[46] It is ironic, to say the least, that Dixon presents himself protesting in the book, upon hearing these claims: "Perfect is a strong expression?" he asks Wolseley. Apparently, he attempts to implicate Wolseley as the main force behind the decision to maintain Ottoman Law in Cyprus. In refusing to disregard Ottoman Law, the high commissioner was not simply eager to make the transition from Ottoman to British rule more gradual, but he believed, in earnest, that Ottoman Law is simply "perfect."

Dixon introduces *British Cyprus*, rather peculiarly, with an epigraph from Horace's Ode 3.26:[47] "o quae beatam diva tenes Cyprum" (oh queen-goddess, you who possess wealthy Cyprus). The epigraph aims to draw a parallel between the goddess Aphrodite, Horace's original subject, and Victoria, the queen who is now in possession of Cyprus. Hence, the island's ancient mythological past collapses, symbolically, into the new historical era of the British possession of Cyprus. But this gesture is not merely symbolic. Although most British travelers in Cyprus commented extensively on Richard the Lionheart's conquest of Cyprus in 1191, implicitly extending the English presence on the island by seven centuries, Dixon is much more explicit on this parallelism between the old and the new. Speaking in the first person plural, Dixon reminds his readers that the British landed on these shores "seven hundred years ago"[48] and freed the island from Isaac Comnenus, the Byzantine emperor whom he describes as "a tyrant, ruling his people with an iron rod."[49] "Having freed the people from his yoke," he continues, "we took them under our protection, giving them as rulers men who were then regarded as the purest of the pure no less than as the bravest of the brave."[50] In another telling conversation with Garnet Wolseley, described in the book's rather exaggerated style, Dixon clearly outlines the significance of this otherwise brief moment of Cypriot history:

> "Our policy, Sir Garnet, should connect our ancient occupation with the new. Whether we will or not, the facts of our former visit stare us in the face. There, for example, you are building your new quarters on the ground once occupied by Lion Heart's men."
>
> "A good idea! I will call that place King Richard's camp."
>
> Richard-Victoria! By these great names we link our second advent with our first. A chain from Richard to Victoria seems long; but England is an

> ancient country, and her sovereigns are connected with each other by unbroken lines.[51]

The British Empire, in Dixon's imperial reasoning, had a legal right to claim Cyprus; it did not merely possess the island but reclaimed it. As in the twelfth century, its duty today is to free its people from tyranny. The claim to the historical, and even legal, right of the British acquisition of Cyprus will be repeated throughout his book in different contexts. In describing Nicosia, Dixon writes that the city "has bent to many lords in turn"; yet, the "present case is somewhat new" since "these newcomers [i.e., the British] are the only men who have stayed away seven hundred years, and then came back to them more masterful than before."[52] In fact, he is confident that "Nicosians, though they never been at school, are well aware that we have been here long ago."[53] When Dixon sees the Church of St. Nicholas in Nicosia, he excitedly, and mistakenly, traces its origins to the Knights of Saint Thomas and emphatically affirms that it is "a piece of English work, that has outlasted Lusignan kings, Genoese governors, Egyptian satraps, Venetian prefects, and Turkish pashas. We ought to get possession of our house again."[54]

The claim to Cyprus is not merely based on unearthing those moments in history, however brief, that emphasize the English presence on the island prior to 1878. In a remarkably misconstrued reading of history, Dixon claims that the right to possess Cyprus is founded on Law. England, he claims, was the legal possessor of Cyprus until Aimery, in the twelfth century, conspired with Pope Celestine and King Heinrich of Germany (Henry VI) and illegally became King of Cyprus. This move, according to Dixon, introduced "religious strife" on the island, between the Latin and the Orthodox Church, "which burned for ages hardly ever ceasing for a day until the Venetian garrisons were expelled from Cyprus by the Turks."[55] Hence, while elaborating extensively on Richard the Lionheart's conquering of Cyprus and the events leading to Aimery's reign (1191–94), Dixon collapses almost four centuries of the island's history into a short paragraph that covers the period from Aimery's rule to the Ottoman conquest of the island (1194–1571). Cyprus, in this narrative, was stolen from the British through treachery and deceit. The legal argument is clear: "England never recognized that transfer of her fief"[56] and "Cyprus, in the view of English king and English council, had never ceased to be an English fief—had never passed legitimately from the jurisdiction of the English crown."[57]

Dixon's popularity, his status as a literary figure, as well as the fact that his reports on Cyprus constitute some of the earliest English descriptions of the island, makes *British Cyprus* one of the most influential books of its time concerning colonialism in Cyprus. About eight decades after its publication, when Lawrence Durrell published his book *Bitter Lemons*, chronicling his life on the island "during the troubled years 1953–56,"[58] Dixon's book featured prominently as a source. In fact, one of the passages Durrell refers to and cites at length, in which Dixon describes the local Cypriots, is one of the most paradigmatic tropes of colonial discourse:

> What they are they were; and what they were they are—an indolent, careless, and mimetic people, but without a spark of Turkish fire, without a touch of Grecian taste. With neither beauty of body nor sense of beauty in the mind—with neither personal restlessness nor pride of origin—with neither large aspirations nor practical dexterity of hand, they live on in a limpid state, like creatures of the lower types, clinging to life for life's own sake; voluptuaries of the sun and sea; holding on by simple animal tenacity through tempests which have wrecked the nobler races of mankind.[59]

Being neither *this* nor *that*, and not possessing any distinguishable characteristics, Cypriots live in an animal-like state; and this "simple animal tenacity" is precisely what has allowed them to survive through the centuries. This line of thinking—which is clearly steeped in the standard differentiation between the civilized English and the uncivilized Orientals—permeates Dixon's entire book and even finds its way in Durrell's perception of Cypriots as late as the 1950s. Whenever Dixon uses the nouns "Greeks" and "Turks," he always puts them in quotation marks so as to distinguish them from proper Greeks and Turks and to underline a fundamental position of his that he expresses from the beginning of the book: "What are the Cypriots? Except in name, they are neither Turks nor Greeks; neither are they an amalgam of these two races."[60] Based on the way they speak, Dixon concludes, "they are of Aryan not Semitic root"; but they lived in isolation for centuries and, therefore, cannot be categorized under the existing racial categories.

In this context, it is not surprising that Dixon is greatly interested in a particular class of Cypriots, the "Linobambaki." These, he explains, are people who change their creed according to their interests; they are "both Mohammedan and Orthodox Christian"[61] or, accordingly, they are "neither "Greek or Turk in duty, yet both Greek and Turk in privilege."[62] They are hybrid,[63] troublesome, comic,[64] "slippery and tricksy people."[65] In order to sustain their protean identity, Dixon writes, "they give their children neutral names" like "Yacoub, Jousouf, and Mousa."[66] The entire description of the Linobambaki in Dixon's book is, in fact, paraphrased from Luigi Palma di Cesnola's book, *Cyprus: Its Ancient Cities, Tombs, and Temples*, which was published a year before Dixon set off for his journey to the island. The extent of this paraphrasing, a common practice between nineteenth-century travelers, is such that Dixon copies even the names in describing the Linobambaki. In Cesnola's book we read that they "adopt such names for their sons as are common to both Christians and Moslem, such as Ibrahim (Abraham), Moussa (Moses), Yusuf (Joseph), etc."[67]

Dixon and Cesnola are echoing here one of the most widespread colonial perceptions of the nineteenth century: that people of mixed races or unidentified origins are particularly dangerous to social cohesion and a threat to civilized societies. As such, the Cypriot Linobambaki bear a striking resemblance to one of the most derogatory terms invented to describe such people: that is, Levantines. "The terms 'Levantine' and 'Levantinism,'" as Gil Hochberg informs us, "have always designated a state of in-betweenness." The Levantines are described as "partly Europeans" or "semi-Orientals," and "culturally impure"; they "lack cultural authenticity and stability" and "possess no distinct national characteristics."[68] It was, in fact, the famous Lord Cromer, whose brother Walter Baring was dispatched to Cyprus to assist Wolseley in 1878, who offered nineteenth-century Victorian readers one of the most detailed and extensive descriptions of "Levantines," branding them as "more or less Orientalised Europeans."[69] Being neither Orientals nor Europeans, "they lie midway between . . . two extremes."[70] Their nationality is "of slight importance" and the "particular Consulate at which the Levantine is inscribed is a mere accident."[71] Like the Levantines, the Linobambaki possess an in-between state in the pseudo-anthropological science of colonial discourse. As converts, they pose a threat to a cohesive perception of identity and they blur the markers of distinction between *us* and *them*: the civilized and the heathens, the Christians and the Moslems, the British and the natives. It is not surprising, given the anxieties linked to this state of non-being, that this small group of people—no more than 1,200 by Cesnola's estimate—make their reappearance in several publications after Cesnola and Dixon's descriptions: from Samuel Baker's and Esmé Scott-Stevenson's travel accounts to magazines and newspaper articles.

Much like other colonized natives, Cypriots, as Dixon describes them, are set apart from the known anthropological categories of identity. As in other colonial situations, this "clearing of the slate" in colonial discourse, allows the colonizing powers to civilize, develop and manage a savage territory inhabited by people of uncertain origins. These islanders are "tame and feeble folk, unlikely to resist";[72] they are a backwards people, stuck in their "pastoral" way of life,[73] and they cannot lead themselves out of misery even if they wanted to (in fact, they "run away from power" which they perceive as evil);[74] in other words, they cannot lead and they must be led. "In time," Dixon proclaims, "we may improve them; but an Oriental race is very slow to change."[75] Speaking of their indifference to ride carts and coaches, he asserts that all Orientals must learn the lesson that wheels save "time and strength": "If lucky in their teachers, they may learn this lesson and acquire this habit in a hundred years. If left alone, they will never learn. The Cypriote peasant has not changed a habit or a garment for a thousand years."[76] Echoing Fallmerayer's theory, which had become popular five decades earlier, and appropriating the quasi-scientific evolutionary theory of the period, Dixon goes so far as to state that Cyprus may have been "peopled earlier, civilized earlier, than Britain" but the "fittest people have not survived" on the island.[77]

Dixon's description of Cypriots is complimented by the presentation of certain emblematic "types" who reside on the island. As Edward Said writes, "(u)nderlying all the different units of Orientalist discourse . . . is a set of representative figures, or tropes. These figures are to the actual Orient . . . as stylized costumes are to characters in a play."[78] Dixon's opening chapter focuses precisely on three such figures whom he describes as "type(s) of Cyprus in the act of passing from the Sultan to the Queen."[79] Stefan, a bearded Christian monk standing beside an "Anlgo-Norman" sarcophagus in the monastery of Bellapaese [*sic*] is the first type; Ali Effendi, a turbaned Muslim, a cadi, who praises the merits of the Ottoman legal system is the second type; Losh, an Arab worker from Lebanon who came to the island looking for a job is the third type. These types serve as prototypes which represent, in an emblematic way, the challenges that lay ahead in the act of passing from Ottoman to British rule: the reclaiming of the island's Englishness, dealing with Ottoman Law, finding workers to assist the British in the reconstruction of the island, etc.

The most "representative figures" in the book—the ones that capture succinctly the meaning of Said's theatrical analogy—are Emin and Creon. The first is a somewhat enlightened Turk, with three wives, kind, gracious, sensible and protective of his private home. Creon, on the other hand, is a pestering Greek who loves to speak about the suffering of his people under the Turks; he hates the Turks, loves the English and considers himself European. In all their encounters, the dynamic between the three (Emin, Creon and Dixon himself) is much the same: Creon, who is susceptible to false historical claims, makes a certain accusation against the Turks; Emin, who is much more knowledgeable, reverses the accusation; and Dixon, who presents himself as the impartial observer, steps in to confirm Emin's claim. When the subject of the "Harem" comes up—Dixon was particularly interested in the subject of polygamy—Creon denounces its existence and describes it as "a cesspool of abominations; a sink of iniquity; a nest of tyrants, eunuchs, concubines and slaves."[80] Emin responds that the harem is not the invention of the Turks but of the Ancient Greeks. Dixon, confirming Emin's claim, informs his readers that the perception that the harem is a Muslim institution is entirely false.[81] It is indeed "Greek in origin and growth," though "it has come to be Mohammedan through adoption."[82] In a similar conversation, Creon expresses his desire to take down the crescent moon, the Ottoman symbol that adorned the Church of St. Sophia in Nicosia; he regards the crescent, he tells Dixon and Emin, "as a symbol of slavery, intolerance, and decay."[83] Emin informs him that the crescent was already there, on the church, before the Ottomans' arrival as it adorned the famous Hagia Sophia in Constantinople prior to the city's Ottoman conquest. Once again, Dixon intervenes to inform Creon (and his readers) that the symbol of the crescent is "intensely and entirely Greek."[84] Throughout these revelations, the "Greek" Creon is described as puzzled, helpless, dazed and completely clueless. On the contrary, Emin, the "Turk," is presented as much more composed, logical and learned. The line that separates the caricatures of the enlightened, exotic Turk and the passionate, yet shallow, Greek, who is clueless on matters of history, is drawn by the civilized representative of British culture: unlike the "Greeks," Ottomans, Dixon tells us, "have no objection to be saved and civilized."[85]

On account of his widely published letters from Cyprus and the announcement of his forthcoming book on the island, Dixon was quickly emerging as an authority on Cyprus at a time when the public was infatuated with the island. A few weeks after his return from Cyprus and a few days before the publication of his book, the prestigious Royal United Service Institution announced that on Friday, February 7, 1879, at 3.00 pm, Dixon would be speaking on the subject of Cyprus.[86] In front of a large audience and with Admiral Sir Henry Frederick Nicholson serving as chairman and moderator, he repeated many of the findings included in his then forthcoming book.[87] He praised Queen Victoria and Lord Beaconsfield for the acquisition of the island and proceeded to eulogize its beauty as well as its potential usefulness for the British Empire. He admitted that there was sickness in Cyprus but not enough to panic or despair; he explained that when he broke his collarbone, the dryness in the air helped him recover speedily and assume his daily routine as if nothing had happened. The climate of Cyprus, he claimed, can cure many diseases, and the island could potentially become a British resort for curing ailments. He suggested that Cyprus could become a line of defense for the Empire and that the port of Famagusta could potentially serve the purpose of hosting the Imperial Fleet.[88]

According to press reports, among the audience in attendance were the distinguished hydrographer of the Royal Navy, Captain Frederick John Owen Evans, whom Dixon mentions in *British Cyprus*, Rev. G. Kirkwood, a Presbyterian chaplain to the 42nd regiment who, like Wolseley, had fought in the Ashanti War in 1873, Admiral Sir Henry Frederick Nicholson, Admiral Alfred Ryder, and others.[89] The discussion following the lecture focused on two subjects that widely preoccupied the daily press: the potential usefulness of Famagusta as a port (whether it had the capacity to host the British fleet, how much it would cost to construct a deep harbour, etc.) and the healthiness of the troops in Cyprus. Dixon's response to the audience's questions constituted, much like his lecture, an emphatic support of the political decision to take over the administration of the island. But once *British Cyprus* was published, on February 15, 1879, it was caught in a cyclone of negative publicity.

If we consider both the media frenzy that followed the possession of the island by Britain, and Dixon's position in England as a travel writer and a historian, it was only natural that *British Cyprus* was reviewed extensively by both mainstream and provincial newspapers and magazines. The clear majority of these reviews were published in the spring of 1879 and, like most reviews in nineteenth-century British newspapers or journals, they were unsigned. Apart from a few reviews in provincial newspapers, such as *The Cornishman*, or minor journals, such as *The Reliquary*, whose editor was, in fact, Dixon's friend, Llewellynn Jewitt, the book was denounced as too Dixonian.[90] "Only Hepworth Dixon could write so much about so little," bemoaned *The Glasgow Herald*, which was represented by Vizetelly in Cyprus, and which pointed out that Dixon's book gives service to the government in trying to convince the readers that the occupation of the island was a good political and strategic decision.[91] In an apparent sarcastic evaluation of the book, *The Saturday Review*, one of the most widely circulated journals in London, mocked Dixon's ornamental language and style and playfully described it as more akin to a theatrical play, rather than a historical book. It pointed out several contradictions and hyperboles, such as Dixon's description of a dry river in Cyprus (i.e., Pedieos) as a "lesser Nile."[92] Criticizing Dixon's criteria in describing Cypriots as Aryan (as opposed to Semitic) and Pelasgians (as opposed to Greek), the journal affirms that the book encompasses some of the wildest notions of ethnology. The most fundamental problem with Dixon's book, it concludes, is the author's "deplorable style": "that style may have its admirers, but it is the bane of a book which would have been very useful had it been written in a calm and simple manner."[93] In a more balanced tone, *The Academy* criticized Dixon's exaggerations and his attempt to draw historical parallels between the occupation of Cyprus and other unrelated historical events.[94] Similarly, *The Literary World* generally described his books as "neither masterpieces of accurate research nor marvels of philosophical observation."[95] They present us with an "ingenious reading of history" and they are meant to last for a season.[96] Even the *Athenaeum*, the journal Dixon had edited for sixteen years, felt obliged to report, in an otherwise balanced review of the book, "that not much can be said for the author's historical disquisitions."[97] Like many of the other reviews, the *Athenaeum*, bemoaned Dixon's negative representation of the Greeks as well as his outlandish descriptions of the histories of the harem and the symbol of the crescent.

The negative reception of *British Cyprus* was not, of course, entirely due to Dixon's historical errors, his exaggerations or his writing style. Much of the criticism he received constituted a continuation of the discussion regarding the extent to which the acquisition of Cyprus, and the terms of the treaty signed with the sultan, were a political and strategic blunder. The conservative Beaconsfield government initially attempted to market the acquisition as a diplomatic miracle but was dealt a severe blow after reality set in and disillusionment with the state of Cyprus became widespread. The Liberals, on the other side, were critical from the onset, pointing out the vague language of the treaty and the harsh conditions on the ground.[98] Many of the reviewers of *British Cyprus*, highlighted the fact that Dixon's positive view of the acquisition was a service to the ruling Conservative party. Commenting, for example, on Dixon's view that the climate of Cyprus is therapeutic, as he claimed after breaking his collarbone, *The North Devon Journal* sarcastically noted:

> Another recommendation of Cyprus, which ought to influence public opinion, is that when Mr. Hepworth Dixon broke his collarbone there, the healing properties of the atmosphere enabled him to go about as if nothing had happened. This is a point which the Government will probably turn to account. "Cyprus and Dixon's collarbone!" should make a good "cry" at the general election.[99]

A year before the UK general election of 1880, which Disraeli's conservatives would lose, Cyprus became one of the most bitterly contested issues. Dixon's position as a self-proclaimed expert on Cyprus placed him at the center of the political debate. Following several heated debates on Cyprus in the House of Commons, the satirical magazine *Punch* suggested the following: "Why don't Honourable Members engage Mr. Hepworth Dixon to give them a lecture on the island he has taken under his pen and his protection, and to set matters to-rights as between Britannia and Aphrodite and their respective isles, for good and all."[100]

One review of Dixon's *British Cyprus* that deserves a closer investigation was signed, contrary to the nineteenth-century magazine practice of submitting anonymous reviews, by John Augustus O'Shea. O'Shea's review of *British Cyprus* was published in the May 1879 issue of *Tinsley's* magazine and bears the title "About Cyprus."[101] It begins, like most reviews of the book, with a sharp critique of Dixon's flowery style and his persistent description of Cyprus in rosy terms. His sarcasm and mockery of Dixon is rather playful, but a few paragraphs into his article, he drops "the tone of playfulness" and explains why he has offensively been calling the author "Dixon" (as opposed to the more polite "Mr. Dixon"):

> Dropping the tone of playfulness assumed so far, and reminding Mr. W. Hepworth Dixon that if I have called him "Dixon" it is only in imitation of an offensive habit of his in speaking of others, many of them my personal friends, I will take the opportunity of pointing out some mistakes into which he has fallen—inadvertently, I do think—in the hope that he may have them corrected in the next edition of his book.[102]

From this point on, everything that O'Shea writes points to the many errors he discovered in Dixon's book: the British flag in Limassol was not hoisted by Colonel Warren, as Dixon claimed, but by Captain Beamish; there is no stream in Messaria [*sic*] and the climate is much hotter than Dixon suggests; the suggestion that the coast of Limassol is unparalleled in beauty by other Mediterranean shores is "rank balderdash";[103] the statement that no milk or beer is to be found on the island is also nonsense (O'Shea informs his readers that he had plenty of both while living there); the famous Black Watch (the 42nd regiment of Royal Scots) did not fight in Coomassie for the first time, as Dixon mistakenly suggests, but was formed much earlier, in 1729. After a detailed enumeration of Dixon's errors, O'Shea concludes his review in a bitterly critical tone. "I began by praising Mr. Dixon's book for certain qualities," he writes.[104] "That praise was meant less in jest than earnest." Dixon, according to O'Shea, wishes to imitate literary masters like Macaulay, Hugo, Carlyle, or all three for that matter. Instead, he is "Bombastes, a book maker *in excelsis*."[105] The reference to William Barnes Rhodes's burlesque tragic opera, *Bombastes Furioso* (1810),[106] aims, of course, to underline Dixon's attempt at imitation: the opera ridicules the bombastic style of late-eighteenth/early-nineteenth-century tragedy, and much like Dixon, in O'Shea's perception, borrows from the language of masters in order to articulate what amounts to an exaggerated, even erroneous, historical account.

Dixon's journey to Cyprus was destined to be the last one he would undertake. He died of apoplexy on Saturday, December 27, 1879, less than a year after his return from the island. Several newspapers attributed his death to two causes: sadness over the loss of his son, William Jerold Dixon, who had passed away two months earlier, in Dublin, and the accident he suffered while he was in Cyprus. "It is probable that he had never entirely recovered from the fall from his horse which he experienced last year," noted one newspaper, "and which no doubt affected deleteriously his nervous system."[107] *The Troubadour* magazine was more blunt in attributing Dixon's death to his Cyprus accident:

> When we last met Mr. Dixon he had just returned from Cyprus, and was full of his impressions of that celebrated, though malarious, island. Amongst other things he told us of his accident, how he had a fall with his horse, how the doctor insisted on his absolute repose and abstinence from solid food for several days, how he declared that he would eat his steak for breakfast that day, and be in the saddle again the same afternoon, and how he did all this in spite of the warnings of the local Aesculapius. We were strangely reminded of this story when some of the papers attributed the cause of his death to the lingering effects of the same accident.[108]

The arbitrary connection between the "malarious island" of Cyprus and Dixon's death, is consistent with the press' representation of Britain's new colony as a pit of pestilence. Apparently, the island was deleterious to such an extent, that even a strongminded and stubborn man, such as Hepworth Dixon, eventually succumbed to its poison. Ironically, as we have seen, Dixon himself, much like John Augustus O'Shea, was rather dismissive of the suggestion that Cyprus was an unhealthy island.

NOTES

1. William Hepworth Dixon, *The Azamoglan* (London: Simpkin, Marshall, and Co., 1845).
2. Dixon published the first two volumes of *The Royal Windsor* but died while revising the manuscripts for the remaining two.
3. For a brief biography of Dixon, see C. Kent, "William Hepworth Dixon," in *Dictionary of National Biography*, vol. 15, eds. Leslie Stephen and Sidney Lee (New York: Macmillan and Co., 1888), 128–30.
4. *Liverpool Mail*, January 3, 1880, p. 9.
5. *Freeman's Journal and Daily Commercial Advertiser*, December 31, 1879, p. 6.
6. *Daily News*, December 29, 1879, p. 2.
7. William Carew Hazlitt, *Four Generations of a Literary Family* (London: George Redway, 1897), 35–36.
8. In a review of Dixon's *New America*, the American journal *Southern Review* describes the book as "decidedly Dixonian, both in the flippancy of its tone and in the flashiness of its rhetoric." "New America," *The Southern Review* 1, no. 2 (April 1867): 462.
9. *Western Mail*, September 25, 1878, p. 2.
10. See *Sheffield and Rotherham Independent*, October 22, 1874, p. 1.
11. Wolseley, *Cyprus 1878*, 100.
12. Ibid.
13. This was not the first time Dixon and Wolseley met. A few months earlier, in March 1878, they were both guests at the "Savage Club," the famous bohemian gentlemen's club in London. See Joyce Emmerson Muddock, *Pages from an Adventurous Life* (New York: Mitchell Kennerley, 1907), 185; Aaron Watson, *The Savage Club: A Medley of History, Anecdote and Reminiscence* (London: T. Fisher Unwin, 1907), 251. Dixon's eldest son, Willie Dixon, was honorary secretary of the "Savage Club."
14. Wolseley, *Cyprus 1878*, 112.
15. Ibid., 115.
16. Ibid., 9.
17. Ibid., 95.
18. Ibid., 119. Admiral Sir Geoffrey Thomas Phipps Hornby was the commander-in-chief of the Mediterranean Fleet.
19. Ibid., 129.
20. Dixon, *British Cyprus*, 68.
21. Wolseley, *Cyprus 1878*, 9.
22. *Western Mail*, October 12, 1878, p. 3.
23. *Western Mail*, November 16, 1878, p. 3.
24. Alexander Palma Cesnola, *Salaminia (Cyprus): The History, Treasures and Antiquities of Salamis in the Island of Cyprus*, 2nd ed. (London: Whiting and Co., 1884), xxiii–xxiv.
25. Ibid.
26. Dixon, *British Cyprus*, 127.
27. *Western Mail*, October 12, 1878, p. 3.
28. *Western Mail*, November 16, 1878, p. 3.
29. *Western Mail*, November 16, 1878, p. 3.
30. This claim is repeated in Dixon's *British Cyprus.* See Dixon, *British Cyprus*, 139.
31. *Western Mail*, December 14, 1878, p. 3.
32. Dixon, *British Cyprus*, 219.

33. Wolseley, *Cyprus 1878*, 116.
34. Ibid.
35. *Times,* October 24, 1878, p. 4.
36. *Times*, October 29, 1878, p. 8.
37. *New York Times*, November 28, 1878, p. 3.
38. *Frank Leslie's Illustrated Newspaper* 47, no. 1211 (December 14, 1878): 243.
39. See William Hepworth Dixon, *New America* (Leipzig: Bernhard Tauchnitz, 1867). Dilke's grandfather, also named Charles W. Dilke, was, like Dixon, proprietor and editor of *The Athenaeum,* from 1829 to 1846. He later assumed the editorship of London's *Daily News*.
40. United Kingdom. *Hansard Parliamentary Debates*, vol. 243 (London: Cornelius Buck, 1879), 637.
41. Ibid.
42. "Law in Cyprus," *The Law Magazine and Review: A Quarterly Review of Jurisprudence* 4, no. 230 (November 1878): 30.
43. "Cyprus and the Capitulations," *The Law Magazine and Review: A Quarterly Review of Jurisprudence* 4, no. 231 (February 1879): 132.
44. Dixon, *British Cyprus*, 172.
45. Ibid., 171–72.
46. Ibid., 172.
47. Dixon misattributes the Ode as 3.25.
48. Dixon, *British Cyprus*, 132.
49. Ibid., 133.
50. Ibid., 133–134. Here Dixon is referring to the Templar Knights.
51. Ibid., 139.
52. Ibid., 156.
53. Ibid., 157.
54. Ibid., 249.
55. Ibid., 137.
56. Ibid.
57. Ibid., 139.
58. Durrell (1957:11).
59. Dixon, *British Cyprus*, 28, and Durrell (1957: 168).
60. Dixon, *British Cyprus*, 19.
61. Ibid., 29.
62. Ibid., 40.
63. Ibid., 84.
64. Ibid., 29.
65. Ibid., 40.
66. Ibid., 30.
67. Cesnola, *Cyprus*, 185.
68. Gil Z. Hochberg, *In Spite of Partition: Jews, Arabs, and the Limits of Separatist Imagination* (Princeton: Princeton University Press, 2007), 46.
69. Evelyn Baring Cromer, *Modern Egypt,* vol. 2 (London: Macmillan and Co., 1908), 246.
70. Ibid., 247.
71. Ibid.
72. Dixon, *British Cyprus*, 57.
73. Ibid., 116.
74. Ibid., 120.
75. Ibid., 116.
76. Ibid., 117.
77. Ibid., 119.
78. Said, *Orientalism*, 71.
79. Dixon, *British Cyprus*, 1–8.
80. Ibid., 211.
81. Ibid., 214.
82. Ibid., 215.

83. Ibid., 221.
84. Ibid., 223.
85. Ibid., 207. Interestingly, Dixon's belief in the potential of the Ottomans went far beyond the ideas expressed in his books. As the *Athenaeum* obituary noted, he had invested all his savings in Turkish stock "with an unaccountable confidence in a hopelessly bankrupt and failing state." *Athenaeum* no. 2723 (January 3, 1880): 20.
86. "Meetings for the Ensuing Week." *Journal of the Society of Arts* 27, no. 1367 (1879): 178.
87. *Daily News*, February 8, 1879, p. 2.
88. *Daily News*, February 8, 1879, p. 2.
89. See *Daily News*, February 8, 1879, p. 2, and *Cambridge Independent Press*, February 15, 1879, p. 2
90. *The Reliquary* published one of the most enthusiastic reviews of Dixon's book. Llewellynn Jewitt, the editor of the magazine, knew Hepworth Dixon well. As he confessed to William Henry Goss upon hearing of Dixon's passing: "I knew him well and the very last time I was in London we dined together. Poor fellow—he has lived 'fast' and died early and suddenly." William Henry Goss, *The Life and Death of Llewellynn Jewitt* (Hanely: Allbut and Daniel, 1889), 344.
91. *Glasgow Herald*, May 16, 1879, p. 4.
92. "Dixon's British Cyprus," *The Saturday Review of Politics, Literature, Science, and Art* 47, no. 1219 (March 8, 1879): 305.
93. Ibid., 306.
94. "British Cyprus. By W. Hepworth Dixon," *The Academy: A Weekly Review of Literature, Science, and Art* 15, no. 358 (15 March, 1879): 235.
95. "British Cyprus," *The Literary World* 19, no. 489 (14 March, 1879): 170.
96. Ibid.
97. "British Cyprus," *The Athenaeum,* no. 2680 (8 March, 1879): 304.
98. For a detailed account of the political turmoil that the acquisition of Cyprus caused, see Chapters 3, 4 and 5 in Andrekos Varnava, *British Imperialism in Cyprus 1878–1915* (Manchester: Manchester University Press, 2009).
99. *North Devon Journal*, February 20, 1879, p. 4.
100. "Punch's essence of Parliament," *Punch or the London Charivari* 76 (April 5, 1879): 155.
101. O'Shea, "About Cyprus."
102. Ibid., 440.
103. Ibid., 441.
104. Ibid., 442.
105. Ibid.
106. The opera wasn't published until 1822.
107. *Nottinghamshire Guardian*, January 2, 1880, p. 5.
108. *Troubadour*, January 3, 1880, no. 2., p. 15.

Chapter Nine

Letters to the Editor

J. L. Haddan's Pioneer Railway and V. L. Cameron's Journey to Cyprus

In previous chapters we investigated the reception of Cyprus's acquisition by Britain through an examination of new plays, literary works, musical compositions, advertisements and, most importantly, special correspondences in both mainstream and provincial newspapers. "Letters to the editor" constitute, perhaps, the most unique of these resources in our effort to ascertain the educated public's response to the occupation. They are essentially part of the reception of or the readers' response to the occupation: they can point to the specific fantasies or the anxieties the acquisition of Cyprus elicited, how the public responded to the special correspondents' reportage, how Britain's new acquisition became part of the existing colonial discourse or, generally, how the readers reacted to the issues surrounding the occupation. In the first months of the occupation, dozens of editorials were published in the mainstream British newspapers by ordinary citizens, distinguished scholars, politicians, explorers, scientists and, more generally, people who wished to participate in the discussion over the state of things in Cyprus and the future of Britain's new acquisition.

Unlike special correspondences, these letters are signed by their authors. The list of people who participated in these debates is indeed impressive and it includes: the eminent engineer J. L. Haddan; the distinguished explorer of Africa, Verney Lovett Cameron; the politician Julian Goldsmid; the physician and the first Linacre Professor of Physiology at the University of Oxford, George Rolleston; the British orientalist and M.P., Edward Backhouse Eastwick; the editor of *The Statesman's Yearbook*, Frederick Martin; the Scottish professor John Stuart Blackie; the Greek writer Dimitrios Vikelas;

the archaeologist Charles Thomas Newton; the antislavery campaigner Edmund Sturge; one of the most famous British explorers of Victorian England, Richard F. Burton; the British M.P. Sir Henry Bernhard Samuelson; the archaeologist Alexander di Cesnola; the diplomat Robert Hamilton Lang; the M.P. Thomas Brassey; the British architect, engineer and archaeologist, John Turtle Wood; the explorer Samuel Baker; the politician and sculptor, Clarence Edward Paget; and many others.

Most of these editorials are representative of the colonial imaginary and the ways it was expressed in a public forum. In other words, they verify the Empire's subjects' view of themselves, their anxieties and their desires. Many of them, for example, express the certainty that, now that Britain has acquired Cyprus, the hitherto neglected island will soon be transformed into the garden of the Mediterranean. This fantasy of the colonized subject ushered from a barbaric state into civilization, is perhaps best exemplified in Rudyard Kipling's *The Jungle Book*, and particularly by the character of Mowgli. In the case of Cyprus, the metaphor used by many British travelers and scholars to describe their new colony, especially since the beginning of the twentieth century, is the story of Cinderella. These editorials, though published in the early months of the occupation, before the popularization of the Cinderella metaphor, largely express the certainty that the island, rendered barren by previous conquerors, and particularly the Ottomans, is now about to be transformed. At the same time, the ontological context in which these writers saw their place in the story of the Empire becomes apparent in the subject matters they choose to present in the editorial pages of British newspapers. In other words, what they were anxious to re-present was their perception of what it means to be a part of what they perceived as the greatest Empire in the world.

While this chapter follows a specific story that was presented through the editorial pages of *The Times*, among other places, some examples of the subjects explored in these editorials are important in illustrating their function in the British colonial imaginary. Reverend J. J. Coxhead, an Oxford graduate and the vicar of St. John's at Fitzroy Square, reminded *The Times*' readers, on July 18, 1878, that Cyprus was "the first country in the world that had a Christian ruler," the place "where the name of Saul was changed to Paul," "the country of Barnabas."[1] This reminder of Cyprus's place in biblical history, constitutes, in fact, one of the two great subjects that fueled perceptions of the island; the other, as we have already discussed, is Ancient Greece. The Scottish professor John Stuart Blackie, a fierce supporter of the Modern Greek pronunciation of Ancient Greek (as opposed to the Erasmian pronunciation), wrote that two-thirds of the population of Cyprus speaks Greek, therefore to understand them means to understand their language. The English, he continued, though honorable and great as administrators, are far inferior to the Russians and the Germans "in their command of living languages."[2] What is especially lamentable is the "factitious and barbarous pronunciation of Greek practiced by the English Universities." The occupation of a Greek island, he concludes, furnishes the heads of universities with a "favourable excuse" for promoting Greek as a living language. No student should be able to pass a Greek course, according to Blackie, if he "cannot read, without a dictionary, any column of a Greek newspaper that may be set before him."[3] In the same context, many archaeologists, scholars of Greek or, simply, Ancient Greece enthusiasts, discovered, in the occupation of Cyprus, an opportunity to further explore and understand the Ancient Greek civilization. W. F. Prideaux, who had donated a large number of antiquities and coins to the British Museum, wrote, on August 2, that "the occupation of Cyprus for the first time affords the English nation a fair field for the systematic pursuit of a most interesting branch of archaeology."[4] Another favorite subject-matter highlighted in the editorial columns of *The Times*, in the early years of the occupation, was the British superiority in the fields of science and technology. Hinckes Bird, a surgeon who would eventually move to Cyprus in 1882 to become a medical officer, wrote, on July 25, that in order to combat malaria, more eucalyptus trees needed to be imported and planted on the island. Even the famous explorer Richard F. Burton thought it prudent to remind *The Times*' readers that science, under the auspices of the government, has made strides in combating the diseases still prevalent in uncivilized lands.[5] With such medical advances, Burton seems to suggest, the miserable condition of the island is inexcusable. Similarly, George Yeates Hunter, a surgeon-major in the Bombay Army, wrote to explain the origins of fever in Cyprus, and the British architect and engineer John Turtle Wood wrote to suggest that, according to his measurements, Famagosta [*sic*] would make the most ideal port on the island.[6]

One of the first editorials published after the acquisition of the island was by the engineer John Lawton Haddan, under the title "Cyprus and the Euphrates Valley Railway."[7] Haddan held several positions as an engineer during his career (in Spain, India, Poland and the Ottoman Empire), including the important position of chief engineer and director of public works for Syria and Lebanon. During his service in the Ottoman administration, he made surveys for the "Euphrates Valley Railway," an ambitious British project which entailed the construction of a railway line that would potentially connect India with the Mediterranean coast or with the European continent, making the transportation of goods from Britain's most important colony more efficient. The ambitious plan of finding "an alternative route to India by the Euphrates valley . . . had attracted attention off and on as early as 1836 and became an object of lively interest in the early seventies."[8] In the context of this "lively interest," and particularly in the final years of his life, Haddan became obsessed with his invention of the Pioneer Railway, an alternative railway system, which aimed "to provide a mode of communication and transport which [would be] cheap, elastic, and efficient" (see figure 9.1).[9] Apparently Haddan was so preoccupied with his invention that at least one obituary commented that he devoted the later portion of his life to the promotion of the Pioneer Railway system and that "over-anxiety in regard to this matter hastened his death, which occurred at the early age of thirty-nine years."[10] In May 1878, just one month prior to the British takeover of Cyprus, Haddan gave a lecture at the Royal United Service Institution, with General Wolseley presiding as chair. Since Haddan was trying to convince the military of the potential use of his Pioneer Railway in cases of war, prior to the lecture he staged a rather spectacular show, in which he invited "10 soldiers sent as a fatigue party from the Grenadier Guards and one or two ordinary unskilled labourers"[11] to construct his railway system at the rear of Whitehall-place in London. His intention was to prove that his invention could be constructed very simply and speedily "without the necessity of surveying, levelling, and passing through the preliminary stages of ordinary railway making."[12] Indeed, as newspapers reported, the railway was promptly put together within four hours. In the evening of the same day, Haddan presented his lecture in the presence of Wolseley and received the endorsement he desired by the general. In cases of war, Wolseley stated after Haddan completed his presentation, "other [railway] systems required good roads, but for a country without the roads, and in rapidity and simplicity of construction, Mr. Haddan's railway would meet an army's wants."[13]

Haddan promoted his invention aggressively, gave several lectures on its merits, and exhibited his railway system as often as he could. He also convinced several well-established personalities to support his invention. General Clifford, for example, called for the adaptation of the Pioneer in the Zululand.[14] In an 1876 letter to the editor of *The Times of India*, the explorer Richard Burton also praised the potential usefulness of the Pioneer; "a system," as he wrote, "invented by my friend Mr. John Hadden" [*sic*].[15] When the occupation of Cyprus was announced, Haddan's invention was at the peak of its popularity, with several journals and newspapers either praising its merits or doubting its usefulness.

What Haddan saw in the occupation was a golden opportunity to move forward, at long last, with the large-scale construction of the Pioneer Railway System, under the auspices of the colonial government of Cyprus. The fact that Wolseley, the newly appointed high commissioner of the island, had seemingly endorsed his invention just weeks prior to the occupation was a welcome blessing. Haddan begins his letter to *The Times* by referring to an "admirable paper" read at the United Service Institution by Sir F. Goldsmid, "on the occupation of Cyprus as a *tête du pont* for the Euphrates Valley Railway."[16] Indeed, Major-General Frederic Goldsmid, a well-established British Army officer, presented a lecture at the United Service Institution, on June 14, 1878, under the title "On Communications with British India under

Figure 9.1. "The Pioneer Railway." ***Source: The Graphic*****, August 3, 1878.**

Possible Contingencies,"[17] in which he underlined the necessity of constructing a railway line that would connect British India to the European continent. Among other possibilities, he suggested the following:

> Let us suppose ourselves [i.e., the British] at some particular spot in the Mediterranean always available, and so situated as to place us within easy reach of the Syrian coast, or a convenient starting-point for a railway to the Persian Gulf. As an island wears an independent look, we may choose Cyprus.[18]

The suggestion for the occupation of Cyprus by Britain was, of course, not new. As George Hill writes, the possession of Cyprus and its use as a naval base was suggested as early as 1818 by Captain John Macdonald Kinneir, who noted, in his *Journey Through Asia Minor, Armenia, and Koordistan in the Years 1813 and 1814*, that "the possession of Cyprus would give to England a preponderating influence in the Mediterranean and place at her disposal the future destinies of the Levant."[19] When Goldsmid delivered his lecture at the United Service Institution, however, the secret Anglo-Turkish treaty had already been signed a few days earlier. Given his powerful family connections and his involvement in politics, it is very likely that he was already informed about the agreement. Hence, his commentary on Cyprus is far from being a general suggestion. In his lecture, he proceeded to give a geographical description of the island, a brief account of its history, the current state of the population, its resources, the state of its public works, the administrative divisions in the island, etc. "I do not see that it is exactly talking politics," he comments after this extensive reference to Cyprus, "to say that Cyprus in the hands of Great Britain would be an invaluable acquisition."[20] His suggestion was that "the possession of Cyprus would facilitate selection of a terminus; for with such resources as are there available we could only require on the mainland a landing place, offices sheds for temporary accommodation of troops, and residence for a small railway staff provided from head-quarters in the island."[21] Eleven days after Goldsmid's United Service Institution lecture, *The Telegraph*, which would soon be credited with breaking the news of Cyprus's occupation, published a lengthy commentary on the lecture and the potential of occupying Cyprus. It is clear, perhaps in connection with its own sources and the rumors that came out of the Berlin Congress, that the newspaper treated the occupation of Cyprus, as early as June 25, not merely as a probability but as an imminent development:

> A name has been uttered lately, and by a high authority on Eastern subjects, General Sir Frederic Goldsmid, which we repeat because we think it possible that it is a name which may be heard frequently in the next few months, and under circumstances very interesting to Englishmen. The word to which we

> allude is "Cyprus," and we are mistaken if a good deal of attention will not soon be concentrated on this fair and fertile island.[22]

The newspaper's elaborate commentary concludes with the hope that Cyprus would soon constitute "a very excellent and profitable terminus and depot of the Indo-European Railway."[23]

Haddan, who was present at Goldsmid's lecture and understood the ramifications of such a development for his own invention, was ecstatic with the suggestion. In an extensive commentary immediately following the presentation, he introduced himself as "late Engineer in Chief to the Turkish Government" and proceeded to describe Goldsmid's suggestion to use the island of Cyprus as an "outpost" as a "golden one."[24] After elaborating on the disadvantages of using a conventional railway line to connect India to the Mediterranean coast, he gets to the gist of his intervention: the obstacles of constructing a conventional railway line through certain countries, he argued, were insuperable "until I designed the Pioneer Railway, some ten years ago." He then proceeded to elaborate on the vast advantages of his railway system in comparison to conventional railway lines.[25]

After the lecture, Haddan writes in his *Times* editorial, he met with Admiral F. Nicolson, Sir Willian Codrington, and Commander Verney Lovett Cameron, to further investigate the proposal; they all concluded that the Gulf of Alexandretta, in Turkey, directly across from Cyprus, would be the best *point de depart* for the Euphrates Valley Railway. In an indirect reference to his Pioneer system, he suggests that conditions in Cyprus are such that the construction of a short railway is essential:

> The summer heat of Larnaca is unbearable, and there is no doubt that an elevated camp will be required, to which a short railway should be made. This and a jetty three-quarters of a mile long will constitute the first public works the British will have to carry out in the island.[26]

In the days that followed, a discussion ensued in *The Times* (between Haddan, Verney Lovett Cameron, and Julian and Frederic Goldsmid, members of the distinguished Anglo-Jewish Goldsmid family), around Haddan's proposal of using Cyprus as a base for the transport of goods, in combination with the construction of the Euphrates Valley Railway. The most significant actor in this exchange was Captain Verney Lovett Cameron, who took it upon himself to travel to Cyprus in order to confirm the possibility for the construction of a railway system in Cyprus.

Haddan had earlier delivered a lecture, under the title "On Overcoming Geographical Obstacles to African Trade by Economical, Animal, and Mechanical Expedients," at the Royal Geographical Society, on March 25, 1878, dwelling upon "the advantages in a country like Africa of the 'Pioneer Railway.'"[27] Present at the lecture were the two famous explorers, Henry Morton

Stanley and Verney Lovett Cameron. In their interventions, immediately following the lecture, both men discussed the significance of Haddan's Pioneer System in improving trade with Africa, with Stanley arguing that more capital is needed to support such projects if the British Empire was to annex the "6,000,000 square miles of territory" lying in wait in the African Continent.[28] Cameron, who had himself designed the more primitive "Cameron Pontoon Cart" (see figure 9.1) for the transfer of goods, praised Haddan's invention, stating that "he had no doubt that if such lines had been laid down the 'Pioneer' Railway would by this time have occupied a very high position in the quotation of shares." He also noted that "Mr. Haddan's Railway . . . entailed only one-sixth of the cost," compared to traditional railways.[29] When Haddan published his editorial in *The Times*, Cameron responded on the very next day, on July 13, supporting his claim that Ayas Bay would be the best possible terminus for the proposed Euphrates Railway Line since it is the "one closest to Cyprus."[30] On August 1, Cameron published yet another editorial, insisting on the absolute necessity of building a railway system from India to the Mediterranean coast, as an alternative to the use of the Suez Canal.[31]

Cameron was already familiar with the Pioneer Railway and had referred to its significance in his most important book, *Across Africa*, published a year before the occupation.[32] In some occasions, Goldsmid, Haddan and Cameron jointly promoted the Pioneer Railway to potential investors and, more specifically, as the appropriate invention that would make the Euphrates Valley Railway possible. One such instance was reported by the press towards the end of July (i.e., two weeks after the occupation of Cyprus), when Goldsmid discussed the merits of the invention with Konstantinos Mousouros, an Ottoman diplomatic officer of Greek descent:

> On Tuesday his Excellency Musurus Pasha spent some hours in critically examining Mr. Haddan's system of steam caravans, designed by the inventor to open up rough countries like Asia Minor and act as test lines for grand undertakings like the Euphrates Valley Railway. Sir F. Goldsmid and his Excellency discussed the best point of departure for his line, and the Gulf of Ayas, as proposed by Captain Cameron and Mr. Haddan, was acquiesced in as by far the best. Colonel Alcock, Mr Rutson, Sir George Campbell, M.P. and others were also present.[33]

By the end of September 1878, Cameron decided to travel to Cyprus and the Middle East, to investigate in person the potential construction of the Euphrates Valley railway and the use of Cyprus as a port for the transport of goods to Great Britain. His experiences and his findings are recorded in his two-volume travelogue *Our Future Highway* (1880). The book begins, in fact, with the event that seemed to have reignited his interest in the region:

> Just before Sir Frederick Goldsmid delivered his lecture on our communications with India at the United Service Institution, and the Duke of Sutherland formed his association for the promotion of the Euphrates valley railway, I had my attention turned to the same regions, being persuaded that the course political affairs were taking in the East would, sooner or later, render the establishment of railway communication between the Persian Gulf (and ultimately our Indian possessions) and the coast of the Mediterranean more and more of an imperial necessity.[34]

He decided to travel to Cyprus, he writes, "to see what were the facilities which might aid, and the difficulties which might stand in the way of, such an undertaking." Cameron had already reached fame with the publication of his book *Across Africa* and had proven his eagerness to assist in the Empire's civilizing mission. In fact, *Across Africa* describes his experience in the "dark continent" after he volunteered to lead the Royal Geographical Society's mission to locate the whereabouts of one of the most famous explorers and missionaries of Victorian England, Dr. David Livingston. It was in this context that his path crossed with another famous explorer of his time, Sir Samuel Baker, who would later, in 1879, provide English readers with the most thorough and detailed description of Cyprus to date.[35] In 1882 he would join yet another famous explorer of his times, Richard Francis Burton, in order to investigate the gold-producing potential of the Gold Coast.[36] Their findings and experiences are recorded in the two-volume *To the Gold Coast for Gold* (1883), jointly written by Burton and Cameron, whom Burton describes as his "energetic and hard-working friend and fellow traveller."[37] "Gold and other metals are there in abundance, and there are good signs of diamond, ruby, and sapphire," Burton writes in the preface;[38] "remains to be seen if England has still the honesty and public spirit enough to work this old-new California as it should be worked."[39] Burton's description of the Gold Coast as of the "old-new California," also summarizes Cameron's position on the acquisition of Cyprus. Despite the harsh criticism in some political circles in England, Cameron was convinced that once the English were allowed to fix all the wrongs that the Ottomans inflicted on the island (the legal system, bribery, corruption), Cyprus was "sure to rapidly increase in prosperity."[40]

Once he arrived in Larnaca, accompanied by a friend he calls Schaefer, Cameron headed for the island's capital, Nicosia, in order to obtain a *firman* that would allow him to travel through the Turkish territories in Asia. The description of his brief meeting with Wolseley shows his admiration for the general's success in the challenging task of governing a new colony:

> We were kindly welcomed by Sir Garnet, Lord Gifford, and the rest of the staff and obtained the firman which was to pass us through the Turkish dominions in Asia. If Cyprus was unhealthy and enervating, it certainly had not made

> its mark on Sir Garnet and those around him, who all seemed as energetic as if only a week from England. He was fully occupied with all the thousand and one matters civil and military entailed by the occupation of a new country, and putting the ponderous machine of Government into motion and maintaining it in working order.[41]

The remainder of Cameron's stay in Cyprus is rather uneventful. After their much-anticipated meeting with the high commissioner, Cameron and Schaefer return to Larnaca, where they meet Castan Bey, a doctor who once worked at the seraglio in Constantinople and who was now exiled, for some unknown reason, to Cyprus. They decide to follow him to Limassol in order to see his "wonderful collection of antiquities."[42] After a cumbersome journey to Limassol, they find that Castan Bey's collection of antiquities, mostly consisting of "large quantities of Phoenician glass," is in total disarray.[43] The description of Castan Bey serves an important purpose in Cameron's narrative. This man, who, from the onset, is described as "an ancient individual" indulging in "numerous eccentricities," is a symbol of the old sickly state of affairs under Ottoman rule.[44] Castan Bey is an Ottoman subject; he has no sense of time, he is a terrible guide who always gets lost, he is mostly concerned with food, and he is, generally speaking, of a rather "comical" disposition.[45] His knowledge of the island's history is completely inaccurate. When he brings the two travelers to a village fountain to show them what he describes as "an ancient inscription," Cameron informs the reader that "the inscription proved to be modern, the date being the latter end of last century."[46] The same is true of practically any sighting of ruins along their way from Larnaca to Limassol: every description Castan Bey gives is perceived as false. But the most telling sign of the man's complete incompetence emerges once the party arrives at Castan Bey's house. Everything there is in "dire disorder," including the much-praised collection of antiquities in his possession:

> Very curious and interesting they were, but no idea of arrangement seemed to have ever entered the head of Castan Bey. Heads, torsos, pitchers, and glass were huddled together in confusion, and not even an attempt had been made at keeping the treasures-trove from different localities separate.[47]

Having decided that they did not have the time or the means to acquire the collection, Cameron is convinced that "it is doomed to reckless destruction by the hands of his Cypriote wife, and still more blundering servant."[48] He also deduces that Castan Bey treats his wife with contempt, much like he treats the maid, and that "she evidently stood in fear and trembling of her lord and master."[49] Once again, this experience—which curiously takes up most of Cameron's time in Cyprus—presents the reader with an emblematic metaphor of the vast cultural and political differences that separate the old Ottoman world from the British civilization. Everything, from the perception of time to the knowledge of antiquity and even family ethics, seems to point to the vast challenges that lie ahead in the British attempt to lead the island out of the dark ages of the past.

Evidently, Cameron had faith in the ability of Sir Garnet Wolseley to awaken the island from its long slumber. His admiration and respect, however, were not mutual. On the contrary, Wolseley's description of his meeting with Cameron, on October 9, 1878, is extremely scornful:

> Commander Cameron who travelled in Africa[50] arrived bringing with him a young Luxembourgh gentleman who was to accompany him on his new travels. He intents crossing from here to Latakia, going to Aleppo and then down the Tigris, across Persia into Ballochistan and our Indian possessions. I suppose he will see something new but the fact is these travellers nowadays have a little too much swagger. They travel for their own amusement and then imagine when they return home they should be worshipped. This little man appeared in the quaintest of costumes. A helmet with a red puggaree, a grey tweed jacket one mass of pockets and pocket flaps, with a very heavy gold chain hanging from one. The jacket had no tails but was nearly met by a pair of long untanned leather boots which reached nearly to his fork. In fact as one looked at the apparition before one it was a huge pair of boots and spurs with a very little man endeavouring to emerge from them.[51]

A similar mocking description is recorded by Wolseley in his journal on the next day. He fancies that Cameron "with his revolvers, two long daggers or knives and several pouches of ammunition added to the watches, barometers etc. etc." is "doing Cook [to] the tourists" rather than going to an expedition.[52] The general's tone is familiar to the reader of his journals, at least in relation to the many travelers who descended upon to the island after the British took over. His scorn is derived from the perception of the vast gap that separates the men of action—men who serve in the army, who fight the Empire's wars and maintain its glory—from the opportunistic men who gain their fame on the backs of military men: travelers, administrators, and politicians. What he persistently sees in all the travelers who come to the island is a kind of empty display, a charade that aims to impress the naïve masses with adventure books.

A good example of the intimate relationship between travelers, administrators, journalists and military men, is the fact that, quite remarkably, Wolseley's private journal entry describing Cameron's attire found its way to the British press. In the gossip columns of *Truth* magazine, we read the following satirical commentary, which was subsequently reprinted by other newspapers:

> I hear that Commander Cameron, who is on his way to survey the overland route to India, has been astonishing the natives of Larnaca by walking about in

> the streets of that town arrayed in the following costume: —A white sun-helmet, red puggaree, light tweed suit, coat cut short, leather belt, with pistols in cases on each hip, cartridge pouches, and heavy hunting knife; and heavy boots, half-way up the thigh, slouched at top.[53]

The anonymous editor was apparently informed about Cameron's adventures in Cyprus by someone who shared the same views, and made the same observations, about him as the high commissioner himself.

Soon after his return from the East and prior to the publication of *Our Future Highway*, Cameron submitted an article to *Macmillan's Magazine*, outlining his plans for the Indo-Mediterranean railway line.[54] On February 20, 1880, he gave a lecture at the Royal United Service Institution on the same subject. In this lecture, he underlined the importance of building the port of Famagusta since it is only six hours away from the proposed railway line. "From Cyprus," he explained, "we could at a moment's notice transport men to stop revolts, barbarities, and atrocities in the greatest portion of Asiatic Turkey."[55] Haddan, who was present at the lecture, praised Cameron for the delivery of an "admirable paper" and stated that those who are critical of the construction of the Euphrates Valley Railway "seem to forget that the bearings of the case are completely changed by the acquisition of Cyprus. It is no longer necessary, from a military point of view, to bring England and India into direct communication with each other—Cyprus being our representative now."[56] Not surprisingly, he also made another effort to promote the usefulness of his Pioneer Railway and its superiority over the conventional railway system.[57]

Cameron's support for the construction of an Indo-Mediterranean railway with Cyprus as a starting point was not received with enthusiasm. The *Athenaeum*'s review of *Our Future Highway* was cordial but merely descriptive, although it concluded by disagreeing with Cameron on the feasibility of such a task.[58] The *Pall-Mall Gazette's* review was less than enthusiastic, and it criticized Cameron for making light of political and financial considerations. *The Western Daily Press* informed its readers that "Commander Cameron's project uniting the Mediterranean with the Persian Gulf by railway has not been received with much enthusiasm, but if anything should come of it the scheme will give this successful and enterprising African explorer a new reputation."[59]

Eight years after his visit to Cyprus, Cameron would recall his experiences there in an article he wrote for the Dutch periodical *Revue Coloniale Internationale*, the mouthpiece of the Dutch Colonial Association of Amsterdam. The article is a summary presentation of the South Kensington Colonial and Indian Exhibition of 1886, which included a section on Cyprus. Repeating the position that he first expressed in *Our Future Highway*, Cameron writes that by virtue of its strategic position, Cyprus is destined to become "a highway of nations."[60] "The exhibits of Cyprus," he continues, resonating with the most common perception of the British position vis-à-vis the island, "show how much she has benefited by being delivered from the incubus of Turkish and Circassian Pashas and intrusted to the care of high-minded Englishmen."[61] Cameron reiterates his pride in belonging to the "Greatest Empire the world has ever seen"; an empire "being ruled with justice and wisdom" and which is "bound in bonds of mutual affection and honesty."[62] Echoing the ideological tune of his times, he concludes his review of the South-Kensington Colonial Exhibition with an emphatic reaffirmation of imperial responsibility:

> [L]et us hope that with that pride was mingled a sense of the responsibility which our great possessions entail upon us, and remember, that though through the virtues and talents of our forefathers we have arrived at our present pitch of greatness, we must not sit down in supine indolence, but that what was hardly won requires to be vigilantly and bravely guarded, lest the mighty structure should fade away and become less than the baseless fabric of a dream.[63]

The trajectory we have followed in tracing the intimate relationships unfolding in the context of colonial discourse, particularly in the case of Haddan and Cameron, point to the many interconnected ways through which colonial imagination was initially triggered and began to coagulate into plans and practices. This particular sequence of events began with Major-General Frederic Goldsmid's lecture in June 1878, where he outlined what is, undoubtedly, a hegemonic colonial fantasy. The fact that he could imagine that there was an island in the eastern Mediterranean, which was simply there for the British to occupy, suggests that there was already a frame in place which rendered the realization of such fantasies possible. From the moment this fantasy became a reality and the occupation of the island was officially announced, the discourse surrounding Britain's newest colony became part of the preexisting colonial imaginary. It seamlessly turned into a significant component in the prospect of actualizing the grand imperial plan of constructing the Euphrates Valley Railway. There were already inventions in place, like Haddan's Pioneer, and, most importantly, there were men who were already prepared (they possessed the knowledge and the skills) to participate in the fulfilment of this colonial project: journalists, military men, explorers, travelers, inventors, entrepreneurs, politicians, engineers. As we have seen, many of these men knew each other; they attended each other's lectures, they participated in the same events, they shared similar fantasies, they were part of that which, to use Cameron's words, "vigilantly and bravely guarded" the Empire's "mighty structure."[64]

In fact, the discussion in the editorial pages of British newspapers after the acquisition of the island exemplifies the attempt to balance the Empire's imaginary perception of itself with the harsh realities in the colony. Sometimes these imperial fantasies were blatantly and unapologetically expressed through statements that fueled the desire for Britain's hegemonic position. Edward B. Eastwick, the British orientalist and conservative M.P., reminded the readers of *The Times* of the words of "an older and more remarkable authority for the value of Cyprus," Alexander the Great: "And Cyprus being in our hands, we shall reign absolute sovereigns at sea, and an easy way will be laid open for making a descent on Egypt."[65] In the same vein that Frederic Goldsmid casually suggested, prior to the occupation, that Cyprus is simply there for the taking, Frederick Martin, the renowned editor of *The Statesman's Yearbook*, remarked that "many millions might be saved by making Rhodes the naval station of Great Britain on the coast of Asia Minor, instead of Cyprus."[66] One of the responses to Martin's suggestion was by a reader who signed his letter with the initials E.P.E.W. Cyprus, he suggested in a similarly arrogant tone, is a better choice than Rhodes for three reasons: (a) if the Empire plans to build the Euphrates Valley Railway, Rhodes would be 600 miles farther away; (b) Cyprus is a larger island; and (c) Cyprus has a larger number of products which naturally means there would be more revenue for the Empire.[67]

This feeling of belonging to the greatest empire in the world was the driving force behind the frenetic attempt to understand the island, to conquer it, to "free" it from centuries of abuse, to make it part of the civilized world. The public exchanges between scholars through the editorial pages of newspapers points, once again, to the ontological frame in which this dialogue unfolded. Several subjects that kept emerging in these discussions: the proper site for a port (the choice between Larnaca and Famagusta), the large waves of emigrants arriving there, the healthiness of the island, its rough Mediterranean climate, the state of its forests, its legal system. These subjects were measured against the Empire's capacity to restore the island to its former beauty, to transform it from its current barren state to its ancient fertility, from sickly to healthy. The perceived ethical, political and technological superiority of the Empire transformed, in these scholars' minds, the colonial project into a noble duty. No matter who was responsible for the island's decline—be it nature itself, the ottomans, or the natives—the British could turn things around. It is not surprising, then, that, by the beginning of the twentieth century, one of the most persistent metaphors used by British scholars to describe Cyprus was the story of Cinderella. The emphasis, in this parallelism to the popular fairy tale of the young woman who moves from misfortune to fortune, is not so much placed on the transformation itself but on the potential for the colony to be transformed into something else. "Today a Cinderella among our colonies," wrote Henry Rider Haggard, one of the most famous British writers who traveled to and resided in Cyprus, "with a little more care—and capital—she might again become what she was of old, the Garden of the Mediterranean, a land of corn and wine, and in fact, as well as figuratively, a mine of wealth."[68] Similarly, Basil Stewart, an engineer who lived and worked in Cyprus at the turn of the century, wrote that Cyprus "may not inaptly be called 'Our Island Cinderella.' Ever since the all conquering Turk besieged its two chief towns and wrested the island from Venice in the latter part of the sixteenth century, neglect and poverty has been her lot."[69] Writing around the same time as Haggard and Stewart, the scholar Arthur H. Beavan similarly described the island, in his book *Popular Royalty*, as the "Cinderella of the Empire."[70] The Cinderella metaphor was also used widely by the press, and it expressed something of the island's conflicting realities: the poor condition of the island and its people on the one hand, and, on the other, the potential that the British saw in Cyprus. But as late as 1934, when Sir Roland Storrs, governor of the island from 1926 to 1932, gave a lecture on the island at the invitation of the Royal Scottish Geographical Society in Edinburgh, the island was still seen as a colony that *could* become something great, but which, in reality, was still the most wretched of the sisters in the Cinderella story. As *The Scotsman* reported at the time, Storrs "accepted the omen [i.e., the frequent characterization of Cyprus as "Cinderella of the British Empire"], for although she started poorly, if ever there was a young woman who got there in the end, it was Cinderella."[71] When George Hill published his four-volume history of the island, the metaphor was so used and abused that, in his 1948 preface to the fourth volume, he wrote:

> The reader will not gather from these chapters any idea of the remarkable progress which has been made, especially in the last fifty years, in the development of what it would no longer be fair to call our Cinderella Colony. Rather will he find in them some explanation of why that progress has not been more rapid; as well as plain speaking about the mistakes that have been made. [72]

What Hill suggests is that, despite the popular characterization of Cyprus as Cinderella, and contrary to Storrs's remarks, the island might have progressed to some extent since the British takeover, but it never quite got there.

NOTES

1. *Times*, July 18, 1878, p. 6.
2. *Times*, July 20, 1878, p. 8.
3. *Times*, July 20, 1878, p. 8.
4. *Times*, August 2, 1878, p. 11.
5. "Now that the secret of "Warburg's Drops" has been bought by Government," Burton writes, "we find in that medicine, a combination of quinine with the diaphoretics used before the discovery of 'Peruvian bark,' the best prophylactic against, and remedy for ague and fever. Perhaps *Tinctura Warburgii* has not been supplied to the medical officers serving in Cyprus" (*Times*, August 30, 1878, p. 3). Warburg's Drops (or *Tinctura Warburgii*) was a medicine used

to treat malaria and other fever-related infections. It was invented in 1834 by the German-born doctor Carl Warburg, in British Guinea. As William Maclean, a doctor, responded to Burton, the suggestion that the recipe for "Warburg's Drops" was bought by the government was erroneous (see *Times*, September 18, 1878, p. 6).

6. *Times*, March 31, 1879, p. 11.

7. *Times*, July 11, 1878, p. 6.

8. Hill, *History of Cyprus*, 269.

9. F. J. Rowan, "The Pioneer Railway, or Steam Caravan, for Undeveloped and Difficult Countries," *Journal of the Society of Arts* 25, no. 1272 (6 April 1877): 462.

10. "Memoirs of Deceased Members: John Lawton Haddan," *Minutes of Proceedings of the Institution of Civil Engineers* 62 (1880): 352–54.

11. *Bristol Mercury and Daily Post*, May 23, 1878, p. 2.

12. *Bristol Mercury and Daily Post*, May 23, 1878, p. 2.

13. *Bristol Mercury and Daily Post*, May 23, 1878, p. 2.

14. *Belfast News-Letter*, June 19, 1879, p. 7

15. Isabel Burton, *The Life of Captain Sir Richard Burton* (New York: D. Appleton and Co., 1893), 534.

16. *Times*, July 11, 1878, p. 6.

17. Frederic J. Goldsmid, "On Communications with British India under Possible Contingencies," *Journal of the Royal United Service Institution* 22 (1879): 675–98.

18. Ibid., 681.

19. John Macdonald Kinneir, *Journey Through Asia Minor, Armenia, and Koordistan, in the Years 1813 and 1814: With Remarks on the Marches of Alexander and Retreat of the Ten Thousand* (London: John Murray, 1818), 185–86. Also see Hill, *History of Cyprus*, 270.

20. Goldsmid, "On Communications with British India," 683–84.

21. Ibid., 684. Frederic Goldsmid's vision of the occupation of Cyprus went beyond its usefulness as a military base. Here is how he describes it in a subsequent lecture (1884): "A few years ago I was requested to read a paper at the Royal United Service Institution, on the lines of communication between England and India; and I argued in favour of a railway from Tripoli to the Euphrates, eventually to become a mere feeder and outlet to the inevitable great railway of the future, uniting Constantinople to Baghdad. But the gist of my recommendation was that Cyprus should become by purchase or otherwise a British possession—a sort of sentinel watching over the railway terminus on the mainland opposite. . . . The geographical site of the new acquisition rendered it a kind of half-way house between England and India for passengers by the Euphrates Valley Railway; and, among many images of its usefulness, I pictured a University in Cyprus at which Indians travelling westward would find the best of European professors, with a genial and customary climate." See Frederic J. Goldsmid, "England's Religious Duties Towards Egypt," in *The Official Report of the church Congress Held at Carlisle*, ed. C. Dunkley (London: Bemrose and Sons, 1884), 429.

22. *Daily Telegraph*, June 25, 1878, p. 4.

23. *Daily Telegraph*, June 25, 1878, p. 5.

24. Goldsmid, "On Communications with British India," 695.

25. Ibid., 696.

26. *Times*, July 11, 1878, p. 6.

27. John Lawton Haddan, "On Overcoming Geographical Obstacles to African Trade, by Economical Animal and Mechanical Expedients," *Proceedings of the Royal Geographical Society* 22, No 4 (1878): 251.

28. Ibid., 253.

29. Ibid., 253–54.

30. *Times*, July 12, 1878, p. 10.

31. *Times*, August 1, 1878, p. 4.

32. Verney Lovett Cameron, *Across Africa* (Leipzig: Bernhard Tauchnitz, 1877), 269.

33. *Hampshire Advertiser*, July 27, 1878, p. 2.

34. Verney Lovett Cameron, *Our Future Highway to India* (London: Macmillan and Co., 1880), 1–2.

35. For the encounter between Cameron and Baker, see Cameron, *Across Africa*, 116; T. Douglas Murray and Arthur Silva White, *Sir Samuel Baker: A Memoir* (London: Macmillan and Co., 1895), 131, 192, 220.

36. Burton and his wife, Isabel, were also familiar with Sir Samuel and Lady Baker and met them on several occasions. As Isabel Burton writes in the biography of her husband, she first met the couple in 1868: "I was very much fascinated with [Lady Baker], and thought her very pretty" (Burton, *Sir Richard Burton*, 284).

37. Burton, Richard Francis and Verney Lovett Cameron, *To the Gold Coast for Gold* (London: Chatto and Windus, 1883), x.

38. Ibid., xii.

39. Ibid.

40. Cameron, *Our Future Highway*, 18.

41. Ibid., 17–18.

42. Ibid., 21.

43. Ibid., 30.

44. Ibid., 20–21.

45. Ibid., 23.

46. Ibid., 28.

47. Ibid., 30.

48. Ibid., 31.

49. Ibid.

50. Wolseley is clearly referring to Cameron's book *Across Africa*.

51. Wolseley, *Cyprus 1878*, 104.

52. Ibid., 105.

53. *Newcastle Courant*, November 8, 1878, p. 3.

54. Verney Lovett Cameron, "Indo-Mediterranean Railway," *Macmillan's Magazine* 40 (1879): 414–23.

55. Verney Lovett Cameron, "My Travels in Mesopotamia, Especially with Reference to a Proposed Indo-Mediterranean Railway," *The Journal of the Royal United Service Institution* 24, no. 105 (1880): 197.

56. Ibid., 200.

57. On December 13, 1878, Haddan attended Hyde Clarke's lecture at the Royal Society of Art, titled "On Railways to India and Turkey" (see Hyde Clarke, "On Railways to India and Turkey," *Journal of the Society of Arts* 27, no. 1360 (1879): 41–58. Haddan, again, talked about his pioneer railway. Interestingly, his path crossed with another major character in the story of Britain's occupation of Cyprus, Hepworth Dixon, who had just returned from his travels to the island. Disagreeing with the construction of Haddan's Pioneer system, Dixon supported the construction of a conventional railway line.

58. "Our Future Highway, by Verney Lovett Cameron," *The Athenaeum*, no. 2732 (6 March, 1880): 310.

59. *Western Daily Press*, September 30, 1879, p. 5.

60. Verney Lovett Cameron, "Colonial and Indian Exhibition South-Kessington," *Revue Coloniale Internationale* 4, no. 3 (March 1887): 224.

61. Ibid., 225.

62. Ibid., 237.

63. Ibid.

64. Ibid.

65. *Times*, July 17, 1878, p. 8.

66. *Times*, July 17, 1878, p. 8.

67. *Times*, July 20,1878, p. 8.

68. Haggard, Henry Rider. *A Winter Pilgrimage: Being an Account of Travels through Palestine, Italy, and the Island of Cyprus, Accomplished in the Year 1900* (London: Longmans, Green, and Co., 1901), 3.

69. Stewart, *My Experiences*, v.

70. "Far away, due east, lay British-ruled Cyprus—Cinderella of the Empire, though of the greatest importance as a naval base—with vast, yet hitherto neglected, facilities for harbours

and docks." See Arthur Henry Beavan, *Popular Royalty* (London: Sampson Low, Marston and Co., 1904), 319.

71. *Scotsman*, December 21, 1934, p. 13.
72. Hill, *History of Cyprus*, ix.

Conclusion

Cosmopolitanism and the Dissection of Native Identity

> I don't like foreigners I am glad to say. I hate their ways and customs but I can forget those, why I really dislike foreigners is on National grounds. If I had ten sons all should be brought up on this feeling.
>
> The more they hated foreigners, the more they would cling to England as their home, the home in which they meant to spend their old age, and the home of their affections and of their deepest feelings all through life, the home that was worth waiting for and for whose honour and in whose interests they would willingly die. . . . These feelings cannot be fostered side by side with new fangled, cosmopolitan, humanitarian, philanthropical sentiments. No man can learn the intense devotion to country that I would wish to see every British subject imbued with, unless he worships his idol so devoutly that all his feelings are absorbed so completely that he should not even care to regard another goddess, he should live his mistress so exclusively that he should have no eyes for another woman, his soul should be wrapt up in her to the exclusion of all or any admiration for others. The man who can live abroad, to whom foreign customs and manners are agreable [*sic*], who is indifferent to where he lives or as to the people of what nationality he associates with, who is in other words, a cosmopolitan cannot be the lover of his country I am and that I would fain see all Englishmen be.
>
> —Garnet Wolseley, *Cyprus 1878*, 49–50

Wolseley wrote these lines in his Cyprus Journal, on August 16, 1878, about three weeks into his administration of Britain's newest colony. In this blatantly colonialist attitude towards "foreigners," by which he means the natives, English patriotism is mixed with a quasi-romantic view of England as an ideal woman who demands absolute devotion from her lovers. A few lines after this long diatribe on foreigners, he will ponder on what appears to be a remarkable coincidence. "Strange to say," he writes, "the Convention handing Cyprus over to England was made and signed on my birthday."[1] He then proceeds to write about the "loathsome . . . inhabitants" of a leper colony in Cyprus; "and yet," he notes, "it is not very long ago since we had lepers in England."[2]

The intimacy expressed in these lines is emblematic of colonialism's *ontological* function that we have traced in many of the pages in this book. This is perhaps the most enduring characterization in Said's description of Orientalism. His most basic definition of orientalism, in fact, is that it constitutes "a style of thought based upon an ontological and epistemological distinction made between 'the Orient' and (most of the time) 'the Occident.'"[3] Epistemology, in this context, refers to the massive production of texts that aimed to study the Orient. Ontology refers to the way in which this knowledge became intrinsically connected with the colonizers' own identity; or in Said's description: "European culture gained its strength and identity by setting itself off against the Orient as a sort of surrogate and even underground self."[4] Hence, in Wolseley's Cyprus Journal, Englishness is measured against foreignness and intimacy is expressed as a tension between the familiar and the uncanny. His despise of the cosmopolitan, as well as its related concepts (humanitarian or philanthropical sentiments), stems from his anxious desire to define what is intimately familiar to him (i.e., Englishness). What is important here, and what emerges in many of the passages discussed in this book, is the intimacy through which this ontological apparatus works. His description is a familial one, if not Oedipal in nature: he imagines a woman, a divine Mother, whom he worships exclusively along with his ten sons. If orientalism, or colonialism for that matter, shares something with mythology or magic, as Said so memorably expressed, it is the "self-containing, self-reinforcing character of a closed system."[5] Hence, Wolseley can imagine Englishness as a stable and diachronic concept whereas the foreign is a marker of instability, perpetual change, and confusion. This fear of the foreign makes him stop and wonder, in what is perhaps the most profound manifestation of this ontological apparatus, why he shares the same birthday with the Anglo-Turkish treaty of 1878. Wolseley was indeed born on June 4, 1833, forty-five years before the signing of the treaty. In this self-containing mythological system, mere coincidences such as this become part of the constant juxtaposition between the familiar and the foreign, the self and the other.

Wolseley's perception of patriotic love as the reverse of cosmopolitanism is, to say the least, ironic, since one of the most common rationalizations in colonialist discourse is precisely the fact that empires provided the foundations for the co-existence of multiple races or religious groups, under the protection of a supposedly "tolerant" empire. As Deborah Starr writes, colonialism "provided the conditions under which cultural, ethnic, and linguistic diversity thrived in port cities of the Eastern and Southern Mediterranean."[6] Indeed, cosmopolitanism, in its most general understanding, thrived under colonialism, particularly in the port cities of the Mediterranean. But beyond the historical reality and the conditions that led to the creation of the thriving cosmopolitan city, the concept also served as a catalyst in both justifying colonialism and demarcating what separated the colonizers from the colonized. Unsurprisingly, in colonial discourse, or in orientalism, the divisions or the pluralism inherent in the notion of cosmopolitanism are often overemphasized in order to differentiate the amorphous mass of the fragmented subalterns from the cohesive and rather distinctive characteristics of the colonizers. Cosmopolitanism, in this context, is founded on a dissection of the native body far beyond the standard racial, linguistic or religious groups living in the colonies. Hence, again and again, nineteenth-century Western travelers, or journalists, who write about Cyprus, tend to divide its inhabitants into distinct groups of people. The Greeks of Cyprus, they all seem to agree, are not quite Greek: their language is a form of corrupted Greek (that even mainland Greeks are unable to comprehend), their characteristics have been altered by centuries of mixing with other races, their church is Orthodox yet autocephalous. The German-English cartographer Ernst Georg Ravenstein, goes as far as claiming, in 1878, that, in Cyprus, the Greeks of the plain differ from those who live in the mountains. The Greeks of the plain are "a mixed race—Syrian, Ethiopian, and Italian blood flowing through their veins."[7] Those who live in the mountains, on the other hand, "are a fine race of men, of noble carriage." Reveinstein took this distinction between mountaineers and plain Greeks, from Franz von Löher's *Cyprus: Historical and Descriptive*, which was translated into English in 1878. In von Löher's version, the Greeks of the sea coast are the descendants of "Italians, Syrians, and Negroes," whereas those who live in the mountains (and specifically the village of Evrychou) are undoubtedly "descended from the old Greek settlers."[8] Also writing in 1878, A. R. Saville notes that it is incorrect to describe the inhabitants of Cyprus as Greeks since their characteristics are different from those of true Greeks. They are not as lively as the Hellenes, they "do not possess any Hellenic aspirations," they are "quiet and docile" and "easily governed."[9] Hamilton Lang, who established himself as a respected authority on the history of Cyprus, during the early years of the occupation, due to his long tenure there as consul, similarly writes:

> But [Cyprus'] greatest isolation from the parent stock [i.e., Greeks in Greece] and her close intercourse with the East modified many of the distinguishing characteristics of the race, and caused the people to lose much of the remarkable individuality which was so pre-eminent in the Athenian Greeks. Climate also may have had an important influence in, as it were, Orientalising the Cyprian section of the Aryan family and toning down the balder and more robust features of the race.[10]

Thirty years later the same description of the "docile" inhabitants would appear in Basil Steward's travelogue *My Experiences of the Island of Cyprus.* Greeks of Cyprus, he writes, are in fact a "separate race."[11] They are easy to manage and their "lack of all desire . . . is probably due to the effect of past ages and through living in a country the climate of which does not induce energy in any form."[12]

Pushing this dissection of the native to the extreme, the distinguished British archaeologist David George Hogarth, who had spent much of 1888 in Cyprus, claimed that the inhabitants of the town of Paphos are of a different descent than inhabitants of other towns or villages. While in Cyprus, Hogarth spent most of his time excavating in Paphos and, as he writes, he got to know the town's inhabitants rather intimately: "their customs, their superstitions, their folk-lore, their racial character," and their "dream-world."[13] His experience led him to believe that "the Paphito is simply the raw material of the old Hellenic stock."[14] Though the inhabitant of Paphos is not as "advanced" as his brothers in "Rhodes, Symi, or Leros," he continues, and though he possesses some of the qualities of the ancient Hellenes, he "possesses but little vitality."[15] Offering a more subdued version of Jakob Philipp Fallmerayer's theory, that the ancient Hellenic race was completely eradicated, Hogarth claims that the "old Hellenic blood" passed down "the road of decay these two thousand years."[16] Yet, "it is not quite wholly extinct" and, therefore, "the new Hellene has to combat in himself a decadent influence, certain ignobler traits being owed by a strange irony to the blood of the same race whose tradition has done so much to ennoble him." This decadent type, as every traveler in the Levant knows, Hogarth continues, is the "graeculus," who, like the Jew, is rather shrewd when dealing with money. He is also "shapely and shrunken, with extremities over small, and teeth close set and level as if filed, and he has a very genius for trifles."[17] Turning to the Paphito, he writes:

> Fortunately for the Paphito, cultured Europe has not made him her spoiled child, nor has emulation of the West induced him to try to disguise the fact that he is by nature an Oriental. His language is an orderly product of his history, untouched by patriotic purists, and he has not learned the savour of the fruit of the Tree of Knowledge. But he has the same quick intelligence and ready adaptability as his more civilised brother, the same fidelity to his kin, the same domestic virtues. And his shortcomings are those of low development, not inherent vice, of one who will steal a sheep and shoot the shepherd, but scorn to commit petty larceny, one who is a very rude child of nature, happy in the blankest squalor, and untaught equally in religious enmity or reverence for priests. His god is a private god, jealous of trivial observances and unreasonable in revenge, ever present in the fields, but to be sought in the church only on a few feast days—, the common god, in short, of all the half civilised Christian or pagan. Like generations of his fathers he lives on in his flea-ridden mud hovel and tills a stony patch of arid land, being always in debt for his

> taxes, and often in prison for his violence, unashamed, unambitious, and wholly unconscious that others can be ambitious or ashamed.[18]

For Hogarth, the inhabitants of Paphos are evidently specimens of the decayed Hellenic race but, unlike the "graeculus type," they live in a kind of natural state, unconscious of the nobility in their blood. What is remarkable in his pseudo-anthropological description is that he sees the inhabitants of Paphos as distinct from the rest of the Greek population of the island, much like Ravenstein and von Löher distinguish between Greeks living in the plain and Greeks living in the mountains. In fact, in his book *Devia Cypria*, Hogarth pushes this dissection even further, claiming that the inhabitants of the small village of Phallia "are of Gypsy origin" and the Marathasiote villagers are "descendants of Phoenician settlers."[19] Furthermore, the peasantry of the Carpas peninsula have a "peculiarly un-Cypriote look: their white skins and frequent fair hair, the beauty of the women, and the use of foreign words . . . suggest that Western influence here is especially present."[20] Hogarth ascribes this "un-Cypriot look" to the Frankish influence on the region.

It is perhaps astounding that, in such a small island, Hogarth sees remnants of past colonizers in the racial characteristics of the natives. Yet, this is precisely the anxiety caused by the cosmopolitan state of the Empire, in which the mutilation and dissection of the natives—from their description as a group (i.e., Cypriotes) to the most minute denomination (i.e., Carpasians, Marathasiotes or Phallians)—creates a social situation where any kind of internal unity is deemed impossible. The only kind of unity that Hogarth and his peers can imagine is under the auspices of the Empire, which, as he claims, had already left a lasting mark on the island in merely two decades of administration. "In spite of fetters, financial and diplomatic," he writes, "our mark has been set on the island, a mark perhaps deeper and more lasting than any other race would have impressed, manacled as we."[21]

Although much of the cosmopolitanism the correspondents saw in Cyprus was induced by the acquisition of the island by England, which had caused a massive migration of people who hoped to profit from the transition of power, they still describe Cyprus as a modern Babel, as if that were its natural or permanent state, prior to the occupation. John Augustus O'Shea characteristically writes, in one of his first impressions of Larnaca, that in this small town he saw "French, Syrians, Armenians, Egyptians, Maltese, Soudan negroes, and Jews from Jerusalem itself; Germans, Italians, Turks, and Greeks beside our own people, with their many diversities, both from the United Kingdom and from India."[22] Cypriots, he further notes, are in the minority. If cosmopolitanism was the precondition of the colonized city, it was also, in a sense, the very condition correspondents, travelers, administrators and military men had to measure their own identity against. Much of their life was spent traveling to foreign lands and, when they returned to the motherland, they spoke or wrote of their impressions, their journeys and their encounters with the heathens, the barbarians and the uncivilized. One of their greatest fears, in these comings and goings from London to the colonies and back, was that of "going native," of becoming Levantines, of being "polluted" by foreign ways and customs. At the same time, the desire to conquer and possess the colonized lands and their inhabitants often led them to the peculiar desire to become just like the foreigners they described. Hence, as we have seen, Archibald Forbes speaks of his longing to "be conversant with the debased Greek patois" of Cypriots and to "put on a fez and a baggy pair of breeches and go among them as one of themselves, and find out all about them, from their songs to their prayers, from their cradles to their graves."[23] Edward Vizetelly did follow through with a similar fantasy when he acquired a yataghan and a blade and joined the irregular Turkish troops to defend the Ottoman Empire against the Russians. "I was now a Bashi-Bazouk," he writes, "or a free lance, or in other terms, I belonged to a regiment of irregular Turkish troops, which is all those words, so ominous to English ears and associated in recent times with such blood-curdling tales of massacre and ruthless rapine, really mean."[24] As Said argues, when Flaubert encountered and described an Egyptian courtesan, Kuchuk Hanem, he essentially "produced a widely influential model of the Oriental woman":

> She never spoke of herself, she never represented her emotions, presence, or history. *He* spoke for and represented her. He was foreign, comparatively wealthy, male, and these were historical facts of domination that allowed him not only to possess Kuchuk Hanem physically but to speak for her and tell his readers in what way she was "typically Oriental."[25]

This desire of knowing, possessing and describing the foreign, or the colonized, was such that sometimes it led travelers or correspondents, as we have seen, to turn into that object of desire or, at least, to express a longing of becoming *just like them*. At the same time, these metamorphoses were dependent upon the safe return of the speaking subject to their authentic identity—the original position of being British—and the dissemination of that transformative knowledge for the pleasures of the British public. If becoming native was foreclosed by the disastrous possibility of being levantanized, then the safest path to possessing the foreign was to "go native" for a brief period of time, and then return to the privileged position that enabled this transformation to begin with.

In these complicated manifestations of cosmopolitanism—which range from the representation of a fragmented/pluralist society to the depiction of a race of undetermined origins—what becomes apparent, once again, is the ontological function of such descriptions. Very often, what these writers have in mind is their own position as British subjects and their own construction of what constitutes British identity in the often-perplexing amalgamation between the English, the Scottish, the Welsh and the Irish. Naturally, in the context of this effort to demarcate Britishness as distinguished from the "foreign," the most dreaded group of people in Cyprus were the linobambaki, a relatively marginal group of people who were perceived as belonging neither to the Greek nor to the Turkish communities. Several authors writing in the first two years of the occupation, including Hepworth Dixon, Samuel Baker, Frederic Henry Fisher, Esmé Scott-Stevenson, and John Joseph Lake, refer to them in their works. Roland L. N. Michell, who had served for many years as district commissioner of Limassol, wrote a lengthy article on the linobambaki in 1908,[26] which was subsequently summarized in the pages of the Scottish *Falkirk Herald* under the title "Practice two faiths: Cyprus Islanders who are both Mahometans and Christians." The newspaper article begins with the characteristic ridicule that accompanied most references to the linobambaki:

> Most persons have made up their minds on religious matters. They do not doubt their ability to select the truth out of a thousand faiths and dogmas. However, there is a sect in the island of Cyprus that follows the principle of the man who when asked whether he believed the world moved from east to west or the other way around replied: "A little of both." These modest believers hold that it is beyond mortal ken to estimate the comparative merits of Mahometanism and Christianity. They refuse to make an exclusive choice, and practice both religions with extreme devotion. . . . As Mahometans they cannot eat swine, but as Christians they are free to enjoy the pig. Being followers of the Prophet, they will not touch wine, while a recollection of Christianity enables them to take a little for the stomach's sake. They are limited to one wife by the practice of one creed and allowed to keep a harem in conformity with the other.[27]

Interestingly, the linobambaki's perceived transitions from one religion to the other, a subject of mockery and ridicule, may be paralleled to the British travelers', explorers' or journalists' desire to turn into "foreigners" in order to report on the character of the natives "from the inside." The fundamental difference between the two states, of course, is that in the case of the linobambaki, this "in-betweenness" was a permanent natural condition, whereas in the case of the British travelers or explorers, it was, in most cases, a conscious and ephemeral choice which the metamorphosed subject could easily and seamlessly shed upon his return to the more stable and recognizable position of being a British subject. If to briefly become the "other" was a precondition of describing, and subsequently possessing, the foreignness of the native, to "go native" was tantamount to levantanization, of becoming indistinguishable from the conquered natives.[28]

In his character sketch of Wolseley, Archibald Forbes offers us a markedly different use of hybridity, in which the combination of national traits make the general the quintessential British subject. "The races are mixed in Wolseley," he writes, "and the cross accounts for the curiously varied traits which his character discloses."[29] From his Celtic blood he gets "his audacity, his *élan*, his buoyancy, his debonair aplomb, his strain of mostly well-timed recklessness, his alert dexterity, his *finesse*, the adroit suppleness . . ."; his Saxon blood "gives him his steadfast constancy, . . . his solid strength, . . . his clam manliness, his almost unparalleled equanimity, his cool steady rancour, . . . his unfaltering fidelity in friendships."[30] In contrast to the confusing cosmopolitanism, which Wolseley despised, or to the great fear of hybridity, Forbes's description of Wolseley is essentially that of a prototypical Britishman who combines all the positive traits that comprise Britishness. Far from the colonial tendency to dissect the native into nonsensical categories, based on pseudo-historical interpretations, national unity is dependent here upon the seamless and cohesive amalgamation of all the positive traits of Britishness in one of the most celebrated warriors of the Empire. Hence, Forbes concludes, in a seemingly contradictory statement, that "no native obscurity could have kept him mute, inglorious."[31]

The sense of national unity, of Britishness, that many of the writers we have followed project in their writings is, as we have seen, in sharp contrast to the cosmopolitan or fragmented state of the colonized subject. After the first few years of the occupation, the Cyprus frenzy eventually subsided and the island fell, once again, into oblivion, in the pages of the British press. The British public would become interested again in Cyprus more than seven decades later, during the anti-colonial insurgency of 1955–59. The "frenzy" of the 1950s was, of course, of an entirely different nature. The Greek-Cypriots that British correspondents, travelers and administrators had once described as docile, lethargic, non-violent, or as a mixed fragmented race of people, would take arms against the Empire and demand Union (Enosis) with Greece. From docile subjects, they now turned into "terrorists." As many of the newspapers reports of the time testify, and as Lawrence Durrell continuously ponders in his celebrated *Bitter Lemons*, it was unfathomable, for many British, why Greek-Cypriots wanted to secede from the Empire and unite with a much poorer country. To many British people's minds, the Greek natives were ungrateful to their colonizers. The British had ushered the island out of centuries of Ottoman rule and into civilization. They were also united in bonds of friendship with Greece, a bond encapsulated in Lord Byron's death in Mesolongi during the war of Greek independence in the nineteenth century and during the greatest conflicts in the twentieth. Cyprus was eventually declared an independent country, in 1960, but the divisive politics that were fostered by the colonial legacy returned, with a vengeance, and defined much of the discussion that ensued after the departure of the British. Many of the subjects that dominated the discussion in the early years of the British occupation, such as the concepts of Greekness, Turkishness, or Cypriotness, and the claims of Greece and Turkey or Britain on the island, became contested issues, and found their way into the first Cypriot constitution. As in the rest of the formerly colonized world, independence from the Empire was a bittersweet resolution that led to further division, conflict and, often, to tragedy.

NOTES

1. Ibid., 50.
2. Ibid.
3. Said, *Orientalism*, 2.
4. Ibid., 3.
5. Ibid., 70.
6. Deborah Starr, *Remembering Cosmopolitan Egypt: Literature, Culture, and Empire* (London: Routledge, 2009), 13.
7. Ravenstein, *Cyprus*, 23.
8. Löher, *Cyprus*, 84–85.
9. Saville, *Cyprus*, 127.
10. Lang, *Cyprus*, 11–12.
11. Stewart, *My Experiences*, 106–7.
12. Ibid., 230.
13. David George Hogarth, *A Wandering Scholar in the Levant.* 2nd ed. (London: John Murray, 1896), 189–90.
14. Ibid., 190.
15. Ibid., 191.
16. Ibid.
17. Ibid., 192.
18. Ibid., 194–95.
19. David George Hogarth, *Devia Cypria: Notes of an Archaeological Journey in Cyprus in 1888* (London: Henry Frowde, 1889), 38.
20. Ibid., 54.
21. Hogarth, *A Wandering Scholar*, 204.
22. *Standard*, August 14, 1878, p. 5.
23. *Daily News*, August 27, 1878, p. 5.
24. Vizetelly, *Bashi-Bazouk*, 83.
25. Said, *Orientalism*, 6.
26. Roland L. N. Michell, "A Muslim-Christian Sect in Cyprus," *The Nineteenth Century and After* 63, No. 375 (May 1908): 751–62.
27. *Falkirk Herald and Linlithgow Journal*, August 12, 1908, p. 3.
28. In relation to this "horror of hybridity and cultural miscegenation," referring to colonial settlers, Leela Gandhi writes, "These anxieties are, in turn, framed by the familiar apprehension that colonial settlers might submit to the civilisational depravity of their victims, or, in other words, 'go native.' Notably, the colonial archive itself records the administrative imperative to—at least—'appear native' in the performance of governmental power." See Leela Gandhi, *Postcolonial Theory: A Critical Introduction* (New York: Columbia University Press, 1998), 133.
29. Forbes, *Souvenirs*, 181.
30. Ibid., 181–82.
31. Ibid., 182.

Bibliography

NEWSPAPERS

Aberdeen Weekly Journal (Aberdeen, Scotland)
Cambridge Independent Press (Cambridge, England)
Frank Leslie's Illustrated Newspaper (New York, U.S.A.)
Hampshire Advertiser (Southampton, England)
Hampshire Telegraph and Sussex Chronicle (Portsmouth, England)
Hartford Daily Courant (Hartford, Connecticut, U.S.A.)
Liverpool Mercury (Liverpool, England)
Lloyd's Weekly Newspaper (London, England)
Naval and Military Gazette (London, England)
New Zealand Herald (Auckland, New Zealand)
Newcastle Courant (Newcastle-upon-Tyne, England)
North and South Shields Daily Gazette and Shipping Telegraph (Shields, England)
Nottingham Evening Post (Nottingham, England)
Nottinghamshire Guardian (Nottingham, England)
South Wales Daily News (Cardiff, Wales)
Staffordshire Daily Sentinel (Stoke-on-Trent, England)
The Bath Chronicle (Bath, England)
The Belfast News-Letter (Belfast, Northern Ireland)
The Bristol Mercury and Daily Post (Bristol, England)
The Cardiff Times and South Wales Weekly News (Cardiff, Wales)
The Citizen (Gloucester, England)
The Cornishman (Penzance, England)
The Daily Express (Dublin, Ireland)
The Daily News (London, England)
The Daily Telegraph (London, England)
The Derbyshire Times (Chesterfield, England)
The Diss Express and Norfolk and Suffolk Journal (Diss, England)
The Dundee Courier and Argus (Dundee, Scotland)
The Durham County Advertiser (Durham, England)
The Entr'acte (London, England)
The Era (London, England)
The Evening News (Portsmouth, England)
The Evening Telegraph (Dundee, Scotland)

The Falkirk Herald and Linlithgow Journal (Falkirk, Scotland)
The Fife Herald (Cupar, Scotland)
The Fifeshire Advertiser (Kirkcaldy, Scotland)
The Freeman's Journal and Daily Commercial Advertiser (Dublin, Ireland)
The Gardeners' Chronicle: a Weekly Illustrated Journal (London, England)
The Glasgow Herald (Glasgow, Scotland)
The Graphic (London, England)
The Hartford Weekly Times (Hartford, Connecticut, U.S.A.)
The Hastings and St Leonard's Observer (Hastings, England)
The Hull Packet and East Riding Times (Hull, England)
The Illustrated London News (London, England)
The Illustrated Police News (London, England)
The Ipswich Journal (Ipswich, England)
The Kent and Sussex Courier and Southern Counties Herald (Tunbridge Wells, England)
The Leeds Times (Leeds, England)
The Liverpool Mail (Liverpool, England)
The Morning Post (London, England)
The New York Times (New York, U.S.A.)
The North Devon Journal (Barnstaple, England)
The Northern Evening Mail (Hartlepool, England)
The Pall Mall Gazette (London, England)
The Scotsman (Edinburgh, Scotland)
The Sheffield and Rotherham Independent (Sheffield, England)
The Sheffield Daily Telegraph (Sheffield, England)
The Sketch (London, England)
The St. James Gazette (London, England)
The Standard (London, England)
The Sunderland Daily Echo and Shipping Gazette (Sunderland, England)
The Sussex Advertiser, Surrey Gazette and West Kent Courier (Lewes, England)
The Times (London, England)
The Weekly Nation (Dublin, Ireland)
The Western Daily Press (Bristol England)
The Western Gazette (Yeovil, England)
The Western Mail (Cardiff, Wales)
The Western Times (Exeter, England)
The Worcestershire Chronicle (Worcester, England)
The York Herald (York, England)
The Yorkshire Post and Leeds Intelligencer (Leeds, England)

WORKS CITED

A Handbook for Travellers in Turkey. 3rd ed. London: John Murray, 1854.
A Handbook for Travellers in Turkey in Asia. 4th ed. London: John Murray, 1878.
Anderson, Benedict. *Imagined Communities*. Rev. ed. New York: Verso, 2006.
"Archibald Forbes and his Reminiscences." *The Review of Reviews* 4 (1891): 295.
Arthur, George, ed. *The Letters of Lord and Lady Wolseley 1870–1911*. London: William Heinemann, 1922.
Baker, Samuel White. *Cyprus as I Saw it in 1879*. London: Macmillan and Co., 1879.
Beavan, Arthur Henry. *Popular Royalty*. London: Sampson Low, Marston and Co., 1904.
Bey, Ali. *Travels of Ali Bey: In Morocco, Tripoli, Cyprus, Egypt, Arabia*. London: Longman, Hurst, Rees, Orme, and Brown, 1816.
Biddulph, H., ed. "Egyptian Campaign of 1882. Contemporary Letters from Lt. Gen. Sir Garnet Wolseley." *Journal of the Society from Army Historical Research* 18, no. 70 (1939): 77–79.
———. "The American Civil War: Contemporary Letters from Lt. Col. G.J. Wolseley." *Journal of the Society from Army Historical Research* 18, no. 69 (1939): 38–40.

———. "Canada and the American Civil War: More Wolseley Letters." *Journal of the Society from Army Historical Research* 19, no. 74 (1940): 112–17.

Biddulph, Robert. *Lord Cardwell at the War Office: History of his Administration, 1868–1874.* London: John Murray, 1904.

Birdwood, George. "The Story of the Ashantee Campaign, by Winwood Reade and Coomassie and Magdala by Henry M. Stanley." *The Academy: A Weekly Review of Literature, Science, and Art* 6 (August 1874): 117–18.

Brackenbury, Henry. *Some Memories of my Spare Time*. London: William Blackwood and Sons, 1909.

———. *The River Column: A Narrative of the Advance of the River Column of the Nile Expeditionary Force, and Its Return Down the Rapids*. London: William Blackwood and Sons, 1885.

Brassey, Annie. *A Voyage in the 'Sunbeam'*. 4th ed. London: Longmans, Green, and Co., 1878.

———. *Sunshine and Storm in the East: Or Cruises to Cyprus and Constantinople*. London: Longmans, Green, and Co., 1881.

"British Cyprus." *The Literary World* 19, no. 489 (March 14, 1879): 170–72.

"British Cyprus." *The Athenaeum*, no. 2680 (March 8, 1879): 304–5.

"British Cyprus. By W. Hepworth Dixon." *The Academy: A Weekly Review of Literature, Science, and Art* 15, no. 358 (March 15, 1879): 235.

Buchholz, H.-G. "Falkland Warren." In *Cyprus in the 19th Century AD: Fact, Fancy and Fiction*, edited by Veronica Tatton-Brown, 207–15. Oxford: Oxbow Books, 2001.

Bulwer, Henry Lytton. *An Autumn in Greece*. London: John Ebers, 1826.

Burton, Isabel. *The Life of Captain Sir Richard Burton*. New York: D. Appleton and Co., 1893.

Burton, Richard Francis, and Verney Lovett Cameron. *To the Gold Coast for Gold.* London: Chatto and Windus, 1883.

Cameron, Verney Lovett. *Across Africa*. Leipzig: Bernhard Tauchnitz, 1877.

———. "Colonial and Indian Exhibition South-Kessington." *Revue Coloniale Internationale* 4, no. 3 (March 1887): 223–37.

———. "Indo-Mediterranean Railway." *Macmillan's Magazine* 40 (1879): 414–23.

———. "My Travels in Mesopotamia, Especially with Reference to a Proposed Indo-Mediterranean Railway." *The Journal of the Royal United Service Institution* 24, no. 105 (1880): 188–206.

———. *Our Future Highway to India*. London: Macmillan and Co., 1880.

Cesnola, Alexander Palma di. *Salaminia (Cyprus): The History, Treasures and Antiquities of Salamis in the Island of Cyprus*. 2nd ed. London: Whiting and Co., 1884.

Cesnola, Luigi Palma di. *Cyprus: Its Ancient Cities, Tombs, and Temples*. London: John Murray, 1877.

Chambers's Encyclopædia. Edinburgh: W. and R. Chambers, 1874.

Clarke, E. *Britain's New Colony: Cyprus, Past and Present*. London: A.H. Moxon, 1878.

Clarke, Hyde. "On Railways to India and Turkey." *Journal of the Society of Arts* 27, no. 1360 (1879): 41–58.

Cohen, Deborah. *Household Gods: The British and Their Possessions*. New Haven: Yale University Press, 2006.

Cowper, Benjamin Harris. *Cyprus: Its Past, Present, and Future* (London: Book Society, 1878).

Cromer, Evelyn Baring. *Modern Egypt*. Vol. 2. London: Macmillan and Co., 1908.

"Cyprus and the Capitulations." *The Law Magazine and Review: a Querterly Review of Jurisprudence* 4, no. 231 (February 1879): 129–41.

Davidson, John Thain. *Cyprus: England's New Possession. Its Place in Bible History*. London: Hodder and Stoughton, 1878.

Davis, Eugene. "Irish writers in London." *Donahoe's Magazine* 29 (1893): 684–88.

Demetriou, Kyriakos. "Victorian Cyprus: Society and Institutions in the Aftermath of the Anglo-Turkish convention, 1878–1891." *Byzantine and Modern Greek Studies* 21, no. 1 (1997): 1–29.

Dictionary of National Biography: Supplement Vol. 2. Edited by Leslie Stephen and Sidney Lee. London: Smith, Elder and Co., 1901.

Dixon, William Hepworth. *British Cyprus*. London: Chapman and Hall, 1879.

———. *New America*. Leipzig: Bernhard Tauchnitz, 1867.

———. *The Azamoglan*. London: Simpkin, Marshall, and Co., 1845.

———. *The London Prisons*. London: Jackson and Walford, 1850.

"Dixon's British Cyprus." *The Saturday Review of Politics, Literature, Science, and Art* 47, no. 1219 (March 8, 1879): 305–6.

Durrell, Lawrence. *Bitter Lemons*. London: Faber and Faber, 1957.

Edwards, Lee M. "Hubert Herkomer in America." *American Art Journal* 21, no. 3 (1989): 49–73.

Ellmann, Richard. *Oscar Wilde*. New York: Vintage, 1988.

The Encyclopaedia Britannica. 9th ed. New York: Charles Scribner's Sons, 1878.

The English Cyclopaedia: Cyprus and Asiatic Turkey: A Handy General Description of our Eastern Protectorate. London: Bradbury, Agnew and Co, 1878.

Fahmy, Shahira, and Thomas J. Johnson. "'How We Performed': Embedded Journalists' Attitudes and Perceptions Towards Covering the Iraq War." *Journalism and Mass Communication Quarterly* 82, no. 2 (2005): 301–17.

Farley, James Lewis. *Egypt, Cyprus and Asiatic Turkey*. London: Trubner and Company, 1878.

Faustmann, Hubert, and Nicos Peristianis, eds. *Britain in Cyprus: Colonialism and Post-Colonialism, 1878–2006*. Möhnesse: Bibliopolis, 2009.

Fearn, Mrs Joseph. *Plain Rhymes for Plain People or Verses on the Five Books of Moses*. London: William Macintosh, 1866.

Fenwolf, Morgan. "Who planted the Flag on the Mess-house at Lucknow?" *The Army and Nave Magazine* 10 (1885): 338–47.

"The Fiasco of Cyprus." *Punch* 75 (19 October 1878): 173.

Fisher, Frederic Henry. *Cyprus, Our New Colony and What We Know about it*. London: George Routledge and Sons, 1878.

Flint, Kate. *The Victorians and the Visual Imagination*. Cambridge: Cambridge University Press, 2000.

Forbes, Archibald. "A War Correspondents Reminiscences." *The Nineteenth Century* 30 (1891): 414–29.

———. *Barracks, Bivouacs, and Battles*. London: Macmillan and Co., 1891.

———. *Memories and Studies of War and Peace*. London: Cassell and Co., 1895.

———. "My Campaign in Pall Mall." *The Universal Review* 3 (1889): 373–85.

———. *Souvenirs of Some Continents*. London: Macmillan and Co., 1885.

———. "The Fiasco of Cyprus." *The Nineteenth Century: a Monthly Review* 4 (1878): 609–26.

Fraser, W. Hamish. *The Wars of Archibald Forbes*. Aberdeen: Aberdeen University Press, 2015.

French, David. *Fighting EOKA: The British Counter-Insurgency Campaign on Cyprus, 1955–1959*. Oxford: Oxford University Press, 2015.

Gandhi, Leela. *Postcolonial Theory: a Critical Introduction*. New York: Columbia University Press, 1998.

Given, Michael. "Corrupting Aphrodite, Colonialist Interpretations of the Cyprian goddess." In *Engendering Aphrodite: Women and Society in Ancient Cyprus*, edited by Diane R. Bolger and Nancy J. Serwint, 419–28. Boston: American Schools of Oriental Research, 2002.

———. "The Fight for the Past: Watkins vs. Warren (1885–86) and the Control of Excavation." In *Cyprus in the 19th Century AD: Fact, Fancy and Fiction*, edited by Veronica Tatton-Brown, 255–60. Oxford: Oxbow Books, 2001.

Goldsmid, Frederic J. "England's Religious Duties Towards Egypt." In *The Official Report of the church Congress Held at Carlisle*, edited by C. Dunkley, 423–30. London: Bemrose and Sons, 1884.

———. "On Communications with British India under Possible Contingencies." *Journal of the Royal United Service Institution* 22 (1879): 675–98.

Goss, William Henry. *The Life and Death of Llewellynn Jewitt*. Hanely: Allbut and Daniel, 1889.

Gourgouris, Stathis. *Dream Nation*. Stanford: Stanford University Press, 1997.

Greaves, George Richards. *Memoirs of General Sir George Richard Greaves*. London: John Murray, 1924.

Haddan, John Lawton. "On Overcoming Geographical Obstacles to African Trade, by Economical Animal and Mechanical Expedients." *Proceedings of the Royal Geographical Society* 22, no. 4 (1878): 251–54.

Haddon, Alfred Cort. *Reports of the Cambridge Anthropological Expedition to Torres Straits: Physiology and Psychology*. Cambridge: Cambridge University Press, 1901.

Haggard, Henry Rider. *A Winter Pilgrimage: Being an Account of Travels through Palestine, Italy, and the Island of Cyprus, Accomplished in the Year 1900*. London: Longmans, Green, and Co., 1901.

Hakki, Murat Metin, ed. *The Cyprus Issue: A Documentary History, 1878–2007*. London: I.B. Tauris, 2007.

Hall, Michael Colin, and Hazel Tucker. *Tourism and Postcolonialism: Contested Discourses, Indenties and Representations*. London: Routledge, 2004.

Harling, Philip. "The Powers of the Victorian State." In *Liberty and Authority in Victorian Britain*, edited by Peter Mandler, 25–50. Oxford: Oxford University Press, 2006.

Hatay, Mete. "Servants, Slaves and Concubines." In *Ottoman Cyprus: a Collection of Studies on History and Culture*, edited by Michalis N. Michael, Matthias Kappler and Eftihios Gavriel, 161–80. Wiesbaden: Harrassowitz Verlag, 2009.

Hatzivassiliou, Evanthis. *Britain and the International Status of Cyprus, 1955–1959*. Minneapolis: University of Minnesota, 1997.

Hazlitt, William Carew. *Four Generations of a Literary Family*. London: George Redway, 1897.

Herbert, St. Leger Algernon. "Our Colonial Policy." *The Fortnightly Review* 35, no. 206 (1884): 241–55.

Hibbert, Christopher. *The Illustrated London News: A Social History of Victorian Britain*. London: Angus and Robertson, 1975.

Hill, George. *A History of Cyprus*. Vol. 4. Cambridge: Cambridge University Press, 1952.

Hochberg, Gil Z. *In Spite of Partition: Jews, Arabs, and the Limits of Separatist Imagination*. Princeton: Princeton University Press, 2007.

Hogarth, David George. *A Wandering Scholar in the Levant*. 2nd ed. London: John Murray, 1896.

———. *Devia Cypria: Notes of an Archaeological Journey in Cyprus in 1888*. London: Henry Frowde, 1889.

Holland, Robert F. *Britain and the Revolt in Cyprus: 1954–1959*. Oxford: Oxford University Press, 1998.

Hook, Gail Ruth. *Protectorate Cyprus: British Imperial Power before World War I*. London: I.B. Tauris, 2015.

Horne, Richard Henry. "Unknown Graves in Cyprus." *Macmillan's Magazine* 38 (1878): 403–4.

Humphrey, Andrew. *On the Nile in the Golden Age of Travel*. Cairo: The American University in Cairo Press, 2015.

Hyam, Ronald. *Understanding the British Empire*. Cambridge: Cambridge University Press, 2010.

Jauss, Hans Robert. *Towards an Aesthetic of Reception*. Translated by Timothy Bahti. Minneapolis: University of Minnesota Press, 1982.

Kent, C. "William Hepworth Dixon." In *Dictionary of National Biography*, Vol. 15, edited by Leslie Stephen and Sidney Lee, 128–30. New York: Macmillan and Co., 1888.

Kinneir, John Macdonald. *Journey Through Asia Minor, Armenia, and Koordistan, in the Years 1813 and 1814: With Remarks on the Marches of Alexander and Retreat of the Ten Thousand*. London: John Murray, 1818.

Kipling, Rudyard. *Selected Works of Rudyard Kipling: The Light that Failed; Plain Tales from the Hills*. New York: Peter Fenelon Collier and Son, 1900.

Kirk-Greene, Anthony. *Britain's Imperial Administrators, 1858–1966*. New York: Palgrave, 2000.

Kochanski, Halik. *Sir Garnet Wolseley: Victorian Hero*. London: The Hambledon Press, 1999.

Koudounaris, Aristides. "Ιασονίδης Ονούφριος του Ιωάννου." In *Βιογραφικό Λεξικό Κυπρίων 1800–1920*, 186–87. 6th ed. Nicosia: n.p., 2010.
Löher, Franz von. *Cyprus: Historical and Descriptive*. Translated by A. Batson Joyner. London: W.H. Allen and Co., 1878.
Lake, John Joseph. *Ceded Cyprus: Its History, Condition, Products, and Prospects*. London: Effingham Wilson, 1878.
Lang, Robert Hamilton. *Cyprus: Its History, Its Present Resources, and Future Prospects*. London: Macmillan and Co., 1878.
"Law in Cyprus." *The Law Magazine and Review: a Querterly Review of Jurisprudence* 4, no. 230 (November 1878): 15–31.
Low, Charles Rathbone. *General Lord Wolseley of Cairo: A Memoir*. London: Richard Bentley and Son, 1883.
Luke, Harry Charles. *Cyprus Under the Turks, 1571–1878*. Oxford: Oxford University Press, 1921.
MacGahan, Januarius Aloysius, and Eugene Schuyler. *The Turkish Atrocities in Bulgaria: Letters of the Special Commissioner of the "Daily News," J.A. MacGahan*. London: Bradbury, Agnew and Co., 1876.
"Major-General Sir Frederick Maurice," *Navy and Army Illustrated* 12, no. 236 (August 10, 1901): 513–15.
Makrides, Diane Weston. *Sendall in Cyprus, 1892–1898: A Governor in Bondage*. Nicosia: Moufflon Publications, 2014.
Mallinson, William. *Britain and Cyprus: Key Themes and Documents since World War II*. London: I.B. Tauris, 2011.
Mallock, William Hurrell. *In an Enchanted Island: Or, A Winter's Retreat in Cyprus*. London: Richard Bentley and Son, 1889.
———. *Memoirs of Life and Literature*. New York: Harper and Brothers, 1920.
Mariti, Giovanni. *Travels Through Cyprus, Syria, and Palestine: with a General History of the Levant*. Dublin: P. Byrne, 1792.
McCalmont, Hugh. *The Memoirs of Major-General Sir Hugh McCalmont*. London: Hutchinson & Co., 1924.
McDonald, John W. *A Soldier of Fortune: the Life and Adventures of General Henry Ronald Maciver*. New York: The New York News Company, 1888.
"Memoirs of Deceased Members: John Lawton Haddan." *Minutes of Proceedings of the Institution of Civil Engineers* 62 (1880): 352–54.
Michell, Roland L. N. "A Muslim-Christian Sect in Cyprus." *The Nineteenth Century and After* 63, no. 375 (May 1908): 751–62.
Moore, Thomas. *The Poetical Works of Thomas Moore*. London: Longman, Brown, Green, and Longmans, 1853.
Morgan, Tabitha. *Sweet and Bitter Island: A History of the British in Cyprus*. London: I.B. Tauris, 2015.
Muddock, Joyce Emmerson. *Pages from an Adventurous Life*. New York: Mitchell Kennerley, 1907.
Murray, T. Douglas, and Arthur Silva White. *Sir Samuel Baker: a Memoir*. London: Macmillan and Co., 1895.
Nakata, Martin N. *Disciplining the Savages, Savaging the Disciplines*. Canberra: Aboriginal Studies Press, 2007.
Nightingale, Florence. *The Collected Works of Florence Nightingale*. Vol. 5. Ontario: Wilfrid Laurier University Press, 2003.
O'Shea, Helen. *Ireland and the End of the British Empire: The Republic and Its Role in the Cyprus Emergency*. London: I.B. Tauris, 2015.
O'Shea, John Augustus. "A Little Dinner in Kiko." *Tinsley's Magazine* 32 (1883): 193–99.
———. "About Cyprus." *Tinsley's Magazine* 24 (1879): 439–42.
———. *Leaves from the Life of a Special Correspondent*. London: Ward and Downey, 1885.
———. *Roundabout Recollections*. London: Ward and Downey, 1892.
———. "The Phantom Piper: a Legend of the Black Watch." *The Army and Navy Magazine* 13 (1887): 168–78.

Ohnefalsch-Richter, Max Hermann. "Dr. Ohnefalsch-Richter's Record." *The Art Collector* 4, no.15 (June 1893): 233–34.

"Our Future Highway, by Verney Lovett Cameron." *The Athenaeum*, no. 2732 (March 6, 1880): 309–10.

Papadakis, Yiannis. "Aphrodite Delights." *Postcolonial Studies* 9, no.3 (2006): 237–50.

Papapolyviou, Petros. *Η Κύπρος και οι Βαλκανικοί πόλεμοι. Συμβολή στην ιστορία του κυπριακού εθελοντισμού*. Nicosia: Cyprus Research Centre, 1997.

Phillips, J. S. R. "The Growth of Journalism." In *The Cambridge History of English Literature. Vol.14: The Nineteenth Century, Part 3*, edited by Adolphus William Ward and Alfred Rayney Waller, 167–204. Cambridge: Cambridge University Press, 1964.

Piesse, George William Septimus. *The Art of Perfumery and Method of Obtaining the Odors of Plants*. Philadelphia: Lindsay and Blakiston, 1857.

Rae, William Fraser. *The Business of Travel: a Fifty Years' Record of Progress*. Leipzig: Bernhard Tauchnetz, 1892.

Rappas, Alexis. *Cyprus in the 1930s: British Colonial Rule and the Roots of the Cyprus Conflict*. London: I.B. Tauris, 2014.

Ravenstein, Ernst Georg. *Cyprus: Its Resources and Capabilities, with Hints for Tourists*. London: George Philip and Son, 1878.

Richter, Heinz A. *Ιστορία της Κύπρου*. Athens: Vivliopolion tis Estias, 2007.

Rideing, William Henry. *Many Celebrities and a Few Others: a Bundle of Reminiscences*. New York: Doubleday, Page and Co., 1912.

Rimmel, Eugene. *Recollections of the Paris Exhibition of 1867*. London: Chapman and Hall, 1868.

———. *The Book of Perfumes*. London: Chapman & Hall, 1865.

Robinson, Philip Stewart. *Cyprus: Its Physical, Economical, Historical, Commercial and Social Aspects*. London: William Clowes and Sons, 1878.

"Romance of War Corresponding." *To-day: A Weekly Magazine-Journal* 16 (1897): 102.

Roth, Michael P. *Historical Dictionary of War Journalism*. London: Greenwood Press, 1997.

———. *The Encyclopaedia of War Journalism 1807–2010*. Amenia (NY): Grey House Publishing, 2010.

Roussou-Sinclair, Mary. *Victorian Travellers in Cyprus: a Garden of Their Own*. Nicosia: Cyprus Research Centre, 2002.

Rowan, F. J. "The Pioneer Railway, or Steam Caravan, for Undeveloped and Difficult Countries." *Journal of the Society of Arts* 25, no. 1272 (April 6, 1877): 462–68.

Said, Edward. *Orientalism*. New York: Vintage Books, 1979.

Saville, A. R. *Cyprus*. London: Her Majesty's Stationery Office, 1878.

Scott-Stevenson, Esmé. *Our Home in Cyprus*. London: Chapman and Hall, 1880.

Severis, Rita. C. "Although to Sight Lost, to Memory Dear: Representations of Cyprus by Foreign Travellers/Artists (1700–1955)." PhD. diss., University of Bristol, 1999.

"Small Talk of the Week," *The Sketch* 28, no. 360 (December 20, 1899): 319–25.

Sophocleous, Andreas. *Συμβολή στην Ιστορία του Κυπριακού Τύπου, Τόμος Α' (1878–1890)*. Nicosia: Ekdotikos Oikos Nicolis, 2008.

Spiers, Edward M. *The Late Victorian Army, 1868–1902*. Manchester: Manchester University Press, 1992.

Stanley, Henry Morton. *Coomassie and Magdala: The Story of Two British Campaigns in Africa*. London: Sampson Low, Marston, Low, and Searle, 1874.

Starr, Deborah. *Remembering Cosmopolitan Egypt: Literature, Culture, and Empire*. London: Routledge, 2009.

Statham, Francis Reginald. *My Life's Record: a Fight for Justice*. London: Gibbings and Co., 1901.

Stearn, Roger T. "War Correspondents and Colonial War, c. 1870–1900." In *Popular Imperialism and the Military: 1850–1950*, edited by John M. MacKenzie, 139–61. Manchester: Manchester University Press, 1992.

Steinbach, Susie L. *Understanding the Victorians: Politics, Culture and Society in Nineteenth-Century Britain*. 2nd ed. London: Routledge, 2016.

Stewart, Basil. *My Experiences of the Island of Cyprus*. London: Skeffington and Son, 1906.

Tennyson, Lord Alfred. *The Foresters: Robin Hood and Maid Marian*. London: Macmillan and Co, 1892.

Thomson, John. *Through Cyprus with the Camera in the Autumn of 1878*. London: S. Low, Marston, Searle and Rivington, 1879.

U.K. Parliament. "Further Correspondence Respecting Complaints made against the Government of Cyprus, C. 2355." In *Parliamentary Papers*, Vol. 54. London: Her Majesty's Stationery Office, 1879.

———. "Correspondence Respecting an Ordinance Enacted in Cyprus, Providing for the Execution of Public Works, C. 2326." In *Parliamentary Papers*, Vol. 54. London: Her Majesty's Stationery Office, 1879.

———. "Correspondence Respecting Complaints, Made Against the Government of Cyprus, C. 2324." In *Parliamentary Papers*, Vol. 54. London: Her Majesty's Stationery Office, 1879.

———. *Correspondence with British Ministers and Agents in Foreign Countries and with Foreign Ministers in England Relating to the Slave Trade. From April 1, 1857, to March 31, 1858*. London: Harrison and Sons, 1859.

Varnava, Andrekos. *British Imperialism in Cyprus 1878–1915: The Inconsequential Possession*. Manchester: Manchester University Press, 2009.

———. "*Punch* and the British Occupation of Cyprus in 1878." *Byzantine and Modern Greek Studies* 29, no. 2 (2005):167–86.

Villiers, Frederic. *Peaceful Personalities and Warriors Bold*. London: Harper and Brothers, 1907.

Vizetelly, Edward Henry. *From Cyprus to Zanzibar by the Egyptian Delta*. London: C. Arthur Pearson, 1901.

———. *The Reminiscenses of a Bashi-Bazouk*. Bristol: J. W. Arrowsmith, 1897.

Vizetelly, Ernest Alfred. *In Seven Lands: Germany, Austria, Hungary, Bohemia, Spain, Portugal, Italy*. New York: Duffield and Co., 1916.

Vizetelly, Henry. *Glances Back Through Seventy Years: Autobiographical and Other Reminiscences*. London: Kegan Paul, Trench, Trubner and Co., 1893.

Walford, Neville Lloyd. *Mr. Archibald Forbes and the Zulu War*. London: Samuel Tinsley and Co., 1880.

Watson, Aaron. *The Savage Club: A Medley of History, Anecdote and Reminiscence*. London: T. Fisher Unwin, 1907.

Williams, James. "St. Leger Algernon Herbert." In *Dictionaty of National Biography*, Vol 9, edited by Leslie Stephen and Sidney Lee. London: Smith, Elder & Co, 1908.

Williamson, C. N. "Illustrated Journalism in England." *The Magazine of Art* 13 (1890): 297–301.

Williams, Stephanie. *Running the Show: Governors of the British Empire*. London: Viking, 2011.

Wolseley, Sir Garnet. *Cyprus 1878: The Journal of Sir Garnet Wolseley*. 2nd ed. Nicosia: Cultural Centre of the Cyprus Popular Bank, 1992.

———. *The Soldier's Pocket Book*. London: Macmillan and Co., 1871.

———. *The Story of a Soldier's Life*. Westminster: Archibald Constable and Co., 1903.

Woods, G. S., "Oliver, Samuel Pasfield." In *Dictionary of National Biography, Second Supplement,* edited by Leslie Stephen and Sidney Lee, 44–45. New York: The Macmillan Company, 1912.

Woolf, Virginia. *The Complete Shorter Fiction of Virginia Woolf*. Edited by Susan Dick. San Diego: Harcourt Brace Jovanovich, 1989.

Yeats, William Butler. *The Collected Works of W. B. Yeats, Vol. 2: The Plays*. New York: Scribner, 2001.

Young, Robert J. C. *Postcolonialism: An Historical Introduction*. Oxford: Blackwell Publishing, 2001.

Index

About the Author

Marinos Pourgouris is assistant professor of literary theory and modern Greek studies in the Department of Byzantine and Modern Greek Studies at the University of Cyprus (since 2010). He has previously taught at Brown University as a visiting assistant professor of comparative literature (2005–10) and at Rutgers University as a part-time lecturer (1998–2005). He is the author of *Mediterranean Modernisms: The Poetic Metaphysics of Odysseus Elytis* (Ashgate 2011/Routledge, 2016), the editor of *Odysseus Elytis: Poetry, Theory, Reception* (Ypsilon, 2014), and the coeditor (with Sanja Bahun) of *The Avant Garde and the Margin* (Cambridge Scholars Publishing, 2006). He has authored several academic papers on topics ranging from modern Greek literature to psychoanalysis, Marxism, and postcolonial theory.

Lightning Source UK Ltd.
Milton Keynes UK
UKHW041124260419
341559UK00005B/30/P

9 781498 576604